DRIVING PAST

A Memoir of What
Made Australia's
Roads Safer

Geoff Quayle

BALBOA.
PRESS

A DIVISION OF HAY HOUSE

Balboa Press books may be ordered through booksellers or by contacting:

Balboa Press
A Division of Hay House
1663 Liberty Drive
Bloomington, IN 47403
www.balboapress.com.au
1 (877) 407-4847

Because of the dynamic nature of the Internet, any web addresses or links contained in
this book may have changed since publication and may no longer be valid. The views
expressed in this work are solely those of the author and do not necessarily reflect the
views of the publisher, and the publisher hereby disclaims any responsibility for them.

Any people depicted in stock imagery provided by Thinkstock are models,
and such images are being used for illustrative purposes only.
Certain stock imagery © Thinkstock.

Print information available on the last page.

ISBN: 978-1-4525-3026-0 (sc)
ISBN: 978-1-4525-3027-7 (e)

Balboa Press rev. date: 08/31/2015

Contents

Acknowledgements.. ix
Preface xi

PART ONE - REMEBERING 1

Recollections 3

   1. How it all began 5
   2. Getting a car and keeping it running in the Fifties 11
   3. Victoria's Bizarre Traffic Laws and Other Oddities 17
   4. A Lifelong Passion 25
   5. The Traffic Commission rewrites the rules............. 29
   6. Limiting Drivers' Blood Alcohol Concentration 33
   7. The problem out of control 37

Revolution 39

   8. New Beginnings 41
   9. Engineering, Medicine and Psychology to the Rescue............ 43
  10. The media lend a hand..51
  11. Record road deaths lead to compulsory seatbelt wearing......... 53
  12. The Final Meeting of the Australian Road Safety Council...... 55

Reform 57

  13. The Expert Group on Road Safety............................. 59
  14. The Road Safety Research Section 61

15. The National Review 65
16. The Expert Group's Report The Road — *Accident Situation in Australia in 1972* 69
17. The Expert Group's Report — *The Road Accident Situation in Australia in 1975* 73
18. The Road Safety and Standards Authority 79
19. Living one's work 85

Reincarnation 91

20. The Office of Road Safety 93
21. Black Spot Programs 97
22. Local Area Traffic Management 105
23. Public Education – a New Way 115
24. Priority Control at Intersections and the T-Junction Rule 125

Relocation 133

25. Along the Road to Gundagai 135
26. The House of Representatives Standing Committee on Road Safety 153
27. Driver Training and Licensing 161
28. Four Principles for Road Infrastructure 169
29. The Lost Cause 175
30. Marginalisation 183

Retirement 191

31. Consultancies and Submissions 193
32. Going Overseas 197
33. The Australasian College of Road Safety 211
34. Together Again 215
35. Letting Go 217

PART TWO - REFLECTING 223

Reflections 225

   36. Australia's Golden Hammer – Automated Enforcement 227
   37. The Meaning of the Yellow Traffic Light............................. 243
   38. Pedestrians at Traffic Lights.. 247
   39. Utility Poles..251
   40. Government Disdain for Private Mobility............................255
   41. The Railways: A Law unto Themselves................................ 261
   42. Compensation without Litigation 269
   43. Uniform Accident Information... 271
   44. Exemplary Drivers... 275
   45. Madcap to ANCAP.. 279

Resolution... 285

   46. The Seasons of Safety.. 287
   47. Vision Zero – the philosophy for the future, not
        just a target.. 295
   48. Protecting the Revolution 301

Appendix 307
Abbreviations 311

Acknowledgements

The assistance provided by the ACT Department of Territory and Municipal Services and the Justice and Community Safety Directorate towards the production of this work is gratefully acknowledged.

The enthusiasm for the project shown by David Quinlan as Manager, Road Safety, in the ACT Department of Territory and Municipal Services has been much appreciated

Thanks go to Robyn Schultz of Checkmate Proofreading who enthusiastically took on the role of midwife to this work, taking me along the final steps that enabled it to reach its final form.

The contribution made by Chris Wilson in dealing with my innumerable word processing problems along the way is also gratefully acknowledged.

Finally, special thanks go to Jennie, my dear wife of 56 years, who, in her own unique way, provided the ultimate incentive for me to finish this work by refusing to read a single word of it until it was finished!

Preface

It had been suggested to me many years ago by my colleagues at the Federal Office of Road Safety that I should write a history of road safety, having been actively involved since 1967. At that time, the toll of death and injury on Australia's roads was amongst the highest in the world on a population basis and getting worse. That was also the time when the revolution in thinking that would lead to the adoption of a scientific rather than a hectoring approach to the road accident problem was just getting under way – truly a watershed time for road safety.

In the years following my retirement, however, I felt that the momentum of the revolution was slowing and public policy was moving away from the concept of doing things *for* people to doing things *to* people. New measures were being directed against the population of drivers as a whole, as if it was just too hard to identify those who do not, will not, or cannot act responsibly. The lack of public understanding on the way the traffic system operated was also allowing the creation of a climate of fear about the road accident situation to justify ever more draconian measures. Perhaps a layman's guide was the way to go. This got as far as a table of contents and the odd chapter before it was interrupted by a number of medical problems.

Clearly what I had was an idea looking for a format. A history would have to be a comprehensive account of everything that had happened whilst there were areas that might not have had justice done to them in a layman's guide. Then I realised that what I could write was a motoring memoir - the story of what was then 55 years of driving written from one driver's perspective, one who had the good fortune to turn a personal interest into a career, surrounded by wonderful people from whom I could learn so much about so many things.

This then is my driving past.

Canberra 2015

PART ONE

REMEMBERING

Recollections

How it all began

Getting a car and keeping it
running in the Fifties

Victoria's bizarre traffic
rules and other oddities

A lifelong passion

The Traffic Commission rewrites the rules

Limiting drivers' Blood
Alcohol Concentration

The problem out of control

Chapter 1

How it all began

My life began in Melbourne just after the Wall Street stock market crash had plunged the world into the Great Depression that lasted through much of the 1930s. The depression delayed by almost two decades the age of mass mobility that had beckoned during the Roaring Twenties. Despite the setback, the same era saw the enclosed 'turret top' sedan replacing the 'tourer' with its fold-back canvas roof and snap-in celluloid windows.

I gained my driver's licence in 1950. By then the situation on the roads in Melbourne was already well on the way to getting out of hand. This was the result of years of neglect of the city by successive Country Party governments and the direction of resources towards the war effort, but in rural areas the situation was no better. As Geoffrey Blainey pointed out in *The Tyranny of Distance*, back in 1967, governments in Australia were more concerned about protecting the state-owned railways from competition by road hauliers than doing anything about the state of the roads; by contrast, privately owned railways in the United States were not protected in this way. To this day, any transport innovation that might induce a demand for travel, no matter how much the consumers ask for it, has been anathema to governments.

Thus, when the end of petrol rationing in 1950 ushered in the age of mass personal mobility, after the false dawn of the late 1930s, roads had fallen into disrepair and traffic controls were minimal. The roads were in fact more suited to the horse-drawn vehicles that were still the norm for the

5

baker, the milkman, the fuel merchant, the iceman and the greengrocer. As an example of the mindset, when clearways were introduced in the 1960s what set them apart was not that one could not stop or park; no, the difference was that one could not drive a horse-drawn vehicle on a clearway!

Even today, more than half a century on, many of the official attitudes to road safety still reflect a time when the general public had to be protected from the few show-offs using their new toy - the horseless carriage - as typified by Kenneth Grahame's Toad in *The Wind in the Willows*. Indeed, the general transport policy debate may have been better if that term had remained in use or even Henry Ford's descriptive term 'gasoline buggy'. Those who could afford it had always enjoyed private personal mobility, courtesy of the horse and carriage. Indeed, the top end of the market was known as 'the carriage trade'. The internal combustion engine simply democratized mobility, something that governments, and the environmental lobbyists, seem not to have comprehended.

When peace returned in 1945, road safety got off to a poor start. Nothing was in place or was put in place that might have prevented the carnage that was to follow and which, within the next quarter of a century, would see Australia in the unenviable situation of having close to the world's worst road traffic accident fatality rate.

The creation in 1946 of the Australian Road Safety Council (ARSC) at the initial meeting of the Australian Transport Advisory Council (ATAC), comprising State and Federal ministers with responsibilities for transport, certainly did little to help. Indeed, with its emphasis clearly on blaming the driver for all that was amiss on the roads, it probably did more harm than good by diverting attention away from the adoption of measures that might have produced positive results. The Council's efforts reached their nadir with the clanger "Don't cross the Styx in '56", as though people went out on the roads with the idea of doing so then or at any time in the near future!

ATAC created two other committees at the same time as the ARSC. The Australian Motor Vehicle Standards Committee (AMVSC) and the Australian Road Traffic Code Committee (ARTCC). The committees were all to be serviced by a secretariat in the Commonwealth Department of Shipping and Transport. The latter would later be renamed the Advisory

Committee on Road User Performance and Traffic Codes (ACRUPTC) reflecting an expanded remit and this was the committee with which I was to become intimately associated.

Before very long I realized that there were things that could be done that would make the roads safer for the people using them. This may seem like a presumptuous attitude for a novice driver, but it took only a little reading and the experience of driving outside Victoria to start asking why things were done so differently elsewhere. I also discovered, for example, that Tasmania had what we now call the T-junction rule.

In South Australia I found that one did not have to pull over to the left if you wanted to turn right, *anywhere*. I found there, too, that Stop signs meant what they did in the United Kingdom and Europe – stop and give way – and, as a result, drivers observed them. I also found that the speed limit in Adelaide was 35 mph [56 km/h], a figure higher than I had been used to. I was also impressed by the foreword to South Australia's Traffic Code booklet where the Commissioner for Police urged everyone to play the game according to the rules. A little more reading, this time of the road traffic accident fatality statistics, showed that despite not even having a practical driving test and a minimum licence age of 16 years, South Australia had the lowest fatality rate in Australia, and by a huge margin at that, but more of that later.

I still remember how I came upon the 1948 United Nations Convention on Road Traffic in the university library. In it I found that there were aids to safety that actually meant something – Give Way signs, and Stop signs like those in South Australia. Give Way signs would come to Australia much, much, later.

By now I had realized that driving could be an art and I devoured every book and motoring magazine article on the subject that I could lay my hands on. Then as I read one such book from the United Kingdom, I was surprised to find that there was no reference to any general rule of precedence at intersections in the United Kingdom comparable to the give-way-to-the- right rule that applied at *all* intersections in Victoria. We shall see later that, at law, not even the presence of traffic lights at an intersection could over-ride it; people may have thought it did but we shall see that the interpretation of traffic law here was literal rather than just, or even sensible.

In the UK most intersections (or junctions as they still call them) had traffic lights, Stop signs or Give Way signs. Even at the few junctions that were not so equipped, drivers were expected to realize which was the major road and if in any doubt to give way. As I was to find out many years later, the wise decision to adopt a major/minor system of intersection priority had resulted from a recommendation from the 1929 Royal Commission on Transport.

Much of Australia would persist with a general give-way-to-the-right rule for the best part of another 50 years, with disastrous results. Indeed, it was not until 1973 that the (advisory) National Road Traffic Code was amended to guarantee the status of priority accorded by traffic signals and only in 1974 did the Stop sign take on its international meaning of stop and give way.

Another source of driving information was the series of articles on the art of driving written by ace racing driver Sir Malcolm Campbell that were serialized in the Australian magazine *Motor Manual* at about the same time. From this source I learned the maxim that a blindfolded passenger should think that every control movement a driver makes is because they choose to make it rather than being forced to make it to avoid a collision. The corollary to this is that the more predictable the driving environment is the more likely it is that drivers will correctly anticipate the actions of others.

Looking back I saw that my mind had been directed towards an interest in roads and traffic even before I was old enough to learn to drive. Two things stand out: first, the distinctive cars owned by relatives even before the war and, secondly, the dangers anyone faced as a driver or a passenger at any of the intersections in the neighbourhood, especially the blind corner two doors down the street from my home.

My favourite uncle who had moved to Adelaide in 1923 drove a 1934 Ford V8 sedan – the first with such an engine. It was also the last with a semi-solid fabric roof. This was replaced on the next year's model by the all-steel roof that was about to become the norm. This represented perhaps the first great advance for safety in vehicle design with occupants now contained within a steel cage for the first time, albeit with dangerous internal projections and doors that could fly open in a crash.

It would be fair to say that I set out later to emulate my uncle's exemplary driving record. Driving every day for more than 50 years, including frequent work trips to the Barossa Valley, he had only two accidents: one in the 1940s and the other not long before he died in 1978.

More spectacular, if less practical, was the monstrous red machine housed in my father's garage for the duration of the war by another uncle. This was a Stutz Bearcat, an American sports car from the Twenties replete with a huge wooden steering wheel, manual [ignition] advance and retard, crank handle, outside handbrake and four cylinders the size of paint pots. My aunt would tell the story of how my uncle had got the Stutz back in working order and as a surprise took it to pick her up after church. Far from being pleased, she roused at him for embarrassing her with the loud putt, putt, putt from the Stutz as it made its way up the steep hill to the church.

By the mid-1960s the results of pioneering research into what was actually killing and injuring people in road traffic accidents were starting to become publicly known. These included the life-saving potential of seatbelts for vehicle occupants and helmets for motorcyclists. The critical role of alcohol as a contributing factor in accident occurrence was also coming to public attention. Research undertaken by the newly established Australian Road Research Board (ARRB) was also starting to make an impact. Insights from psychology about how road users perceived situations were starting to be taken into account. One notable instance of this related to the first stage of Melbourne's first freeway, opened in 1964: when its signage was critically examined in a study by Colin Cameron and numerous deficiencies were uncovered. This perhaps marked the start of a new approach to communication with road users that led over time to the establishment of an Australian Standard for road signs and signals. ARRB also sponsored Australia's first in-depth study of road accidents conducted in Adelaide in the years 1963 to 1965 that would have far-reaching effects on the way the road accident situation would be handled.

On 2 August 1967 I left the Australian Broadcasting Control Board (ABCB) where I worked for some years as a statistical officer having decided that I would either have to grow old there or move on. The position that I took up the next day with the then Department of Shipping and Transport (DST) was again of a statistical nature providing information to the ARSC. I had seen the position advertised a couple of years before but had decided not to apply on that occasion because I did not want to work for an organisation that was so ineffectual and misguided, but more on that later.

Chapter 2

Getting a car and keeping it running in the Fifties

Around age seven I suffered an accident that resulted in my parents becoming over-protective, so much so that I was never allowed to have a bicycle. In return, however, I was promised that when I was old enough they would buy a car.

The big day arrived towards the end of 1950. The brand-new moss green, fully imported, Austin A40 we had chosen was the first all-new car to be produced in Britain after World War II. It had independent front suspension by coil springs and a four-cylinder 10 hp overhead valve engine of 1200 cc capacity.

Being technically advanced for its time, however, presented problems for its owners, notably its inability to run smoothly on the poor quality petrol at the time. This had been quite suitable for cars of pre-war design and even for the new Holden – marketed as "Australia's own car" - that had been released in 1947. Indeed, the truly classic and still modern-looking 850 cc Morris Minor, on which I learned to drive, retained a pre-war side-valve engine, a new version of which was even used in the larger six-seater Morris Oxford introduced in 1949.

The A40 featured a compression ratio of 7.2:1 that was exceeded only by the MG TD roadster. Although low by today's standards, the compression ratio was high for its time and was meant to enhance performance and fuel economy, but not when it had to contend with 68 octane (yes 68!) petrol. In those days there was no 'super'. By comparison, today's standard fuel is 92 octane. It only occurred to me very recently that the problem in 1950 was that the technology had simply outstripped the available fuel.

The A40 engine was therefore prone to the phenomenon known as 'pinging' when straining to climb a hill, a sign that the engine timing was not right. To avoid damage it was necessary to change down on hills that today's cars would barely notice. Moreover, unburnt fuel built up on the tops of the pistons and fouled the spark plugs. Another problem was that the petrol was often dirty. Grit would block the jets that supplied the carburettor in which petrol was mixed with air to fuel the engine. Taking the bowl off the carburettor, cleaning it and blowing through the brass jets was a regular chore. So was scraping the hard carbon build-up off the spark plugs and then resetting them to the correct gap with a tool called a feeler gauge. This consisted of a graduated series of thin flexible metal strips of different thicknesses that one matched to the required spark plug gap. What was beyond the knowledgeable amateur, however, was the legendary 'de-coke' that involved taking off the cylinder head and scraping the carbon build-up off the tops of the pistons. Over its first 60, 000 km the family A40 required this on five occasions and it was not cheap.

Today, too, we take it for granted that if one pushes the clutch pedal in and moves the gear lever to the selected position the gearbox will change up or down. It was not always so. The modern gearbox has a system of parallel gear shafts along which run gears of the appropriate ratio ready to be slotted into place in a split-second – the 'synchromesh' gearbox. Indeed, these have been standard since World War II.

After the invention of synchromesh the previous form of manual gearbox was colloquially referred to as a 'crash box', for reasons that will become obvious in a moment. Before the synchromesh gearbox if one wanted to change down one had to push in the clutch, rev up the engine to what you *hoped* was the right speed, re-engage the clutch and move the gear lever through the 'gate'. This procedure was called 'double-declutching'. Although no longer needed routinely, the skill was regarded as worth cultivating and some drivers would show off by double-declutching. The synchromesh gearbox may have become standard but it still did not cover first gear, as this was regarded as the gear you only used to move the car off. Nevertheless, the performance of some small cars in the early 1950's was so poor that it could still be necessary to double-declutch from second gear down to first to get up hills if the car was fully laden. Indeed, I recall seeing a 1000 cc Ford Prefect being reversed up Queens Park hill in Geelong in 1955 because it could not climb the road in first, reverse being lower geared.

All this meant that if you wanted to keep the car running reliably you had to learn a fair bit about how it worked. It is a tribute to modern automotive engineering that so many people can drive around without having any idea of what is going on under the bonnet.

How many people even know, or are taught, or even care, that the clutch is a device for connecting something (the engine) that is going around very fast to things that are stationary (the wheels). It certainly would have saved me and probably other learners a lot of embarrassment if someone had explained to me that this was what a 'clutch' was for. Basically, the clutch enables the driver to slowly bring the large plate at the front end of the gearbox that is not moving into contact with the large plate at the back of the engine that is moving very fast so that you can move off smoothly. Usually the two plates are kept together by powerful springs except when you press down on the clutch pedal, as you need to do when changing gears. Pressing on the clutch pedal separates the two plates which you must now bring together again by gradually reducing the pressure on the clutch pedal (Somewhat confusingly, this is known as letting the clutch 'in' when you are actually moving your foot out). Unless the uptake is done very smoothly the car will jerk or, worse still, the sudden shock will stall the engine, which does it no good at all. I had enormous difficulty with the clutch and did so-called 'kangaroo hops' every time I wanted to move off. Once I got the hang of it, however, I could fully engage the clutch while the car moved forward only 25 cm.

Today we often speak of 'modifying a car', providing of course that it is legal to do so. This tends to mean things like lowering the suspension, putting on 'widies' or fitting sports 'shocks'. In earlier times, however, it was more likely to involve enhancing performance. A University friend got into this big time, undertaking the not unsubstantial task of 'polishing the ports' (the valve seats) to improve airflow through the engine and 'planing' the underside of the cylinder head to make it thinner so as to increase the compression ratio. All his efforts produced an A40 that, flat out, could do 125 km/h (as opposed to an unmodified A40's 115 km/h). When a Holden straight out of the showroom could do 130 km/h without being touched, this seemed like a lot of effort for very little result. There was a saying among the enthusiasts of the day - 'Give me the cubes', a reference to cubic capacity – the bigger will be better. I learned a valuable lesson from this. There were indeed better things to do around cars than think about performance or do more than attend to the basics.

Long before I joined DST I had taken steps to make my Austin A40 a bit safer. When I became aware that the protruding sharp-edged glove box knob in my Austin A40 could cause unnecessary injury in a crash I promptly removed it. Not long after I put in an element-type plug-in demister (cars even then had cigarette lighters!) and a set of windscreen washers.

Another thing I had done to the A40 to make it safer was to equip it with what were known as 'safety rims'. This involved modifying of the wheel well, into which the tyres fit, by having a groove cold-rolled into the wheel that matched the profile of the tyre wall. In conventional rims of the time it was only the pressure of the air in the tyre that held it in place. In the event of a blowout, much more common in the days of cross-ply tyres, the tyre would slip out of the well and roll around this way and that under the rim making control all but impossible, especially if the blowout involved a front tyre. In one notable case the former champion Australian swimmer John Marshall died when a front tyre blew out on a country road in Victoria. The safety rim is now the accepted form of rim and my uncle from Adelaide probably owed his survival in a blowout on the open road in the 1960s to being able to retain control of his Mark 7 Jaguar. It is quite a contrast to earlier times that the new low-profile tyres can in fact be run flat for a time!

Among the better things to do around cars was to learn how to be a good driver, a theme to be taken up shortly. Suffice to say at this point that it was at the very beginning of my driving career that I began to realise that the emphasis placed on mastery of clutch and gears was putting manipulative skill ahead of learning how to interact with other road users and the driving environment.

The next car, an original 1960 XK Ford Falcon, the epitome of the modern light six with a 2.4 litre in-line engine, was notable for its very large "deep-dished" steering wheel. This feature was shown in the first Adelaide in-depth study of 1963 to 1965 to produce significantly fewer chest injuries in crashes, in comparison to a conventional wheel, which in combination with a rigid steering column was indeed 'a spearing wheel'. Energy-absorbing (or so-called collapsible) steering columns would be developed later on.

Not long before joining DST I had fitted the Falcon with six seatbelts, a move assisted by the public spirited offer of free fitting at Ampol service stations in response to the toll of death and injury that was spiralling out of control. I would soon be glad to have installed the seatbelts when an improperly closed rear door sprang open during a left turn and only the wearing of a seatbelt saved one of my children from falling out of the car. I had in fact been sensitised to that danger by an incident on a street near where I grew up when a young woman fell out in similar circumstances and died from her injuries.

Anyone fortunate enough to have been protected by the change in steering wheel design owes it to Robert S McNamara (yes that one!) who a few years earlier had been head of the Ford Division of the Ford Motor Company. McNamara had taken seriously the mounting evidence that the means existed to reduce the toll of death and injury in automobile accidents by modifications to vehicle design such as the deep-dished steering wheel, better door locks, the 'padding' of instrument panels with energy-absorbing material, and the installation of seatbelts.

The rest of the automotive industry resented the intrusion of safety into their comfort zone and General Motors in particular led the charge with the now well known line that "in 1956 Ford sold safety but Chevy sold cars", something that sales data would later show to be incorrect. This controversy was seminal, however, to the debate, marking as it did a sea change in the way the industry looked at safety.

Events and attitudes of the time were what led consumer rights activist Ralph Nader to pen his historically significant expose of the US motor vehicle industry *Unsafe at Any Speed,* published in 1965, and cited by the journal *Science* as "Likely to be the *Silent Spring* of traffic safety". Not only did Nader excoriate the automobile industry but he also pointed to the *unholy alliance* between that industry, the National Safety Council and government that let the industry 'off the hook' by putting the whole accident problem down to driver error and poor attitude.

Chapter 3

Victoria's Bizarre Traffic Laws and Other Oddities

Imagine a place where if you wanted to turn right you had to move to the left and wait until all traffic from in front and from behind had gone by; a place where you had to get out of your vehicle and go around the back to turn on your tail light; where trams had no rear lights; and where you could only park on the left in a one-way street.

Victoria was indeed a strange place to drive a car in the early 1950s. Some of its traffic laws were unique, not just in Australia, but in the world. Indeed, one of Britain's leading motoring journals devoted an entire article to the subject. An echo of that time can be seen in the Melbourne CBD to this day in the form of the so-called 'hook turn', which disappeared from the rest of the world in the late 1920s. In short, Victoria was a laughing stock.

So grave was the situation that the Melbourne City Council brought one of the most respected traffic engineers from the United States, D Grant Mickle, to advise on what might be done to improve the situation. It might be noted that it was not the state government but the city council that took the initiative. Here is what he had to say about the situation, as reported in the *The Argus* newspaper of 12 October 1954,

> The laws governing traffic were often confusing and
> ambiguous. Contradictions appeared as law was piled

upon law without the cancellation of previous ones. Laws governing traffic should be simplified and made more uniform. There should be adequate understanding of the problem amongst influential groups to ensure public support for changes.

Turning on tail-lights from outside the vehicle

I mention this first because it was the most ludicrous, being both overtly dangerous and having nothing to do with road safety. The law required that any tail-light switch inside a motor vehicle be disconnected and a switch fitted at the rear of the vehicle. The reason: so that burglars and other miscreants fleeing from crime scenes would not be able to turn off the tail-light and evade capture! Despite drivers being crushed between vehicles at dusk the rule persisted into 1954. Moreover, unless a vehicle was parked near a streetlight, both the parking lights and the tail-lights had to be left on. At this time there were no such things as reflectors.

The story of how rear reflectors came to be required is one of the most tragic in the sorry history of road travel in Australia. Five young people were killed when the Austin A40 in which they were travelling slammed into the rear of a tray truck parked on the Nepean Highway at night without lights. I had particular reason to remember the incident as a friend of mine had been with them earlier in the night. It should be remembered that at this time the highway, if it could be dignified by that name, consisted of a single strip of bitumen marked into three lanes with no street lighting. The public outrage that followed led quickly to a requirement for the fitting of red rear reflectors and the simultaneous repeal of the law that prevented tail-lights being switched on from within the vehicle.

With street lighting remaining poor throughout the 1950s I found myself stopping on my way home to wipe clean the reflectors on one particular truck that was regularly parked at night without lights. Continuing problems with truck illumination led, later, to the fitting of the now familiar rear marker plates on heavy vehicles. Nevertheless, the contribution that has been made to road safety by improved street lighting, commencing in the 1960s, is rarely ever mentioned, though more on that later

Hook turns

For those not familiar with Melbourne, a hook turn requires a driver wishing to turn right to move into the extreme *left* lane and remain there until traffic coming from *behind* as well as from the opposite direction passed before turning. In 1950, this was the rule *everywhere* in Victoria, but there was one exception. As it happened, this was only a short walk from where I grew up: the intersection of Dandenong Road and Warrigal Road in Oakleigh where the road layout at the time rendered hook turns impracticable.

Today, although puzzling to visitors, hook turns are still required at a few intersections in the heart of Melbourne where tramlines intersect. This is the remaining carry-over from the time in 1954 when the hook turn rule was changed in most places in Victoria but initially retained where there were intersecting tramlines.

The rule's most bizarre manifestation, however, was at the intersection of Wellington Parade, the eastern continuation of Flinders Street, and Brunton Avenue, the road that runs alongside the MCG. Until the first section of the South-eastern Freeway was opened in 1964 Brunton Avenue carried much of the traffic heading to and from the southeastern suburbs. Until the law was changed to allow right turns from the centre of the road, traffic going straight ahead would be held at a red light while cars turning right from next to the kerb moved across their path on a green arrow.

No parking on the right in one-way streets

It also happened that the first one-way street system in Melbourne outside the CBD was introduced in the Oakleigh shopping centre. I was therefore able to follow, in the local *Caulfield and Oakleigh Times*, the bizarre administration of parking regulations. At the time, there was no provision in the traffic laws for parking on the right-hand side of a one-way street, nor signs that might have allowed it. So, (in the days before Traffic and Parking Infringement Notices) at each sitting of the Oakleigh Court of Petty Sessions there would be a regular procession of drivers who had parked on the right-hand side of the street. The charge was of having *parked more than ten inches from the kerb,* the left-hand kerb that is! (Ten inches [25 cm], not one foot, was the maximum distance out from the kerb specified in the law).

It might be mentioned that at this time there were few parking signs, as we know them today. Parking controls were either set out in the general traffic law, such as not parking close to intersections, or location-by-location in local council by-laws with signs erected accordingly. This is in contrast to the 'sign post law' we have today. How this change came as part of a general traffic reform process will be picked up in another chapter.

No specific speed limit in built-up areas and a *prima facie* limit elsewhere

Administration of such speed regulations as there were was equally bizarre. At this time there was no speed limit in built-up areas Prosecutions for driving too fast depended on a regulation that one could not drive through an intersection faster than 25 mph (42 km/h). Enforcement, as it still is today, was directed to main roads and the offence of driving too fast was prosecuted on the basis of having passed through or, as was more often the case, past a side street at a speed in excess of 25 mph.

It was not until 1954 that a general speed limit of 30 mph (48 km/h) was applied in built-up areas as defined by the presence of provision for street lighting.

Under the new laws there was some provision for speed zoning to 40 mph. Residents along the roads concerned often resented this. On two well-publicised occasions citizens literally took the law into their own hands chopping down the offending signs. Photographs of two such incidents found their way onto the front page of *The Argus*, the long-established morning daily newspaper that ceased publication in 1955. (When The Argus building in Elizabeth Street was converted into offices, I worked there during the 1960s.)

It might be noted that on the open road in Victoria, and in a number of other states, there was a speed limit of sorts – prima facie limit of 50 mph (80 km/h) and this was maintained for many years after the 30 mph limit was applied in built-up areas. A driver might escape conviction for exceeding 50 mph if they could show that their speed was reasonable having regard to all the circumstances. Such a defence rarely succeeded. I recall one notable case reported in the *Geelong Advertiser* in 1955 when I was working and living there. A police motorcycle patrol officer had followed a driver for some miles on the Melbourne-Geelong Road one morning and had then apprehended him for travelling in excess of 50mph. When the case came to court the constable gave evidence that there was little traffic at the time and that the driver had done nothing to endanger anyone. The magistrate, a Mr Steedman, nevertheless imposed a hefty fine! More than fifty years on one must question whether the near-zero risk of crashing on the safest rural roads, the grade-separated rural freeways, receives any consideration when speed limits are being set.

Bear in mind also that in the 1950s and for decades later, there was no priority control at intersections in Victoria other than traffic lights, and minimal traffic control elsewhere. Indeed, the situation was much the same in most of Australia, but that too is a story to be taken up later. The consequences of having drivers racing through local street intersections at even 25 mph without slowing down and going even faster through rural cross-roads, however, were frightening and inevitably contributed in large part to Australia being declared by the World Health Organisation in 1966 to have the world's worst road traffic accident fatality rate, per capita.

Not making a third line of traffic

As I said earlier there were few road markings other than centre lines in the 1950s and certainly no lane lines. In such a situation, overtaking presented no problem, but at that time when roads usually had only one lane in each direction, the idea of ranging up alongside a vehicle that was already overtaking so as to make a third line of traffic time would indeed be downright dangerous. As usual, there were situations where the rule itself was simply nonsensical. By 1956, the year of the Melbourne Olympic Games, Wellington Parade, the major route for traffic heading towards the main stadium, the MCG, had been made one-way. I well remember sitting in my office in Spring Street and hearing police loudspeakers reminding drivers that it was an offence to make a third line of traffic, despite there being ample room. No doubt the embarrassment this caused, and the coming of lane lines, forced the repeal of the rule.

No overtaking on the left

In the absence of lane lines, this rule too made some sense, but not where traffic had to queue at traffic lights. If one driver had already pulled up a car's width from the kerb no one was allowed to move into this space, and so on back down the queue. My first driving licence test was abruptly terminated when I did just that as I arrived second at the red light and pulled up alongside a car that was already there.

Trams without rear lights

Whether or not one thinks trams are a good idea or not, Melbourne has them and is likely to have them for the foreseeable future. Back in the 1950s, however, they presented a frightening hazard during the hours of darkness. Alone among road vehicles they had *no* tail-lights, not even the light left on in the empty driver's cabin. Many years would pass before the issue of visibility of Melbourne's trams would be addressed. What made this even more remarkable was that the State Electricity Commission of Victoria, the operator of the tramway systems in Geelong, Ballarat and Bendigo, all since closed, had responded much earlier. Their trams had black and yellow diagonal striping, above and below the driver's window and along the bumper bar. A white band was also painted directly above the single headlight, which was illuminated by concealed lighting as appropriate to the direction of travel.

It would take the investigation of a perplexing series of accidents where vehicles had driven *head-on into oncoming trams* to shift the Melbourne and Metropolitan Tramways Board (MMTB), under its legendary chairman Sir Robert Risson, from its stance that it had no responsibility to make its vehicles more visible from the rear.

The peculiar nature of the accidents engaged the interest of researchers at the newly established ARRB. While it was known that a number of the car drivers involved had consumed alcohol in the time leading up to their crash, the researchers delved deeper, looking to see what other factors may have contributed. The clue to the true nature of the problem lay in the fact that most of the accidents had occurred in strip shopping centres, common in the suburbs. This led to a remarkable conclusion: that a driver following a tram would mistake the *interior lights* of the tram seen through the windows on its *right-hand-side* (that nearest the centre of the road) for the lights of *shop windows on the left-hand side* of the road. Thinking, mistakenly, that they could be too close to something on their *left*, drivers would move to the *right*, directly into the path of any oncoming tram.

The problem was then how to get the MMTB to light the rear of its trams. How this was achieved was a good case of knowing the right people. In 1970, there was to be a ceremony to open the first section of the Tullamarine Freeway, to which all the usual dignitaries were invited. The chairman of the construction authority, the then Country Roads Board, arranged the seating so that the Executive Director of the ARRB would be seated next to Sir Robert and the rest as they say is history. Trams were fitted with tail-lights and the crashes stopped. .

Innovative Traffic Signal Designs

A distinctive feature of street furniture in Melbourne suburbs in the 1950s was the Marshall (brand) traffic lights. In addition to the usual red-yellow-green displays there were large circular clock-faces mounted high above the control cabinet, one for each direction, around which a hand moved with a light corresponding to the segment of the clock-face – green-yellow-red. The Marshall signals were popular with drivers because they knew exactly when their green phase was coming to an end. In addition to their use at intersections, the pedestrian-operated traffic signals outside the Aspendale, Edithvale, Chelsea and Bonbeach train stations were of this type and pedestrians also benefited from knowing exactly how much time they had to cross the road. The big drawback of the Marshall signals was that they could not be incorporated into co-ordinated signals systems and they gradually disappeared from the scene.

In Geelong in the 1950s there was another form of traffic signal. Suspended above the centre of the main intersections in the CBD were signals consisting of green and red horizontal bars. As with the Marshall signals, they were popular with the public but suffered the same incompatibility with co-ordinated systems and they too disappeared from the scene. Strangely enough, all these years on, a 'countdown' system of bars is under consideration to improve the compliance with pedestrians with 'walk/don't walk' signals

The user-friendly nature of the Marshall and the bar signal designs that gave drivers and pedestrians exact information about how much longer they had to cross before the red signal appeared provides a stark contrast to the harshness with which the law relating to the yellow indication is enforced today.

Red and yellow on together in traffic lights

On a lighter note, older readers may recall a British radio comedy in which a not very bright character complains that being able to see the lights of Balham is about the only thing that gives him any pleasure: "green, yellow, red, red and amber".

Visitors to the UK will have noticed that this is indeed the sequence of traffic lights in the UK. The red and yellow (as we now call amber) 'get ready' indication was actually used for a short time in Victoria in the mid-1960s and was appreciated by drivers who did in fact get away slightly earlier, so improving traffic flow. Some drivers probably moved off too early, leading to the practice being discontinued. The years since have seen the general adoption of the all-red inter-green period at traffic lights. This reduces the likelihood of danger should a driver move off too early. Perhaps this is why the red and amber is still used in the UK.

Chapter 4

A Lifelong Passion

There could hardly have been a better place to develop in interest in roads at an early age than the suburb of Oakleigh lying ten miles (16 km) southeast of Melbourne. Originally it had been the place where the stagecoaches that linked the eastern province of Gippsland to Melbourne would stop for fresh horses to be harnessed for the next *stage* to Dandenong, nine miles further on. The original village had grown up not at a crossroads, which was more common, but around a hotel that had first been located by a spring on nearby Scotchmans Creek to serve the market gardening and fruit growing community, but was moved up the hill when the road went through.

With the arrival of the motor age the stagecoach route became part of what is now Princes Highway East, but still referred to as Dandenong Road. My parent's house was only a block away. At the other end of our street was the Gippsland railway line with its attendant 'Trespassers prosecuted' sign. The railway, having come later, simply sliced the existing street in two. The coming of the railway also had a significant influence on the layout of the suburb-to-be.

It had been expected that the railway between Caulfield and Oakleigh would follow Dandenong Road taking it through the village. Dandenong Road had been surveyed as a 'three-chain' (60 metre) road, one of many in the then rural areas around Melbourne. These generous reservations, as wide as a modern freeway, were to prevent the situation ever occurring again whereby the grand boulevards Robert Hoddle had placed in early Melbourne ran into notoriously narrow and increasingly congested streets in the first ring of suburbs, such as Sydney Road in Brunswick.

Oakleigh benefited from this new policy and its wide main street, replete with central plantation, received the name Broadwood Street, and later Broadway, rather than being called Dandenong Road. Oakleigh was approached from Melbourne in a sweeping curve to intersect with what is now Warrigal Highway. In the early days Warrigal Road ran through small-farming and orchard country from Box Hill some six miles to the north and the same distance south to the beach at Mentone, passing through market gardens in the 'sand belt', now famous for its golf courses.

In the event, the railway took a different course and with it the village. By the time I was old enough to remember, Broadway was something of a time capsule, albeit a major traffic artery. There was still the odd shop, a large bakery, two pubs, the ice works and a bank, to show what it had been. A kilometre to the south was the new Oakleigh, centred on the railway station and laid out in a grid of what would be thought of today as fashionably narrow shopping streets, a feature that still makes it a rarity in the Melbourne of strip shopping centres.

The Oakleigh environment provided the ideal setting for someone who would later spend half his adult life in road safety. It certainly did not take long to learn what an accident sounded like and what it looked like. Paddington Road, where I lived, was a convenient shortcut off Dandenong Road to Warrigal Road that avoided the major intersection. Two doors down from the family home was Euston Road that remains a convenient east-west route to Hughesdale shopping centre and railway station. Crashes at the corner were a regular phenomenon, almost as common as the visits of the Salvation Army band that played there on some Sunday evenings. On two successive mornings, as I was going to the station on my way to work, the same two cars missed each other by inches. In those days traffic control devices on side streets were unheard of and that would remain so until the mid 1970s.

I was also alerted early to the virtues of higher-standard street lighting. Dandenong Road was lit by sodium vapour (yellow) lights, but only as far out as the corner where Chadstone Shopping Centre (built on the site of the Convent of the Good Shepherd) now stands. On foggy winter nights, aircraft could be heard circling around, perhaps taking their bearings from the end of the bright lights.

The intersection of Dandenong Road and Warrigal Road, just up the hill from the original hostelry, was notable for a particular reason. Only at this one intersection in the whole of Victoria was one allowed to turn right from the centre of the road. The geometry of the intersection at the time made compliance with the hook turn rule all but impossible for drivers travelling from Melbourne and wishing to turn right down Warrigal Road. From Caulfield, some six km away, the centre carriageway of Dandenong Road was flanked by two service roads used only by local traffic. On the other side of the intersection, Broadway had a wide central reservation. The hook turn rule tended to be honoured in the breach until frequent, and sometimes fatal, accidents rendered the situation intolerable and traffic lights were installed in 1953.

Because of the heavy volume of traffic turning into Warrigal Road in both directions, three-phase lights, a rarity at the time, were installed. On two approaches were large black-on-yellow signs, announcing on Dandenong Road 'Right turn from centre lane' and on Broadway 'Right turn from right lane'. Also of note was that the traffic lights were vehicle-actuated with vehicles passing over pneumatic detectors set into the road surface – forerunners of today's induction loops - rather than operating to fixed cycles.

It is not difficult to see the accident potential of Oakleigh's grid pattern shopping centre, with its numerous blind corners, in the days of the give-way-to-the–right rule. The local council therefore created the first one-way street system outside of the Melbourne CBD. It is still in place today, with Eaton Street now a mall.

On the northern edge of the shopping centre, Atherton Road was the site of one of the first sets of pedestrian-operated traffic lights in the metropolitan area, near its intersection with Eaton Street. There had been an earlier set outside the Middle Brighton Baths but they had been removed after their misuse by children played havoc with motor traffic and the trams that then ran along St Kilda Street. By a remarkable coincidence, the baths were where students at the small middle school I attended were taken for swimming lessons and the long bus trip familiarised me with parts of Melbourne that I would not otherwise have seen. I even encountered what I think would have been a unique set of railway crossing gates on McKinnon Road at McKinnon station – they literally folded up.

The influence of these antecedents in the development of my career as a road safety practitioner will become evident as the story of my driving past unfolds.

Chapter 5

The Traffic Commission rewrites the rules

Looking back it is hard to believe the number of people who died on Victoria's and indeed Australia's roads in the 1950s when motorisation ran at a fraction of what it is today, but with the number of vehicles growing each year. Moreover, such was the severity of these accidents that the radio broadcasts usually referred to the victims having been 'killed instantly' rather than 'died at the scene' or 'were dead on arrival at hospital'. It was not unusual for car doors to fly open because of the poor design of the latches, especially when both side doors were hinged on the pillar beside the driver. It is not surprising that the medical profession would soon be at the forefront of the clamour for something to be done.

By 1956 the Victorian government was moved to establish the Traffic Commission appointing as its chairman a well-regarded member of the Country Roads Board (CRB), Mr J D Thorpe, with Mr J G Westland, previously a city engineer, as deputy. (For many years the Country Roads Board's jurisdiction had continued into the metropolitan area where State highways were concerned).

Jack Thorpe proved to be a skilled administrator and changes were soon in evidence. At his farewell address as retiring chairman he recalled how the then premier, the redoubtable Henry Bolte (later Sir Henry), gave him his riding orders which were "to do something about the road toll without spending any money". Easier said than done, but Jack Thorpe was equal to the task.

The first step was to introduce what he referred to as 'signpost law', a concept taken for granted now, but new at the time. First to be tackled were parking restrictions. It is hard to believe now but at that time, at least in Victoria, the beginning and end of every parking zone along a street had to be individually notified in accordance with council by-laws. I have already referred to the farcical situation with regard to parking on both sides of a one-way street in Oakleigh.

Next on the reform agenda were the traffic laws themselves that were scattered over a number of pieces of legislation. These were soon organised into one Act of parliament and popularly referred to as the Victorian Traffic Code. So successful was the consolidation that its format would soon be adopted as the model for the National Road Traffic Code (NRTC) then under consideration by the Australian Road Traffic Code Committee (ARTCC) that operated under the aegis of the ministerial council, ATAC.

I have already referred to one remnant of 'the bad old days' that still finds a use today, namely the hook turn. Initially the hook turn was prescribed for all intersections where tramlines intersected. Compliance with that rule required an encyclopaedic knowledge of the tramway system if one was to be able to approach an intersection along a tramline in the correct position to make a right-turn. The rule was soon relegated to a small number of intersections in the Melbourne CBD where it still applies.

The power to regulate traffic on a day-to-day basis that used to reside with the various municipal councils (except for state highways) was gradually transferred to the Traffic Commission that had set about developing 'warrants' by which the need for traffic lights at individual intersections could be dealt with on a uniform basis. Later this would be extended to cover 'major traffic control devices' that in the fullness of time would come to include regulatory signs.

In an important development in terms of safety the Traffic Commission was also empowered to administer a new subsidy scheme for traffic lights. The take-up, however, was patchy but I was fortunate to live in an area whose council acted ahead of time on traffic lights, something I will return to later.

One notable 'turf war' that persisted for years was between the Traffic Commission and the Melbourne City Council, whose jurisdiction extended well beyond the CBD into North Melbourne and East Melbourne, that in the 19th century were originally known as Hotham Hill and Eastern Hill. South Melbourne, however, had its own council until 1994 and this led to some interesting confrontations over the effect of the Westgate Bridge and its approaches.

The Traffic Commission, however, did not have the power to compel other councils to act on traffic control matters. Perhaps the most notable example was how the installation of traffic lights at Camberwell Junction was held up for years because the council that had authority over one side of Burke Road, a major shopping strip, would not give up the parking spaces that would have had to go if traffic lights were installed. Camberwell Junction epitomised the chaotic state of Melbourne's roads when I started to drive: an unsignalised six-way intersection with five of the legs carrying tramlines. Indeed, that situation persisted into the 1970s.

Even an organisation with no direct responsibility in traffic control matters could frustrate attempts to improve safety. In one such case, the electricity authority denied the use of its poles to carry the cable needed to co-ordinate the operation of two adjacent sets of traffic lights. These were in place where the 20 km-long major north-south traffic artery, Warrigal Road (that I referred to earlier), ends at a T-intersection with Canterbury Road and traffic has to turn to reach Union Road to continue north.

When Jack Thorpe retired Jim Westland took charge and was in that position when I joined DST. In 1983, in line with the greater powers that the Traffic Commission had been given by that time, it was retitled the Road Traffic and Safety Authority (RoSTA). Some years later RoSTA was itself absorbed into the roads authority now known as VicRoads.

On the retirement of Jim Westland his position was filled by Peter (A P) Vulcan who, as we shall see, had a pivotal role when, in 1970, the federal government appointed the Expert Group on Road Safety to spearhead its new, more widely focussed, role in the field. It is to get ahead of the story, but nevertheless typical of Peter's collegial style of leadership, that his first step upon taking up his role as head of RoSTA was to visit every city and shire in Victoria in order to gain their support for the initiatives he had in mind.

Chapter 6

Limiting Drivers' Blood Alcohol Concentration

Long before I joined DST I was only too well aware of the problem posed by drink-driving and the difficulties involved in proving it in the event of an accident. I recall listening to the 9pm news on the radio when an aunt was visiting and we heard that a neighbour's son had been killed in a collision in rural Victoria. It was thought that the other driver was under the influence of alcohol, but the case against him was dismissed.

These were the days when people could only be convicted of drink-driving if they showed physical signs – 'rolling drunk' – with subjective evidence, such as the inability to walk a straight line or slurred speech, all that could be presented as evidence.

The situation in Victoria was not aided by the fact that it was possible for 'bona fide travellers', but not others, to be served alcohol on a Sunday if they had travelled more than 20 miles. The hotel on the Princes Highway at Hallam just beyond Dandenong, for example, became a favourite destination for serious drinkers. The combination of six o'clock closing and the absence of anything like adequate street lighting was a lethal combination, especially in the winter months.

What made the biggest difference was the development of a reliable device for assessing a person's blood alcohol concentration (BAC) by means of a breath test rather than a blood test. This was the 'Breathalyzer' invented by Dr Robert F Borkenstein, Professor of Police Administration at the University of Indiana, USA. His work also showed the sharp rise in the likelihood of crashing once BAC exceeded 0.08 gm of alcohol per 100 ml of blood.

Evidence of noticeable impairment in driving performance at a BAC above 0.05 was later provided by a study conducted by two psychologists from the University of New South Wales, Professor S H Lovibond and Mr K Bird. This involved a sample of rally drivers and drivers drawn from members of the public - the Warwick Farm Project - named after the Sydney racecourse where it was conducted. Impairment at the 0.05 level was particularly noticeable in the less skilled non-competition drivers, but the rally drivers had lost their skill advantage by about the 0.06 level.

I had become aware early of how alcohol consumption could be a problem for pedestrians as well when a neighbour of my parents was killed crossing the road after leaving a pub on Broadway in Oakleigh, one of which I mentioned earlier. That was in 1955, almost ten years before the notorious 'six o'clock swill' would be ended with the coming of 10 o'clock closing. Good street lighting that may have made the accident less likely was virtually non-existent in most parts of the cities.

One name stands out in the history of how the drink-driving problem was finally brought under control – the Victoria Police Surgeon, John Birrell, who died only a few years ago. He was indeed at the sharp end of the problem.

Legislation was soon put in place that in 1966 saw Tasmania and then Victoria take the unprecedented step of setting a maximum *prescribed blood alcohol limit* for drivers. This made it an offence to operate a vehicle on the road with a blood alcohol concentration in excess of 0.05 in Victoria and initially 0.08 in Tasmania. Other jurisdictions followed, generally specifying 0.08. In 1976 Victoria also introduced random breath testing, well in advance of the other states and territories. In the years since, additional restrictions have been placed on drivers' BAC for different classes of driver, a process started by Tasmania with novice drivers. The level is generally 0.02 or zero.

The path to reform of the laws relating to drink-driving, however, was not an easy one. A *Four Corners* special on the drink-driving problem screened about the time that the New South Wales government was considering following Victoria's lead in setting a maximum BAC limit on drivers, showed dramatically the casual attitude of patrons in a suburban Sydney pub that it was all right to "have a few drinks" and still drive. "One for the road" took a long time to disappear from popular parlance.

The coming of random breath testing, and the hospital testing of accident participants, however, gave real teeth to BAC legislation and has resulted in a dramatic fall in alcohol-related accidents.

Chapter 7

The problem out of control

Despite the reforms that the Traffic Commission was able to put in place, the number of people killed and injured on Victoria's roads, and indeed Australia's roads continued to rise in line with the level of motorisation as measured by the number of motor vehicles per thousand of population. In the years leading up to the introduction of compulsory seatbelt wearing the correlation between road accident fatalities was almost perfect. The first reaction when I mentioned this was "what's that got to do with it?" Then I showed the graph of the two and that was taken seriously.

This was a time when Professor R J Smeed in the UK was putting a great deal of effort into trying to establish mathematically why some countries had higher or lower numbers of road deaths as measured against some kind of international average. My reaction to this may have been brash but I felt that if it really were possible to predict the number of fatalities there wouldn't be a problem because we would know enough about it to be able to solve it.

As I have said already my main task upon joining DST was to provide statistics for the ARSC to use in its publications, the most prominent of which was entitled, somewhat incongruously I felt, *The Grim Facts*. Various ways of looking at the data were called for at particular times, for example in the Christmas-New Year period and Easter. In the period leading up to the holiday seasons, references would be made to the toll of deaths in the same period the year before with solemn warnings issued on the media reminding people that, for example, "Death is so Permanent." This always reminded me of the line penned by the great American cynic H L Mencken that it was as though people were being expected to go out there and kill themselves so that the numbers would come out right. All states and territories would dutifully submit running totals of the numbers of fatalities that were in fact occurring.

The yearly totals of fatalities were bad enough, but after every weekend the media would report the number of fatalities over the weekend. These figures were even more chilling, the more so because of the almost matter of fact way in which each would get half a dozen lines in the column announcing the count. In fact the numbers were worse with only half making it into the papers.

It seemed in the 1950s and 1960s that everyone knew someone who had been touched by tragedy on the roads. I recall a contemporary of mine who lost his father, when young, and then his wife, both struck by cars. The father of a fellow school student was killed when a car came out of a side street and rammed his car into the side of a tram he was overtaking. I have already referred to the tragic loss of life when a car hit the back of an unlighted truck. I was also made aware of the vulnerability of pedestrians when a friend, with whom I am still in regular contact all these years on, suffered extremely serious head injuries when he was struck by a car in the university grounds, injuries that put an end to his studies.

From today's perspective it is all but impossible to believe that on an *average* weekend *eight* people died in road accidents in Victoria in the late 1960s, with a *low* of four and a high of an incredible 16. Total deaths for the year 1970 in Victoria were 1071 and 3798 for Australia as a whole. In short, the problem was out of control.

One of the paradoxes in roads accident statistics is that generally the *fatality rate* in terms of numbers of vehicles tends to *fall* as motorisation increases. This is likely to be the result of increases in vehicle numbers calling forth more sophisticated systems that make driving safer. ***In Australia this fall in the accident rate did not happen*** and later chapters will spell out the failings that led to Australia in 1970 having the highest per capita fatality rate in the world.

Revolution

New beginnings

Engineering, Medicine and
Psychology to the Rescue

The media lend a hand

Record road deaths lead to
compulsory seatbelt wearing

The final meeting of the Australian
Road Safety Council

Chapter 8

New Beginnings

One event defined the start of the modern approach to the problem of reducing the toll of death and injury on the roads of Australia. This was the Australian Study Week on Road Safety Practices that ran from 29 May to 1 June of 1967. It was a joint initiative of the Institution of Engineers Australia and The Australian Graduate Federation in Medicine. The alliance between engineering and medical science was to become the cornerstone of the new scientific approach that would herald the first spectacular fall in the toll of death and injury on Australia's roads. That toll would reach its notorious climax just three years later in 1970 when a record 3798 people were killed in road traffic accidents.

It was serendipitous in the extreme that I should have made my way at that time into the field that would consume me for the rest of my public service career and into my retirement. The date was 3 August 1967, just a month after the Study Week. I had not known about the event but when the papers were published in four bound volumes I fell upon them with delight. But I get ahead of myself.

The position of Senior Research Officer Grade 2 that I filled had become vacant when the original occupant moved on. The main duty of the position was to provide statistical information to the Executive Director of the Australian Road Safety Council (ARSC), the secretarial and technical support for which were provided by the Department of Shipping and Transport with the positions located in the Land Transport

Section at 35 Elizabeth Street, Melbourne. The section also provided secretarial and technical support to other committees established by the ministerial Australian Transport Advisory Council (ATAC) in 1947, as well as to ATAC itself. Other administrative functions included roads funding and liaison with the Commonwealth Railways.

The position had been advertised some three years earlier. I was interested in the transport area in general and urban public transport in particular and had thought that it might be nice to be around if the Commonwealth ever decided to interest itself in urban affairs. Nevertheless I had no desire to be associated with such an ineffectual body as the ARSC. Despite all its propaganda campaigns addressing driver attitude including clangers such as "Don't cross the Styx in '56", the road toll continued its inexorable march in line with the rise in motorisation.

When the position came up again towards the end of 1966 I decided to apply. I was spurred on by what I was reading in the press about new ways of looking at the road accident problem. Among these were the first in-depth studies to gather data at the sites of accidents to determine what was actually causing the injuries to victims, as well as collecting data on the road environment at the scene. There was also damning evidence emerging that drivers did not have to be drunk, or staggering, to be a menace to themselves and others on the road.

The decision to act this time around was also influenced by one particular issue of Current Affairs Bulletin, a slim fortnightly publication produced by the University of Sydney. Each issue dealt with one topic - social, economic, geo-political - to name just a few areas. Each topic was examined in a closely written and equally closely set essay by an anonymous author. The one entitled *Traffic Accidents* set out in detail how the road accident problem could be handled more effectively by putting the driver, the vehicle and the road into their proper perspective as areas to be studied and acted upon.

Here was a new vision for the future and I wanted to be a part of it.

Chapter 9

Engineering, Medicine and Psychology to the Rescue

The general failure of governments to do anything effective about the escalating road toll during the 1960s can be seen to have brought forth individuals from the fields of medicine, engineering and psychology. These individuals would become the major drivers of action. I have singled out just a few and also mention in passing the contribution of others who worked with them.

John W Birrell

One of the greatest contributors to reducing the toll of death and injury from road accidents was the then Victorian Police Surgeon, John Birrell. Dr Birrell had seen at first hand the consequences of driving when ability was impaired by the influence of alcohol. A master communicator, he addressed many conferences and seminars and was instrumental in convincing the Victorian Government to introduce legislation making it an offence to drive a vehicle on the road with a blood alcohol concentration (BAC) above 0.05 gm of alcohol per 100 ml of blood. Yet, not long before the last meeting of the ARSC, a sub-leader in the Sydney Morning Herald questioned the justification for such a measure. Later John Birrell would also play an important role in the advocacy for compulsory seatbelt wearing by vehicle occupants

Michael J Henderson

In line with the leading role that the medical profession had played in the road safety revolution of the 1960s it was a young medical man from the U K that the New South Wales government chose to head the Traffic Accident Research Unit (TARU) it established in 1969. As it happened, Michael Henderson was also a motor sports enthusiast. He famously ended a debate about whether young drivers should be denied access to so-called super cars by pointing out that a stock-standard Toyota Corolla was more than capable of a speed that would make a crash non-survivable. In the previous chapter I mentioned the seminal influence of reading the Current Affairs Bulletin (CAB) on *Traffic Accidents*. I have a feeling that Michael Henderson may have been the author.

The research program of TARU took in all aspects of road accident and injury prevention and the scope of its activities would not be out of place in 2014. Reports I particularly recall were by engineer Gordon Messiter on high speed approaches to traffic signals (particularly appropriate in today's Canberra) and on the railway level crossing problem, which in New South Wales was confined almost entirely to rural areas and provincial centres. TARU was equipped with all the necessary equipment for crash barrier testing of vehicles and for performance testing of several types of occupant restraint devices. Researchers such as Dawn Linklater and David Saffron also did valuable work in relation to child safety and novice drivers. In particular the work of TARU definitively established that children had to be at least eight years of age to cope with the traffic light task, let alone the road-crossing task.

David C Herbert

Among the list of notable contributors David Herbert ranks highly. Inspired by what was becoming known from work in the United States about the importance of occupant restraint, David Herbert, who was Safety Officer for the Snowy Mountains Hydro Electricity Authority, convinced the chairman of the authority William Hudson (later Sir William) that the best way to reduce the then horrendous toll of death and injury to workers operating vehicles in the treacherous conditions of the Snowy Mountains was to make the wearing of seatbelts compulsory. Sir William decided to do just that although it had never been done anywhere in the world. The effect of the measure was dramatic and from then on there were no more fatalities for vehicle occupants on the project. It might be noted that the belts concerned were not the three-point belts of today but simple lap belts.

Following the resignation of Michael Henderson as head of TARU David Herbert was appointed to the position, although for reasons unknown its status was reduced and retitled as 'superintendent'. In particular, and for reasons we should have learnt long ago from US research, he had no time for driving range training. At one stage in the 1980s, also, some people were advocating a reduction on the speed limit for semi-trailers on the premise that this would reduce accident severity to which he replied that there are some collisions, most notably cross-median events, that were simply non-survivable at any semi-trailer speed above 35 km/h!

A J (Jack) Mclean

As a young engineering graduate from the University of Adelaide Jack McLean [as in clean] was one of the team of three that conducted Australia's first in-depth studies of road traffic accidents collecting data on circumstances and injury patterns on-scene across Adelaide. The team leader was Professor J S Robertson, from the university's school of medicine. Their study, conducted from 1963 to 1965, was sponsored by the newly established Australian Road Research Board. The findings of the study would have wide-ranging consequences for the better understanding of what was behind the toll of death and injury on Australian roads.

Jack furthered his studies at the world-renowned Highway Safety Research Centre at the University of North Carolina studying road accidents as but one part of the wider public health issue to which the epidemiological approach had direct relevance.

Jack's career remained firmly in Adelaide where he was able to establish the Road Accident Research Centre within the University of Adelaide, supervising research in a wide variety of areas, notably with regard to speed as a contributing factor to accidents and injuries. Less well known was the case he felt could be made for vehicle occupants to wear a specially designed helmet to lessen the likelihood of brain injury.

Just as I was putting the finishing touches to this work I read of Jack's retirement from his position at the Centre, so closing a distinguished career of service to road safety spanning more than half a century.

Ronald W Cumming

Perhaps the most revered figure in the emerging field of 'Human Factors' research as it related to driving was Ron Cumming. Formerly an engineer with the Aeronautical Research Laboratory in Melbourne, a part of CSIRO, his entire team famously followed him to the Mechanical Engineering Department of the University of Melbourne in the late 1960s when funding for their research into human factors in aviation was cut. In a presidential address to the Australian Psychological Society he had this to say about how he came to think about the principles that applied to the work of pilots,

> I became concerned about the proportion of [aviation] accidents attributed to 'human error' or 'pilot error'. Working on the assumption that the people concerned were neither incompetent nor suicidally inclined, I started asking questions about how pilots do their job, the demands of their job, and the circumstances in which the demands of the job might exceed the capacity of the pilot at that time. Specifically I became interested in studying judgments pilots make on approach to landing.
>
> I believe I can claim that this was the first organized programme in Australia in the new field of human factors where engineering and engineering psychologists work together as a team.

The relevance to road safety was obvious and in 1966 Ron Cumming wrote an article in the journal of the Australian Road Research Board with the title *The Analysis of Skills in Driving*. His influence, with that of Dr J.C. Lane, Director of Aviation Medicine within the then Department of Civil Aviation (DCA), brought about the creation of a Human Factors Committee within the Australian Motor Vehicle Design Advisory Panel that was established by ATAC. Professor Cumming went on to train many of the people who later became influential in applying human factors research to the road safety problem. Among those known to me were Wendy McDonald (nee McGill) and later Ian Johnston, with whom I would soon find myself working.

John C Lane

Dr Lane's name was familiar to me long before I joined DST having worked with someone who had worked under him in DCA. To John Lane the scope for applying the same principles of the new field of ergonomics – adapting the machine to man rather than the other way around - that were proving highly successful in aviation were applicable on the roads was blindingly obvious even if it was not to others! His lack of patience with such people was legendary.

Gordon W Trinca

Dr Gordon Trinca, then head of the emergency department of the Preston and Northcote Community Hospital, better known as PANCH, played a major role in involving his profession in road safety research. In a variant on the theme of in-depth studies, Gordon Trinca set up a Study of Injury Patterns in road accident victims admitted to hospitals in Melbourne under the aegis of the Royal Australasian College of Surgeons (RACS) combining hospital data and police accident reports. The results of the RACS study confirmed the importance of occupant restraint wearing on reducing the severity of injury in accidents.

The RACS was prominent as one of the coalition of professional bodies pushing the case for greater action on the part of the Commonwealth Government in the field of road safety. Its report entitled *Road Accidents: the Unnatural Epidemic* placed the road accident problem firmly in the sphere of public health issues.

Kenneth G Jamieson

Had he lived longer, Brisbane neurosurgeon Ken Jamieson would have made an even greater contribution to the field of road safety. Well liked and an excellent communicator, he had with John Tonge from the University of Queensland faculty of Medicine conducted an in-depth study of accidents in Brisbane around the same time as the Adelaide study that somewhat overshadowed it. Largely due to his lobbying, the Queensland government introduced limits to drivers' BAC and the compulsory wearing of helmets by motorcyclists (pioneered in Victoria in 1961) and the compulsory wearing of seatbelts in motor vehicles (also pioneered in Victoria in 1971).

Peter N Joubert

The wartime experience of being left hanging upside down held only by his seatbelt when a light aircraft flipped after a rough landing was enough to turn Peter Joubert into a strenuous campaigner for the need for seatbelts in cars and their use to be made compulsory. By 1970 he was a professor in the Mechanical Engineering faculty of the University of Melbourne and had already advised the all-party parliamentary committee, that had been appointed to inquire into what could be done to stem the tide of death and injury on Victoria's roads, to recommend mandatory seatbelt use.

In 1970 Peter Joubert took deputy premier Arthur Rylah on a tour of the quadriplegic ward of the Austin Hospital. When Mr Rylah asked how many of the seriously injured patients would have been there had they been wearing seatbelts, he was told "none". This can be credited with convincing Mr Rylah to make seatbelt-wearing compulsory, a measure for which Victoria would achieve world renown.

JHW Permezel

I have left referring to John Permezel until the end of this chapter because he is the only one of this distinguished group that it was my good fortune to have worked with. Indeed my job interview with him for a position in the Land Transport Section of DST, which he headed, marked the start of my career in road safety. Quite coincidentally, his name and initials were familiar to me from my days at Wesley College in Melbourne as captain of athletics in 1942, just before my time there.

Engineer John Permezel can be credited with developing the concept of the Australian Design Rules for Motor Vehicle Safety (now referred to simply as the ADRs) during the 1960s. These would lay down specific safety requirements to protect vehicle occupants in crashes with compliance with these requirements to be demonstrated by manufacturers in accordance with precise scientific testing. It was because of his tenacity in the face of what was at times considerable opposition that the system was put in place. The 1965 decision to mandate these requirements in fact predated similar action in the United States. John was appointed to chair of the Australian Motor Vehicle Design Advisory Panel established by ATAC and was chief technical adviser to the Australian Motor Vehicle Certification Board, until he took up a senior position with the Road Traffic Authority in Victoria in 1981, retiring in 1986.

Chapter 10

The media lend a hand

From the early years of my driving career Melbourne's newspapers had taken a great deal of interest in the road accident problem, as did the motoring magazines: in the UK *Autocar* and *The Motor* and in Australia the *Motor Manual* and later *Wheels*. In the years before it folded in 1954, *The Argus* had given a great deal of prominence to traffic matters generally with calls for reform. It would be remiss therefore not to acknowledge the part played by the media in bringing a thoughtful, rather than a sensational, approach to the mounting social problem of road traffic accidents.

Most remembered, however, was how, in 1971, *The Sun,* under its dynamic editor Harry Gordon, joined the battle for change. This culminated in a sustained campaign to attack the problem that took as its title the number of deaths on the roads for 1970, the *1034 Campaign*.

Other newspapers also took up the call for action. I especially remember the five-part series published in *The Australian* in the last week of October 1971 for its thoughtful exposition of all aspects of the problem.

Importantly, the coverage given to the road accident problem was generally notable for the scope of its analysis, no longer laying all blame on the driver, but drawing particular attention to the deficiencies of road network, a term I use advisedly as it certainly could not have been called a system. There is no doubt that the large often dramatic, sometimes horrific, photographs of individual accidents never allowed readers to become complacent about the horrors that were occurring on the roads almost every day.

Harry Gordon's relentless '1034 campaign', as it became known, is credited with getting the Victorian community sensitised to the idea of making the wearing of seatbelts compulsory. The dramatic announcement that the Victorian government was about to make the wearing of seatbelts compulsory was made just before Christmas 1971 and 22 December 1971 became a red-letter day in the history of road safety in Australia and indeed around the world. Other states and territories followed suit in 1972.

Television also played a part in sensitising the community to the vital role that seatbelts could play in reducing the toll of death and injury on the roads. For me the clincher had been a short film screened on television at the time entitled *7/10 of a second* (the usual duration of a crash). A barrier crash test showed that *the crashing vehicle was actually moving **back** from the barrier when the unrestrained dummy moved off the seat and on through the windscreen.* A seatbelt would hold you and thus you might escape injury.

A specialist voice was even added to the media scene when the Traffic Accident Research Unit commenced publication of a monthly magazine *Autosafe* that for some years went on sale alongside other motoring magazines to communicate the safety message to a wider audience.

It should be emphasised that by the time wearing of seatbelts was made compulsory around some 75% of vehicles already had seatbelts fitted for the driver and front seat passenger as a result of the requirements under the Australian Design Rules for Motor Vehicle Safety, the first of which came into effect in 1967. Independently, South Australia had already required the fitting of seatbelts by vehicle manufacturers in that State.

As we have seen, a coalition of professionals would soon add their voice and, more particularly their special expertise, to the call for action to do something about a problem that was truly out of control. In fact, 1970s fatality count in Victoria was 1071, even higher than the figure Harry Gordon had used. The Australian total today is less than half of that in 1970 with almost three times the number of vehicles on the roads. In fact the total number of fatalities Australia-wide for 2013 was lower than at any time since 1924. (It was only in that year that deaths from 'road traffic accidents' were first distinguished in the Australian statistics from 'other crushings'.)

Chapter 11

Record road deaths lead to compulsory seatbelt wearing

Australia's place today as one of the world leaders in road safety has arisen largely as a result of the decision by the Victorian government to make the wearing of seatbelts compulsory. There can be no doubt that the community wanted to see something, anything, done to stem the loss of life on Victoria's roads as the problem spiralled out of control. The dramatic announcement that the Victorian government was about to make the wearing of seatbelts compulsory was made just before Christmas 1971. Other states and territories followed suit in 1972.

Evidence had been mounting on the vital role that occupant protection could play in making road usage safer. Work started as early as the 1940s, especially in the US by the Cornell Aeronautical Laboratory and in the UK by the Road Research Laboratory. These efforts built on the pioneering work of US Air Force Colonel John Stapp whose rocket-sled deceleration experiments, with him as the seat-belted subject, had shown the feasibility of 'packaging' people to absorb the 'G' forces involved in crashes. It is to the credit of those involved that a Special Subcommittee on Traffic Safety of the US House of Representatives conducted an inquiry that led to a recommendation for installation and use of seatbelts as early as 1957.

Having had no part in the lead-up to the government's decision I can only pay tribute to those who amassed the evidence. A committee of the Victorian parliament was so impressed by the testimony of police surgeon John Birrell and Peter Joubert of the Mechanical Engineering department of the University of Melbourne that it recommended that seatbelt wearing be made compulsory after a two year period of public education about the benefits.

A clincher for many was the Volvo study from Sweden that showed no fatalities among properly restrained car drivers or passengers in Volvo cars at speeds of less than 96 km/h. I often wonder whether the extent to which the speed/injury ratio has moved to the right has been adequately taken into account when the safety establishment looks at speed limits, bearing in mind that the current open road speed limits were put in place prior to seatbelt wearing being made compulsory.

The benefits of the measure were immediately apparent with road deaths falling by 13 per cent over the next twelve months.

Chapter 12

The Final Meeting of the Australian Road Safety Council

The final meeting of the ARSC was held in Sydney on 20 May 1970. The major item of general business was whether the Council would support making the use of seatbelts compulsory. Also on the agenda was the question of whether the ARSC was still the relevant body to be advising ATAC on road safety matters, at least in its current form.

In the morning the meeting heard an inspiring address on the seatbelt issue by the Chairman of the Snowy Mountains Hydro-electric Authority, Sir William Hudson. The reaction within the meeting to the proposal that seatbelt wearing be made compulsory throughout Australia was mixed to say at the least. The National Health and Medical Research Council representative, Professor J S Robertson of the University of Adelaide, who had directed the groundbreaking in-depth accident study in Adelaide, enthusiastically supported it. Also in support was P G Pak-Poy, a pioneer of traffic engineering in Australia. The most vociferous opposition came from the head of the Australian Automobile Association who said that he would give up driving if seatbelt wearing were to be made compulsory.

Not surprisingly, emotions ran deep and this so exasperated the chairman, Sir James Darling, that he angrily adjourned the meeting for lunch and stormed out into the winter chill, muttering that the members were acting like schoolboys, an apt description given his time as headmaster of Geelong Grammar School. His fury paid off and in the afternoon session the Council agreed to support compulsory seatbelt wearing.

By the time the debate began on the future of the ARSC itself, the whole mood of the meeting had changed. Indeed, members had accepted that the ARSC might no longer be the appropriate body to direct public education on behalf of ATAC. For some time there had been a growing feeling that the council's primary function of hectoring the public to take more care on the roads was increasingly irrelevant in the light of the findings of in-depth studies. These had shown that the more effective approach was to find out what was actually causing the deaths and injuries in the crashes themselves rather than concentrating solely on prevention.

All this led to the somewhat surprising, though very sensible, decision that the Council should recommend its own demise with its public education activities to be carried out by a new committee. This would comprise the current State and Territory representatives of the ARSC and report to ATAC in the same way as the ARSC had.

The recommendation for a new committee was duly endorsed by ATAC at its next meeting and named the Publicity Advisory Committee on Education and Road Safety. PACERS might have been catchy acronym but it may not have been the most appropriate short title for a road safety committee given that it was already the name given by the Chrysler Company to its high performance coupe, in competition with the Holden Monaro and the Ford GTS.

A role was soon found for the remaining, specialist, members of the ARSC including its chairman, in the formation of a new body, outside the ATAC structure, to advise the Commonwealth Minister for Shipping and Transport on road safety matters more generally. The story of the formation of the Expert Group on Road Safety is taken up in the next chapter.

Reform

THE EXPERT GROUP ON ROAD SAFETY

THE ROAD SAFETY RESEARCH SECTION

THE NATIONAL REVIEW

THE EXPERT GROUP'S REPORT –
THE ROAD ACCIDENT SITUATION IN AUSTRALIA IN 1972

THE EXPERT GROUP'S REPORT –
THE ROAD ACCIDENT SITUATION IN AUSTRALIA IN 1975

THE ROAD SAFETY AND STANDARDS
AUTHORITY 1975-1977

LIVING ONE'S WORK

Chapter 13

The Expert Group on Road Safety

The end of the ARSC came at a time when the Commonwealth Government was coming under mounting pressure to do something to stem the rising toll of death and injury on Australia's roads. Leading this pressure were The Institution of Engineers in a resolution from their Australian Study Week on Road Safety Practices May 1967; the Australian Medical Association in their Policy on Road Safety, November 1968; the Society of Automotive Engineers, Australasia, arising out of their Convention, October 1969; and the Royal Australasian College of Surgeons (RACS) at their Seminar on the Management of Road Casualties also in October 1969.

This was also the time when a new federal approach to highway safety was emerging in the United States. Hearings of the US Senate Subcommittee under Senator Rubicoff in 1965-66 had shown how little was being applied of what was known about how to make cars and the road environment safer.

The Commonwealth's response to ATAC was that a new committee should take over the public education role formerly undertaken by the ARSC while it would establish an Expert Group on Road Safety (EGORS) to advise its Minister for Shipping and Transport to determine what should be done about the road accident situation in Australia.

EGORS was distinguished from the committees that had gone before it as it was not composed entirely of road safety experts as might have been expected. Instead it comprised men, each eminent in their own field, whose task it would be to review the results of the research that was needed to make sense of the road accident problem. The members were therefore more akin to a Board of Directors.

The natural choice for chairmanship of EGORS was Sir James Darling who had been the last chairman of the ARSC and who had established a reputation for being open to new ideas and opportunities. His deputy was a Judge of the Supreme Court of New South Wales, the Honourable Mr Justice C L D Meares, who had chaired that State's Law Reform Commission with distinction. Three other members of EGORS had been members of the ARSC, two of whom brought with them a direct practical interest in road safety.

Professor J S Robertson, Professor of Pathology in the University of Adelaide, had been the senior member of the team that had conducted Australia's first in-depth study of road accidents in Adelaide from 1963 to 1965. Mr P G Pak-Poy was a transport, planning and operations research consultant, also from Adelaide. The third member from the ARSC was Mr P J Kenny, past president of the RACS. These men were logical inclusions in EGORS, because of their previous involvement in road safety, the remainder less so. They were Brigadier E.F. Campbell, consulting psychologist; Mr S E Solomon, statistician; and Mr M F Sweeny, mechanical engineer and market researcher. After a year, Jack Brabham, the renowned racing driver and vehicle engineer, joined the Expert Group. Sir James, however, retired as chairman of EGORS after it presented its first report in late 1972 and was succeeded by Mr Justice Meares.

At its first meeting EGORS agreed that an extensive program of research covering all aspects of the road accident problem should be conducted. To this end the Road Safety Research Section (RSRS) was established within DST. Given their expertise in the key aspects of the fields involved, Professor Robertson and Mr Pak-Poy were put in charge of overseeing the development of the action plan with a view to producing a comprehensive review of the road accident situation by the second half of 1972.

Chapter 14

The Road Safety Research Section

In line with previous practice with Commonwealth-State committees, at least in the transport area, the Commonwealth was to provide the technical and administrative support for both the bodies that replaced the ARSC. Applications for the positions in the Road Safety Research Section (RSRS) that was to service EGORS were called and interviews conducted in November 1970 with promotions, including mine, finalised in early 1971.

How much it had to do with the favourable impression I had made on Sir James I do not know, but I was told that he had been keen to see me as a member of the new RSRS team. In particular, and perhaps as a reflection of his having been the headmaster for many years of the prestigious Geelong Grammar School, we shared the belief that there was something amiss with setting the minimum driving age, at least in Victoria, at age 18, which was also the minimum age for the purchase of alcohol. Moreover, it coincided with the sharp rise in sexual awareness among young males - and consequent showing off. Sir James had also paid me the compliment of asking me to write the entry on road safety that he had been asked to contribute to the Australian Encyclopaedia.

When the staff of the RSRS had been appointed, the first task undertaken was to put in place the research program recommended by

EGORS. A total of 24 literature reviews were to be carried out under contract by outside research bodies and business firms working to specifications drawn up by the RSRS.

The first head of the new section was Dr Peter (A P) Vulcan, a biomechanical engineer from the Vehicle Structures Safety Branch of DST. A year or so before he had completed a PhD at Monash University in Melbourne on the tolerance of the human body to the forces involved in crashes. He was also personally familiar with the research work being done in the United States in that area and his contacts with researchers there and in the United Kingdom would prove invaluable.

The 2 IC of the section, Bob Ungers, came from the Transport Research Section of DST, as did another team member, Peter Milne. I brought with me an enthusiastic young research officer from the Land Transport Section, John McPherson.

The initial team was rounded out by two support staff whose enthusiasm for the task ranked with that of the research team: Pam Thomas who came to us from the departmental library and Laura Golino, section typist and Peter's secretary, fresh from school.

I remember well the first time the staff of the Road Safety Research Section got together. Peter Vulcan made it clear that as this was to be, as he put it so well, "a non-ranked team" in which everyone would be valued and hard work expected, and so it remained to a degree that was still in evidence over thirty years later when we got together again for a reunion.

Such was the rapport in the section that when Pam left, her replacement, a snappy young dresser from the department's registry, George Inglis, described the place as 'the greatest show on earth' despite the sometimes frantic pace, especially in the later years when the central office of the DST was split between Melbourne and Canberra as a precursor to full transfer. In fact, Peter was by then running the section from there. Rushes to make the 'five o'clock departmental bag' were legendary.

The writing of the specifications for the National Review was an exacting task, which we took to with great enthusiasm. One staff member would be given responsibility for developing the draft specifications for one of the 24 reviews. The draft would then be discussed by a meeting of the whole section. We must have had done our job rather well because one prominent researcher from the Mechanical Engineering Department of the University of Melbourne was moved to comment that "You might not know much about road safety but you sure know how to ask the right questions".

Chapter 15

The National Review

The first task that the Expert Group on Road Safety (EGORS) undertook in late 1970 was to set out a framework for the investigation into what worked and what didn't across the whole spectrum of road safety measures. A similar overview study had been conducted in the United States by Arthur D. Little and Associates some years before, but the road accident situation in Australia was clearly desperate and needed to be investigated separately. Indeed, some problems were unique to Australia. The idea of conducting the review is credited to Kevin Cosgrove, then First Assistant Secretary, Land Transport Policy Division, DST.

Three members of EGORS acted as a Research Committee whose first task was to develop the framework and timelines for a national review of the road accident situation in Australia. Two members had direct professional experience in road safety and had been 'specialist' members of the former Australian Road Safety Council. Mr P G Pak-Poy and Professor J S Robertson. The third, Brigadier E F Campbell, had been Director of Psychological Services in the Australian Army.

A perhaps unusual requirement in the research specifications was that the contracted researchers were not to approach universities, other research bodies or State departments for information or access to data. In establishing the Expert Group the Commonwealth was breaking new ground and it was considered essential that relations with State bodies were not jeopardised by contractors making requests for information.

There was also another less obvious advantage to that requirement, namely that the recommendations for action made by EGORS would be based on information that was available in the *public domain* but which had clearly not been acted upon, so bringing about the crisis that had led to the creation of the Expert Group. We were new kids on the block and had to build up trust with the State authorities since it was they who would be called upon to take the new initiatives that would be recommended.

This may have been the era of critical path analysis, but spreadsheets had yet to arrive on the scene and it was on a metre-wide engineering-style dyeline sheet that the steps from conception to report were set out.

The head of the Road Safety Research Section, Peter Vulcan, worked directly with the Research Committee in developing the framework and timelines for the national review. Once the 24 areas for study had been identified it would be the task of the RSRS to develop detailed project briefs for each topic that would be then be let out to competitive tender. Tenders were called for in the weekend newspapers around the country. Strict timeframes were set for the conduct of the research - as short as six weeks from the time of letting the tender.

As each review was received the staff member responsible for the area would prepare a summary of the review and its recommendations. This would be subject to a similar review process to that concerned with the drawing up of the specification. Once agreed, the draft recommendations for each portion of the EGORS report would be put to meetings of its Research Committee. Following the consideration of them, draft chapters would be written and subjected to a similar process of scrutiny and agreement before being put to full meetings of EGORS.

It was during one of these review sessions that we were able to witness one of the most remarkable phenomena in the history of Melbourne. Suddenly, Pam burst in the door of Peter's office where we were assembled telling us to look out the window. When we did not immediately respond, she said with more urgency – "No, you really must!" Thus urged, we got up and looked down on the great flood of Elizabeth Street and saw water rushing down, up to the level of the kerbside rubbish bins. The iconic image of a car with water rushing over its roof was captured just up the street at the corner of Little Collins Street. We were on the corner of Flinders Lane. The date was 17 February 1972.

Whilst the contracted researchers had not been permitted to approach State Authorities whilst undertaking their projects, it was obvious that these same bodies had undertaken research and evaluation of their own programs. The next step in the process was, as we put it, to get such research out of the filing cabinets and into the public arena. To this end the first National Road Safety Seminar was held in Canberra over three days from 14-16 March 1972, with papers presented by invited experts in particular fields.

Immediately following the seminar the Road Safety Research Section would gain a new member who would go on to forge a distinguished career in the field of human factors in road safety, Ian Johnston. Ian had just completed his PhD entitled *Visual Factors in Locomotion* under Ron Cumming at the University of Melbourne. A major aspect of Ian's thesis was the determination of just where it is that people are looking when in charge of a motor vehicle – the 'focus of expansion'. His work no doubt influenced the placement of the now ubiquitous 'high-mounted' tail-light at about the level of the bottom of the rear window of a sedan. As 'the oldest inhabitant', I have been able to see Ian's career go from post-graduate student to Professor Emeritus.

We were also joined during 1972 by Bob Heacock who had trained as an aeronautical engineer in the United States. He brought with him expertise with regard to street lighting, the topic of his MESc thesis. It was from him that I learned that the big advantage of yellow (sodium vapour) street lighting over blue (mercury vapour) was that it put more output into the visual part of the spectrum. Not surprisingly, he was also concerned with making the roadside environment (including its utility poles) more forgiving.

The mere fact that no less than 24 areas were deemed necessary to be studied in detail was indicative of a new scientific approach to the road accident problem that stood in stark contrast to simply hectoring people to 'drive safely' and all would be well in an unchanged and unchanging environment. The topics, with some combined from two into one, are those of the chapter headings in the first report of the Expert Group that is the subject of the next chapter.

Chapter 16

The Expert Group's Report The Road — *Accident Situation in Australia in 1972*

Two years of intensive work by the Road Safety Research Section culminated in the tabling in Federal Parliament, by the Minister for Shipping and Transport, of the Expert Group's first report in September of 1972, in the last days of the McMahon Coalition government.

The forward-looking approach and the continuing challenge it presents to entrenched positions even today has never been better expressed than on the first page of the report which was entitled *The Road Accident Situation in Australia – a National Review.* It introduced its basic findings with the words,

> Road accidents are rarely caused by a single factor. They represent failures in the operation of the interacting components of a large and complex transport system involving the vehicle, the road environment, the road user and his social environment.
>
> The behaviour of the road user is nearly always the final link in the chain of circumstances that leads to a road

accident. Because of this fact there is a widely held belief that the most effective way to reduce road accidents is to modify human behaviour by more driver education and training and by intensive road safety publicity. In practice these efforts have proved only minimally effective.

Although the driver may appear primarily to be at fault in many accidents, there is clear evidence that in the shorter term making the road and/or the vehicle safer is often more effective in reducing both the incidence and severity of accidents than are attempts to modify human behaviour.

Forty years on, the import of the third paragraph seems to have become lost as the current generation of road safety administrators focus on changing driver behaviour through the use of punitive measures, and attendant publicity, that impact on all road users whilst having minimal effect on the recalcitrant minority. I shall have much more to say on that issue later.

The report was divided into six chapters under which the twenty-four study areas could be conveniently considered.

> **The Road User:** Alcohol and Road Accidents; Education and Training; Road Safety Publicity; Driver/Rider Licensing; Legislation and Enforcement
>
> **The Vehicle:** Vehicle Design to Reduce Accidents; Vehicle Design to Reduce Injuries; Vehicle Inspection; Cycles and Motorcycles
>
> **Town Planning and Road Design:** Town Planning; The Roadway; The Roadside; Streetlighting; Railway Crossings
>
> **Traffic Management:** Intersection Rules; Traffic Control; Speed Control; Pedestrian Protection

The Post-crash Phase: Emergency Services; Insurance; Accident Information

The Institutional Framework.

The report made 100 recommendations for action and research with studies recommended in all of the categories considered. The recommendations for action and research would to a large extent occupy the Road Safety Research Section for the next three years after which a second report would be produced setting out what had been achieved and what still needed to be done.

Chapter 17

The Expert Group's Report — *The Road Accident Situation in Australia in 1975*

At the conclusion of its first report, *The Road Accident Situation in Australia in 1972*, the Expert Group made 100 recommendations on what needed to be done to improve the situation. Its second report, *The Road Accident Situation in Australia in 1975*, was an examination of what had happened in the intervening three years on the part of the Commonwealth and the states. This covered the areas that had been identified for action in the first report, including the comprehensive research program it had recommended. EGORS, however, did not leave that matter there and, reflecting the optimistic tenor of the times, made further strong recommendations for action in specific areas.

The format of the second report differed from the first report in that its major recommendations came first and it is instructive to look first at what has come to pass in regard to them. Indeed, it is a matter of regret that more than thirty years on a number of these have still not been acted upon.

The preface to the report noted that the base upon which future actions could be built had been broadened by two specialised seminars held with the assistance of the Australian Department of Transport.

Some 200 magistrates, judges, criminologists, police and others associated with traffic law and its enforcement attended the first seminar, *Road Safety and the Law,* in August 1973. A presentation that made a lasting impression on me was on understanding the motivations and feelings that underlie the actions of young drivers. The presenter used stick figures and simple line drawings to illustrate these feelings and one depicted 'Fred' at the wheel on a box labelled 'anger' as the seat – 'Fred sitting on his anger!'

The second seminar, *Road Accident Information,* in March 1974, brought together the suppliers and users of road information to stress the need for, and to stimulate progress in, the provision of more adequate data urgently needed to understand and control road accidents. Pessimistic, it may be, but it was pointed out at the seminar that mass data collections for the most part are a *by-product* of the enforcement system.

Chief among the developments to have taken place over the previous three years that were noted in the report was the establishment of the Road Safety and Standards Authority (RSSA). In its first report EGORS had made a recommendation for a National Authority (Co-ordination and Research) to be created. In June 1973 the Expert Group gave evidence before the House of Representatives Select (later Standing) Committee on Road Safety to reinforce the findings of the National Review and, in particular, to stress the need for a national road safety body. The Committee recommended the establishment of an independent statutory body, and developed detailed terms of reference. In October 1973 the Australian Government [by then the preferred form of reference to the Commonwealth] announced its decision to create the RSSA along the lines suggested.

Not surprisingly, a key feature of the Expert Group's second report was the emphasis it placed on the need for a nationally consistent database with which to tackle the complex issues surrounding road safety. The language may seem quaint today but the import of the recommendation is clear, namely that,

The Australian Government should, therefore,

> Provide financial and technical assistance to the states for
> the establishment of integrated statistical systems using

the most modern electronic data processing facilities. These systems should work to common guidelines and should incorporate information covering accidents, licence holders, motor vehicle registrations and indices of exposure to risk.

Intensify its efforts, through its co-ordinating role, to promote uniformity in the information gathered by the States.

It can only be a matter of deep regret that integrated data systems operating to common guidelines are still not in place in all states and territories. One is tempted to ask whether the speed camera has militated against the use of such data to elucidate the true state of play and why even in Queensland, where such a database exists, has no research based on it been made public.

The Expert Group saw a major role for the RSSA in the area of accident information more generally and recommended the creation within it of a central information hub. The difficulty of obtaining up-to-date information about what was happening in the area of road safety research had been a major stumbling block during the preparation of the consultants' reports that were the basis of the first EGORS report. As a result of this recommendation the Road Accident Information Section was created within the Road Safety Branch of the RSSA.

The report also noted that its recommendation from the first report that the Commonwealth should fund a program for the remedial action at accident black spots had borne fruit. The Traffic Engineering and Road Safety Improvement Program (TERSIP) had operated during 1973/74 and funding was to continue from 1974/75 to 1976/77 with a new category of funding under the Commonwealth roads grant legislation – Minor Improvements for Traffic Engineering and Road Safety (MITERS).

The body of the report was divided into five chapters and it is worth noting the placement of each topic within them and in particular the prominence given to accident information. There can, however, be no doubting the primacy given to actions designed to reduce the problem of alcohol as a contributing factor and the need to modify driver behaviour in this regard. Indeed, the *first* recommendation from the report was that the Australian Government,

> Provide substantial funds for the implementation of and controlled evaluation of comprehensive and co-ordinated programs to counter the use of alcohol by road users.

Significantly, the report reiterated the message from the opening chapter of the first EGORS report, that generalised appeals for safe behaviour are ineffective. It then went on to stress the importance of publicity programs being based on reliable and valid information and to be carefully designed to achieve specific objectives.

Also notable is the inclusion of the young driver as a topic separate from licensing. Reference is also made to insurance in the context of the cost of accidents; this found expression in the decision of the then government to work towards the introduction of a national 'no-fault' insurance scheme. The chapter headings were,

Accident Information

The Road User: Alcohol and Drugs; Traffic Law and its Enforcement; Licensing, The Young Driver; Education and Training; Road Safety Publicity

The Vehicle: Vehicle Design to Reduce Accidents; Vehicle Design to Reduce Injuries; Vehicle Inspection; Motorcycles and Pedal cycles

Roads and Traffic: Town Planning; Roads; Traffic Management

Post Crash Factors: Emergency Services; Insurance

Summary of Recommendations: Australian Government Action; Road Safety Measures; Studies.

The report went on to recommend a greatly expanded research program and an increase in the technical and other support services in the areas of vehicle safety standards, traffic codes and education and publicity.

The report concluded with a number of appendices,

A. The Objects and Functions of the Road Safety and Standards Authority
B. The Road Safety Research Program of the Australian Government [completed and in progress]
C. Accident Statistics
D. Australian Design Rules for Motor Vehicle Safety
E. Town Planning Guidelines.

Chapter 18

The Road Safety and Standards Authority

In 1974, the ALP government led by Gough Whitlam had before it two important documents urging upon it the creation of a national road safety body. These were the 1972 report of the Expert Group on Road Safety and the First Report of the House of Representatives Select Committee on Road Safety that had endorsed the recommendation of the Expert Group in relation to the need for a national road safety body. The government accepted the recommendation of the committee and set out the main functions of the Road Safety and Standards Authority (RSSA) as being to,

- Advise the Minister for Transport on road safety including proposals for financial assistance to the States for this purpose.
- Formulate, in consultation with the relevant State and Australian Authorities, proposals in respect of:

   motor vehicle standards involving emission control and consumer protection as well as safety standards;

   road safety standards in respect of highway engineering, traffic management, roadside furniture and town planning; and

   uniform traffic codes

- Certify compliance of motor vehicles and motor vehicle components with approved standards
- Prepare road safety impact standards in respect of transport and urban development programs being financed to a significant degree out of Australian Government funds
- Conduct road safety research on a multi-discipline basis by the use of outside bodies and persons and of its own staff and facilities
- Collect and disseminate road safety research information
- Consult and disseminate,in consultation with the Australian Bureau of Statistics, national statistical information required by workers in the various disciplines relevant to road safety and relating to such topics as drivers, vehicles and accidents etc. on an Australia-wide basis
- Conduct road safety education and publicity campaigns and co-ordinate State and Territory efforts in this field.

The Vehicle Structures Safety Branch and the Road Safety Branch of the Department of Transport had been performing some of these functions for some years, but the RSSA had a clearer focus. Relevant staff members were transferred to the Authority under the leadership of Frank E Yeend, formerly head of Air Safety Investigation in the Department of Civil Aviation that had been subsumed into the integrated Department of Transport. The part-time members were Alderman Clem Jones, Lord Mayor of Brisbane, and Professor R W Cumming.

The creation of a new, independent, road safety body fitted neatly into the Whitlam government's plans for decentralising urban development to a number of regional growth centres, the foremost of which was the border conurbation of Albury-Wodonga. A body similar in function and title to Canberra's National Capital Development Commission was established to oversee the planned development of the enlarged growth centre, including new towns, on the Canberra model. In the event, only one such district eventuated – Thurgoona, east of Albury, now home to a campus of Charles Sturt University.

The growth centre was to be the location for the RSSA and a site on the Hume Highway at Barnawartha, just west of Wodonga, was selected. There was profound symbolism in having the authority located in a growth centre straddling two States – the hope that it would signal the start of a new era of co-operation between the States. Even the siting of the authority alongside the nation's major interstate road artery, the Hume Highway, was significant in the light of the Whitlam Government's commitment to federally fund designated National Highways.

In order to further symbolise the importance of the RSSA and its siting, one of the last meetings of the Expert Group was held in the Wodonga Civic Centre. The meeting was also attended by the Minister for Transport, the Hon. Charlie Jones, who addressed the meeting reading a speech that I had the pleasure of preparing, taking up these themes as signifying the start of a new era in road transport safety in Australia.

In the minds of the staff of the Authority, the relative proximity of Albury-Wodonga to Melbourne made relocation there a far more attractive proposition than the possibility of relocation to Canberra that was always at the back of the minds of people in the central offices of Commonwealth departments.

It had been intended that a major focus of the new Authority would be the provision of appropriate road safety information, the lack of which on any sort of nationally organised basis had been highlighted during the preparation of the Expert Group's first report. The absence of a central source for such information had caused difficulties for the consultants commissioned to prepare each of the twenty-four literature reviews upon which the report was to be based. The establishment of a central information unit was a major recommendation of the Expert Group's report. Emphasis was to be given to information on the conduct and evaluation of research, the application of findings and the application of new developments and strategies.

The holding of a seminar specifically addressing the topic highlighted the importance placed on accident information. This need was picked up in the second report of the Expert Group presented to the Minister in November of 1975, hardly a propitious time for it to have received the consideration it deserved. The number-two recommendation of the report bears repeating in full,

The Australian Government should therefore provide financial and technical assistance to the States for the establishment of integrated statistical systems using the most modern *electronic* data processing facilities. These systems should work to common guidelines and should incorporate information covering accidents, licence holders, motor vehicle registrations and indexes of exposure to risk.

The report also recommended that the Australian Government, Intensify its efforts, through its co-ordinating role, to promote uniformity in the information gathered by the States.

To this day, neither of these recommendations has been taken up on an Australia-wide basis. Indeed, only in one State, Queensland, is the cross-referencing of accident and offence records possible, whilst there is still not even a common core of accident data. It is true, however, that at the national level common data can be assembled in respect of fatal accidents.

The victory of the Liberal-National coalition in the December 1975 election that followed the dismissal of Gough Whitlam as Prime Minister put paid to the RSSA as well as the Albury-Wodonga Development Commission. Protests from the same bodies that a few years earlier had urged the Commonwealth to take a greater role in promoting road safety measures were of no avail and the *Road Safety and Standards Authority (Repeal) Act* was passed early in 1976.

To be fair, however, the incoming government continued with many of the initiatives of the former government. These included federal funding of national highways and inclusion of the Minor Improvements for Traffic Engineering and Road Safety (MITERS) category in federal road funding legislation. To take the place of the RSSA the government established the Office of Road Safety as a separate division in the Department of Transport (minus the vehicle testing facilities) with Canberra as its ultimate location.

Extensive planning of facilities for the RSSA had taken place during 1974 and 1975 that were to include a full-scale vehicle-testing laboratory. It was always felt that had the bulldozers been set to work on the site earlier, the decision to abolish the RSSA might not have been made. For many years the rumour also persisted that the Fraser Government Razor Gang had misread the construction cost of the RSSA facilities ($90m) as the amount to be saved each year from the abolition of the authority.

Even in adversity the Australian sense of humour came to the rescue of the dispirited RSSA staff. A wake for the Authority was held in the courtyard garden of the restaurant in the refurbished Gordon House at the top end of Melbourne. Copies of the abolition Act were reduced to ashes in the barbecue pit and yours truly delivered the eulogy in Irish brogue.

Perhaps the saddest commentary on the short life of the RSSA lies in the form in which the report of its operations was presented to Parliament - eight pages of very ordinary-looking folded paper with an equally ordinary-looking pale green paper cover. No one was even interested in retaining the records of the authority and I took it upon myself to take them into my care with the intention that they should go to the National Archives.

Chapter 19

Living one's work

Even the choice of a place to live when Jennie and I married seems to have resonance with my career path. Generally, at that time, young people moved further out from where they had grown up. Hence, in 1962 we had a display house, the cheapest on the market, built in White Street, Mt Waverley, eleven miles out on the Glen Waverley line. White Street was off Stephensons Road just at the start of its steep descent to the newly reconstructed intersection with the curiously named High Street Road.

At this time and for many years later, the government or the municipal councils only took responsibility for providing a sealed surface on highways and declared main roads. This situation was, like so much in Victoria then, unique in Australia. Like all the other so-called 'private' streets, White Street was a quagmire in winter, lacking even side drains - just another 'heartbreak street'. So widespread was the problem that it was estimated at the time that it would be forty years before all the heartbreak streets could be surfaced. In our street everyone regularly pitched in to buy road metal and hire a grader to provide a trafficable surface. A friend in Gwynne Street, the next street down, even bought a load of second-hand bricks to fill the remains of a gully that bisected the street, and cut off direct access to Stephensons Road.

The whole area on that side of Stephensons Road and up the hill in High Street Road had been sub-divided in the 1850s and named the Township of Waverley, a name influenced by the popularity of the novels by Sir Walter Scott. None of the blocks was built on, however, until the 1950s. Not far away on the other side of the railway that came through in 1930, years ahead of any suburban development, lay what we called 'great concrete estate'. Here was a little slice of Canberra, all kerbed and guttered, that lay fallow until the 1950s, save for the original farmhouse, and one house dating from 1946 - the Glen Alvie Estate, constructed in the era of optimism just before the great depression of the 1930s.

The one-mile grid of main roads common in Victoria during the pioneering days took no regard of topography. As a result, the intersection of High Street Road and Stephensons Road lay at the bottom of a deep gully that led back to Damper Creek and ran diagonally through the intersection. The existence of the gully meant that both arms of High Street Road diverged to the south giving the intersection a torturous reputation and its name 'The Devils Elbow'. This alignment remained in place for the best part of a century until the approaches were regraded to their present configuration so that intersection is approached *uphill* from the west, not *downhill* as it had been. In the 1970s both sides of the gully became reserves, the larger on the northwest corner becoming known locally as Bellbird Corner. The approach from the south in Stephensons Road, however, remains as steep as ever. In the early days it was known locally as 'Eighteen Penny Hill' a reference to its 1:6 gradient (1/6 being the way of writing one shilling and sixpence in the days before decimal currency).

Stephensons Road eventually became a major route servicing the broadacre industrial estates in Clayton and Notting Hill to the south. Semi-trailer drivers would wait at the top of the hill until the traffic lights turned green at High Street Road before commencing their descent, knowing that they have no chance of stopping if the lights were to change. The success of this strategy was evidenced by the fact that, in my time, there was never an accident involving a semi-trailer at the intersection. To stand on the traffic island beside the lights as the semi-trailers thundered past a metre or so away, however, was an unnerving experience.

Coming down the hill from the Mt Waverley station in the evenings and looking for an opportunity to cross further up made be aware of a characteristic of traffic flow – that a period of non-stop movement will most likely come to end and usually just after one has been tempted to 'make a dash for it'. Indeed, I would often marvel at the silence. That there'll always be a gap applies almost equally for drivers as for pedestrians and my elder son often reminds me of this when he sees people becoming impatient.

As far as I am aware the combination of 'street' and 'road' in the name High Street Road is unique. It was quite literally the road that led from the market gardening and orchard country to the east of Melbourne to High Street which started at Warrigal Road and led west to the St Kilda Road and on to the markets in the city. High Street Road even had a tollgate at Warrigal Road as early as 1864. Waverley Road, one mile to the south, also had its tollgate not far from where it is now crossed by the Monash Freeway. There is nothing new about people closer in complaining about traffic from further out.

One hundred years on from the era of tollgates, High Street Road had become a major traffic artery. Neither this, nor the notorious corner nearby deterred Jennie and me when a house we had long admired, two doors up the hill, came on the market in 1964. The long block sloped all the way down to the gully referred to earlier giving it a bush outlook in the heart of suburbia. There was a downside, however, especially when I became involved in road safety. Although the location proved an ideal vantage point from which to observe traffic operations over the years, I found myself literally living my work. Only on weekends when I spent the afternoons playing tennis at a club in the long-established suburb of Camberwell could I really put work out of my mind.

First, there was the sheer volume of traffic. By the time we left for Canberra in 1981, when my job was transferred there, High Street Road was carrying 22,000 vehicles a day and Stephensons Road, fifty metres away, 19,000. The sheer volume itself was not the major problem: it was the acceleration noise, especially from the semi-trailers and other trucks that had stopped at the lights at Stephensons Road and then had to climb the hill past our place. Much more worrying was the potential for 'right turn against' accidents involving vehicles turning right off High Street Road into Stephensons Road to go south; this saw drivers being unsighted by vehicles coming down High Street Road and turning in the opposing direction. One would hear the acceleration noise as the lights changed and then literally wonder whether a crash would come during this phase, or the next. Before a fifth lane was fitted in to give right-turners a better view, there was an accident a week.

That was also the era when traffic lights would be put into flashing mode from about 11.45 pm so that drivers would not have to stop if there was nothing coming. One knew when that hour had come because the screech of brakes would disturb the night air as drivers braked to avoid collisions. We breathed a big sigh of relief when the traffic lights everywhere were left to operate normally 24 hours a day.

What was particularly interesting was the ignorance of the fact that traffic lights are vehicle-actuated responding to demand as vehicles record their presence by passing over induction loops under the road surface. If the programming of the lights in response to demand is operating as intended, drivers will barely have to stop before the lights change in their favour. Indeed, on one occasion, in a quiet time around midnight, I watched the lights change thirty times in a ten-minute period.

At the location I have been speaking of there was also the potential for out-of-control accidents on the long grade down High Street Road. A truck laden with sand actually ended upside down in the downhill neighbour's front garden having gone over the steep wall below the footpath on our properties. This led to the installation of a guardrail to prevent a re-occurrence. This so impressed my small son that, while being read a story from Richard Scarry's book *What do People do all Day?* in which one character, a terrible driver, drove off the road and over the edge, he asked, "Why don't they put in a gail?" (guardrail). "Out of the mouths of babes and sucklings cometh wisdom" as the Bible says. Although blindingly obvious to a three-year-old, it would be years before road improvement programs would routinely include this measure to reduce the incidence of death and injury in hazardous situations.

Within the 'Township of Waverley' subdivision there was a hill even steeper than the one on Stephensons Road. That was the one on Gwynne Street. Once it had been properly paved it provided thrills for our elder son. He would take his Presley-purple bike up the hill and over the cross street at the top to start the run down. Making sure there was nothing coming, he would accelerate to the top of the hill before careering down the slope to the bottom of the gully. This left him plenty of time to pull up before reaching the main road. On his last recorded run he wound the speedo off its stop; it only went to 80 km/h! Jennie and I had never heard about this activity. Thrill seeking was then transferred to the hill out the front, screaming down on his billycart and around the bend into Stephensons Road. This was even more hazardous than the other activity given what lay ahead at the bottom of the hill if he misjudged the turn. I soon put a stop to that and the activity was transferred to the backyard that had an equally attractive slope. All that was missing was the noise.

The steep approaches to the busy intersection nearby put a premium on the lights not failing and the early hours of New Years Day was certainly not a good time for this to happen. Yet it did happen. I realised there was nothing to show drivers who were not familiar with the area that a busy intersection lay ahead, unless I did something about it. With Jennie being a preschool teacher, there was always coloured card around and soon a black-on-yellow diamond sign was in place on the utility pole outside the house. All went well.

People who lived in the area gained great benefit from the commitment to traffic safety of the Waverley Council. In the years I am referring to municipal councils received a subsidy from the Road Safety and Traffic Authority when they installed traffic lights on roads under their control. Some councils would not act without the subsidy. Not so the City of Waverley (now part of the City of Monash). Every major, and some not so major, intersection had traffic lights installed and for only one of these did the council wait for a subsidy before acting. That case was of interest because it involved the replacement of a set of pedestrian signals outside Ashwood High School by a full set of traffic lights at the adjacent intersection of High Street Road and Vannam Drive. The same thing was done at Holy Family School on Stephensons Road adjacent to the hump bridge near Mt Waverley train station.

A further indication of the local council's commitment to road safety was the employment of four crossing supervisors, one for each approach, to shepherd children across the slip lanes at the busy intersection of High Street Road and Stephensons Road used by my children to get to the primary school up the hill on Stephensons Road and the local high school in a street nearby.

I have dwelt on the pro-active stance of the local council because it leads neatly into my giving great credit to the Victorian government for the fact that *almost all* pedestrian crossings on arterial roads in the major centres in the state were replaced by pedestrian operated signals decades ago. It was the death of a youngster struck by a car while crossing busy Bell Street in Preston near his school that highlighted the need for action on school crossing safety. This saw, first, the introduction of flagged school crossings and then the move to pedestrian-operated traffic lights. I am surprised that the government in New South Wales has not done likewise in view of the many well-publicised fatalities that have occurred in such situations and indeed that it is only in the last few months of 2013 that the decision was made to install flashing yellow lights at pedestrian crossings.

Reincarnation

THE OFFICE OF ROAD SAFETY

BLACK SPOT PROGRAMS

LOCAL AREA TRAFFIC MANAGEMENT

PUBLIC EDUCATION - A NEW WAY

PRIORITY CONTROL AT INTERSECTIONS
AND THE T-JUNCTION RULE

Chapter 20

The Office of Road Safety

After the demise of the Road Safety and Standards Authority things back at the office went on much the same except that we had lost the promised vehicle testing facilities. Within the Road Safety Branch – the non-vehicle area of the Office of Road Safety – things in fact got even better when the department decided that the branch should take over the secretarial and technical advice support for the Advisory Committee on Road User Performance and Traffic Codes (ACRUPTC) from the area of the department that had traditionally performed those functions.

In the Road Safety Branch (RSB) we thought all our Christmases had come at once. Now we had a direct conduit into the deliberations of ACRUPTC and were free to prepare documents on all the areas that were important to us. Our aim was simple: to advance the adoption of best practice on a uniform basis. As had been the case with the National Review we were 'the new kids on the block' but neither were we burdened with the demands of running a department that was dealing with issues raised by the public on a day-to-day basis. Fortunately, the members of the committee quickly accepted us. On numerous occasions the local knowledge I had gathered over the years again proved helpful. Moreover, the regulatory aspects relating to signs and signals fitted neatly with the administration of the black spot program that the branch retained.

As with other ATAC committees, any recommendations for action would have to be reviewed by a co-ordinating group of officials drawn from the higher echelons of the state and territory departments with responsibility for transport matters generally. This higher body was serviced by the ATAC secretariat within the Department of Transport. For much of the time that I was involved with ACRPUTC this higher body went by the name Motor Transport Group. This meant that there was liaison both sideways within the department and outwards with the state and territory members of ACRUPTC. Amendments to the model National Road Traffic Code, endorsed by ATAC in 1962 as a model for uniformity, would first be given legislative shape by ACRUPTC's Drafting Sub-committee; and as technical adviser to the main committee I was convenor of this sub-committee. Matters relating to the licensing of drivers and riders also fell within the committee's ambit and I was also convenor of its Driver Licensing Sub-committee. As well as chairing meetings this also involved the preparation of position papers and background documentation.

Speed control was one particular area that exercised the minds of legislators in the traffic field. The setting of general limits in urban areas and rural areas demanded information about levels of compliance and to this end a number of Australia-wide speed surveys were conducted. I was glad to be put in charge of the development of a set of guidelines that would ensure that as far as possible data would be collected on a uniform basis across the wide variety of road configurations that are encountered in the states and territories. In this task I received valuable assistance and advice from Keith Hastings, the engineer from the CBR, with whom I worked on the implementation of the first accident black spot program. It was particularly gratifying some years later to hear a senior traffic engineer describe the guidelines that were developed as being 'the best off-the-shelf guidelines around'.

I have already mentioned that Peter Vulcan left the department to take up the chairmanship of RoSTA, but most of the original group remained with the ORS and others joined as the activities of the Road Safety Branch (RSB) expanded.

It was at this time that I encountered someone who over the years would become not only a loyal colleague but also a true family friend, Kevin Larkins - who had formerly been with the transport area of the Department of Supply. Kevin had a way with people that made him an ideal choice as the secretary for ACRUPTC, a task he fulfilled with distinction.

New areas of activity for the ORS arose directly out of recommendations in the EGORS reports. These included setting up a Road Safety Information Service (RSIS) that would serve as a computerised one-stop shop. It is hard to think back to the time before the internet when consultants had difficulty locating and accessing source material. The RSRS and the RSB were living proof of the Nobel laureate physicist Richard Fyneman's saying that "You don't have to be solemn to be serious". The member of staff who ran the service advertised his office as being "Andrew Carter's fiche and chip shop". The RSIS was not a browsing library, but one where holdings held on microfiche were accessed by computer. The system went by the acronym LASORS, standing for Literature Access Service Office of Road Safety, and produced regular catalogues of its holdings.

The RSB attracted talented people from other institutions. Some would later go on to bigger things. One such researcher was Carol Boughton who came to the RSB from the ARRB and I had met her there under her maiden name, Carol Watkins. As I recounted in an earlier chapter she had made her name when researching the truly mysterious series of accidents involving Melbourne's trams. Eventually, Ian Johnston, by then branch head, gave her, as he put it, 'a run on the ball' to use a phrase from his footballing days - this was Melbourne after all - and her career was away and running up the departmental ladder.

The RSB took up many areas that had been identified as in need of attention in the second EGORS report. Some were in areas where I had interest or experience. These will be discussed in the following chapters.

Chapter 21

Black Spot Programs

The idea for the first accident black spot program arose out of work done in the late 1960s by the Commonwealth Bureau of Roads (CBR) detailing the state of Australia's roads. The Bureau had been formally established during 1964, but was not constituted until 1966 and not fully operational until 1967. Its purpose was to provide the necessary information to the Federal Government upon which a *needs-based* allocation of federal roads funds could be made to the States. Previously various formulas had been used. The Bureau's first report, entitled *Report on Roads in Australia, 1973,* would include a recommendation for a separate category of road funding for minor traffic engineering and road safety improvements.

The Expert Group on Road Safety (EGORS) had of course been aware of the work of the CBR and embraced the idea with enthusiasm. Its first report tabled in 1972 included a recommendation for,

> A special program of financial assistance to the States for low cost traffic management and other improvements at locations with poor accident records should be introduced. Initially, $5 million a year should be made available on a dollar for dollar basis for this purpose.

The Australian Government responded with a special unmatched grant to the States of $3 million under the Traffic Engineering and Road Safety Improvement Program for the year 1973/74.

In order that the maximum benefit would result from the program, the likely effectiveness of each of a long list of project types was determined in a study commissioned by DST and undertaken by P G Pak-Poy and Associates. Because there were significant differences between the States as to what constituted a reportable accident, it was decided that the potential for reducing *accidents involving casualties* would be the basis for a ranking in terms of cost-benefit when measured against project cost.

Road authorities in each State, as well as the Road Safety and Traffic Authority in Victoria and the Brisbane City Council, were invited to submit projects from the list of project types for consideration. An allocation of funds between the States was not to be made until the evaluation process had commenced, which meant the States were in effect making competitive bids for funding that greatly exceeded the amount available. Projects were evaluated and ranked on a cost-benefit basis taking into account their accident reduction factor and cost. Strangely, the allocation of funds for the Traffic Engineering and Road Safety Improvement Program (TERSIP) ended up being made on the classic formula under the Commonwealth Aid (Roads) formula with equal weighting for area and population. The States were then given the flexibility to choose projects from a list of projects up to four times their allocation.

It was during the process of examining the consultant's report on accident reduction factors that I was able to advance the case for the provision of *raised reflective pavement markers (cat's eyes)*. The consultant's report had shown that such markers in use overseas could reduce accidents by between 10 and 20 per cent on the roads where they were installed. The failure to use raised reflective pavement markers in Australia despite them having been invented in England in 1934, nor to use retro-reflective material on warning signs, was of course indicative of a prevailing attitude fostered by bodies such as the ARSC that accidents were all the driver's fault and that was that. Realising that the States were competing for funds and having regard to their low cost, I succeeded in getting the accident reduction factor for raised reflective pavement markers set at the higher figure. This resulted in New South Wales putting forward a number of roads for such treatment including the Great Western Highway as far as Lithgow. Letters of appreciation flooded into the Minister's office and their use has subsequently become standard practice.

The State authorities were not always happy about the Australian Government seeking to direct their expenditures, but the programs were all discussed with them on their home ground. On these visits, I was accompanied by Keith Hastings from the CBR. In the course of these liaison visits Keith and I visited every State capital city in less than a fortnight, flying somewhere on ten nights out of a consecutive thirteen. As the Commonwealth representatives, we would make the point that accidents were occurring and if the Australian government could prevent them by directing expenditure it would do so. Nevertheless, when I had referred to "federal funds" and the government's right to control their use, Keith reminded me that the funds in question were contributed by people from the States and therefore the States needed to be accorded proper consideration.

One notable exchange occurred with the Chief Engineer of the NSW Department of Main Roads (DMR), a Mr Willing. He had told me that "everything we do is safety", to which I replied that that was interesting because I had a list of projects for NSW totalling $3 million that had a benefit-cost ratio of 19:1. As we walked to the lift after the meeting Keith told me that chief engineers were not used to being spoken to like that. Nevertheless the point had to be made.

News of a similar exchange in Sydney during discussions about the next iteration of TERSIP, namely the roads legislation's category Minor Improvements for Traffic Engineering and Road Safety (MITERS), spread quickly. In the case of NSW, although the state programs were co-ordinated by the DMR, they could also include projects on roads that were not under direct state government control. The Australian Minister for Transport, however, had given the public the opportunity to nominate locations where remedial action might be taken.

One such nominated location was brought to attention by a Sydney resident who had meticulously documented the scores and scores of accidents that had occurred on a notorious downhill bend on Homer Street in Undercliffe. This was a 'local road' and we were told that there was no funding mechanism by which MITERS funds could be directed to it. "That's interesting", I said. "What did you do when it had a double tram track down the middle"? By a remarkable coincidence I was familiar with the location from the time when I was doing public opinion surveys with the ABCB. I had seen where the tram tracks had been covered over after the demise of the tram system a year or so before. "We'll look into it" came the reply, astonished that someone from Melbourne would have that degree of local knowledge. They did take action and a project for grooving the road to improve traction on the bend was undertaken. The success of the project was such that it was featured in a professional journal not long after.

The first entry of the Commonwealth into specific-purpose road funding, at least at the level of individual projects, was attended by an acute awareness of political sensitivities and, in particular, the need for the spread of projects over electorates to be seen as even-handed. In order to dispel any doubt, a decision was made that each electorate would receive at least one TERSIP project. One public school in the seat of Hume even got a set of pedestrian-operated traffic lights that way. There was also much poring over electoral maps to see in just which seat a project in a mountainous area was located, and to questions such as – "Where *is* the seat of Ryan – it hasn't got a project".

The states too had to play a similar game. In Queensland the state government decided that each local government area had to receive a project. In the outback this produced a hilarious result when Birdsville Shire, not surprisingly, failed to figure in the initial allocation. A solution, however, was at hand. One of the project types recognised under TERSIP (and of course MITERS) was intersection channelisation to separate traffic streams. But in Birdsville Shire? You're joking! Look closely at a photo of the Birdsville Hotel and you will see concrete kerb and gutter. Thanks to TERSIP.

Sometimes, however, the right hand in a state did not know what the left hand was doing. When the first announcements of TERSIP-funded projects were being made we had still heard nothing from Victoria. We were therefore astonished when the state Minister of Transport let forth a tirade in the press that Victoria had been slighted. We were aware that the Victorian program was being co-ordinated by the Road Safety and Traffic Authority, which was responsible to the Chief Secretary's Department. Investigation of the matter led to the envelope containing the Victorian project documentation being found on a mantelpiece in the Chief Secretary's office because no one knew what to do with it.

Provision of funding for black spot improvements continued with a MITERS category included in subsequent roads legislation. Funding continued under the Fraser government, elected after the dismissal of the Whitlam government in 1975. Funding for black spot programs remained as part of the ALP platform, but funding ended soon after the election of the Hawke government in 1983. Funding, however, resumed under the Howard government that took office in 1996. I often wonder whether support under Coalition governments results in part from the horrific nature of many accidents in rural seats at sites that might not otherwise be treated, except as part of comprehensive reconstruction works.

The renewed black spot program was evaluated and a report produced in 2002. This provided very strong evidence that the program achieved its aim of improving safety at locations with a history of crashes involving death or serious injury and yielding an overall benefit-cost ratio of 14:1. Measures that were particularly effective in the capital cities were roundabouts, traffic lights (even those not incorporating turn arrows), medians, non-skid surfaces, traffic islands and indented right and left hand turns. In regional areas, signs, traffic lights with arrows, medians, shoulder sealing, edge lines and improved lighting also improved safety. In general, urban areas gained the most benefit from works under the program with a benefit-cost ratio of 18:1. The report also made the comment that data availability, timeliness and quality issues had limited the usefulness of the evaluation. The report noted that one state had even ceased to produce crash diagrams as part of the accident reporting process.

Funding continued under the Rudd and Gillard ALP governments as part of the Auslink/Nation Building Program and is continuing under the Coalition government. The last program under the previous government provided for a 33 per cent increase per year Australia-wide. Administration of the program that had formerly been with the ORS became a function of the Department of Infrastructure and Transport as a part of general road funding programs. There is, of course, an upper limit on what constitutes a 'low cost' project and a choice has to be made between doing a few big projects or a larger number of smaller projects.

A development noted in the 2002 report was the inclusion of funding for projects that had been identified as potential black spots by what are known as 'road safety audits' that cast a lay user's view over the locations in question. The current black spot program has provision for up to 30% of a state or territory's funding to be use on projects identified in this way. This stands in sharp contrast to 'tombstone safety'- doing nothing until tragedy strikes. It is to the credit of state governments that a number have instituted their own black spot programs.

A feature of federally funded black spot programs since their reintroduction has been the establishment of Black Spot Consultative Committees to consider each state or territory's project recommendations under the chairmanship of a senator or member from the party in federal government. The committees comprise representatives of relevant departments, state, territory and federal, plus user groups. I am privileged to represent the Australasian College of Road Safety on the ACT Panel. Members of the public can also nominate sites for consideration under the program by writing or emailing their local federal member. This is not a new idea. I have already shown how one case was successfully brought to attention.

Whilst the distribution of funds made available under the federally funded black spot program takes place independently of how state and territory governments distribute state funds to local government bodies, there remains the issue of how such funding fits in with the capital works budgets of the states and territories. It was for this reason that, from the inception of black spot funding, the states were required to certify that federal funds had not been used in place of, or in substitution for, other funds. Certification was also required on completion that such works had been carried out in compliance with relevant technical standards.

Work at particular locations, however, may be high on the list for funding under the federal black spot program *and* on the state or municipal works program. One such case occurred in the ACT only recently. Installation of traffic lights at the top priority intersection for treatment under the federal black spot criteria was held up because they were included in work being undertaken along one of the roads concerned as part of the ACT Capital Works program. Sadly a fatality occurred at the site in the interim. This is a matter of special importance where new housing or other developments are taking place on the edges of existing urban areas that already have their own problems in need of remedial action.

In other cases, especially in rural areas, major roadworks may be in progress, or being planned, that will eliminate a black spot completely or make a location less likely to be black spot in the future. Special care needs to be taken to ensure that the risk of accidents at such locations is minimised in the meantime. At work, we would often make wry observations about having to wait for 'the grand solution' to solve problems at one location or another, a section of the old Hume Highway near Black Dog Creek north of Wangaratta being one example.

In the light of the success of accident black spot programs that have an *immediate and continuing* influence on driving behaviour, requiring no more than normal maintenance, it is small wonder that I am distrustful of safety *campaigns* directed at the entire driving population that require continual reinforcement and whose efficacy has rarely, if ever, been objectively proved.

Chapter 22

Local Area Traffic Management

It will be clear from the tenor of this book that I regard the motorcar as a beneficial invention, not as something to be disinvented, but as something to be *managed*. Nowhere is this more so than in the local street system. I have referred already to the experience of having grown up living close to a dangerous cross–intersection and close to a major traffic artery. I was therefore receptive to the notion that traffic in the local street system needed to be subject to some special sort of control.

I had long observed that most intersections along main roads, at least in Melbourne, took the form not of crossroads but of T-junctions. I was therefore interested to learn, not long after joining DST, of the work of Harold Marks reported in *Traffic Quarterly* in 1957 in an article entitled 'Subdividing for Traffic Safety'. His work in the United States showed that T-junctions had a significantly lower accident record than cross-intersections.

Much closer to home, came the pioneering work of the City Engineer of the City of Woodville, in suburban Adelaide, Jan Vreugdenhil, who had become alarmed at the increasing number of accidents at its intersections. Like most of Adelaide at that time, the area concerned had been laid out on a geometric grid. He decided to take matters into his own hands and introduced Australia's very first system of street closures and other measures that would ultimately become known as *local area traffic management*.

It should be remembered that at this time there were *no* traffic control devices in place to control priority at intersections in Australia (except in Tasmania) that overrode the notorious *give-way-to-the right* rule, apart from traffic lights. Actually, even the status of traffic lights in that regard would remain in doubt until the 1970s. Risk-taking at cross-intersections was endemic as I knew only too well and I joined the department determined to do all that I could to change the situation, but more of that later.

At around the time that Jan Vreugdenhil was doing his work in Adelaide, the City Engineer of the City of Box Hill in suburban Melbourne, Brian Harper, saw the opportunity to pursue the same line of research as Harold Marks. Accordingly, he studied the accident and traffic flow records for an area just off Union and Belmore Roads in Box Hill North. (Their intersection was the site of one of Melbourne's first roundabouts.) Brian Harper's results confirmed those of Marks and were presented in an unpublished paper to the Highways and Traffic Engineering Branch of the Institution of Engineers Australia under the title 'Design of the Local Street System' in July 1966.

In Canberra similar results were evident. This was the time when the National Capital Development Commission was developing the modern Canberra in line with the best of town planning practice in Australian and overseas. A comparison study was made between the older suburbs - with their grid layouts to the north of Lake Burley Griffin and the circles to the south - with the newer suburbs that featured T-junctions, curvilinear alignments and cul-de-sacs. This showed that the new suburbs had significantly lower accident rates. Indeed, accidents had virtually been eliminated from the local street system.

Changing the meaning of the 'Stop' sign in Australia to what it had always meant everywhere else in the world, i.e. stop and give way, following a change to the National Road Traffic Code in 1974 gave town planners and traffic engineers another tool for their kit. As well as enabling control of access to main roads, Stop signs could be used to reduce the speed of approach at cross intersections in the local street system, in combination with Give Way signs which were more appropriate at sites with better visibility. Alternating priority at intersections on long local streets laid out on a grid could also reduce speeds – so-called egg-crate priority. At local street cross intersections, where traffic volumes warranted it, small roundabouts soon found a place and have become a notable feature of the urban streetscape.

In the 1970s and 1980s the freeway fighters still believed that Australian cities, once again alone in the world, could survive without even a skeletal system of freeways and influenced timid governments, reluctant to spend the necessary money, accordingly. At this time too, those groups who would gladly have seen motorcars disappear altogether started to apply the term 'traffic calming', to what was correctly called Local Area Traffic Management (LATM). Indeed they saw it primarily as a means of at least taming the 'evil' motor car, quite ignoring its safety benefits.

Australia's capital cities, with one exception, have now accepted that inner city bypasses and cross-metropolitan freeways are an essential part of the urban fabric to cater for the cross-suburban and regional traffic, and particularly the heavy vehicle traffic that should not have any place on the modern surface street system. In Melbourne, for example, roads that formerly carried four lanes of through traffic are now marked with one general traffic lane and a cycle lane in each direction while through traffic passes safely by on the adjacent freeway.

In a recent twist, LATM is now being applied to rescue some of Canberra's newest suburbs from the deleterious effects of New Urbanism. To the New Urbanists cul-de-sacs, curvilinear alignments and loop streets, despite their safety benefits, are anathema – as indeed is the suburban city in general. They see straight streets and grid patterns as standing in contrast to what they perceive as the environmental excesses of suburbia. For curved streets and cul-de-sacs they have coined the term 'cul-de-sac cancer' in a derogatory reference to the modern suburbs in American cities such as Phoenix which employ such devices within a one-mile grid of dual-carriageway arterials.

It is no surprise to see LATM devices such as speed hump having to be routinely included on the long straight streets of Canberra's newest suburbs. The same trend is evident elsewhere and examples of the two types of layout can be seen alongside each other in the new suburb of Wyndham Vale in the outer west of Melbourne.

In a paper delivered to a Nature and Society Forum in Canberra in 2000 on 'Personal Mobility in a Pollution-free Environment', however, I argued that promoting an urban form that is most suitable for public transport may not only be unnecessary once non-polluting private vehicles are developed, but also inequitable since those with the highest incomes will tend to gravitate to the places where their transport costs are minimised, to the detriment of those less well-off or with families. This theme was elaborated on in a paper I presented to the ACT Chapter of Independent Scholars Association of Australia during 2014 reflecting on the minority ideology that appears to be influencing the land planning and transport policies of the current ACT government.

One cannot leave the subject of LATM without returning to the city where it all began – Adelaide. *Alone in the developed world for a city of its size, Adelaide has no freeways that penetrate the urban fabric.* One has been built across the outer northern suburbs to carry industrial traffic, but is called an expressway; another exists in tandem with a surface arterial in the outer southern suburbs (with the dubious distinction of being the only tidal flow freeway in the world) and the one through the Adelaide Hills terminates abruptly at Glen Osmond on the urban fringe. The result is a horrendous mix of trucks and cars with too few traffic lights to break up the flow of traffic, and every grid-pattern side street used as a 'rat run' to avoid the main roads.

The national fatality statistics reveal that in the 1950s when Stop signs in South Australia meant what they do today, the State's urban speed limit was 35 mph, higher than in other capital cities, and there was no practical driving test, South Australia had a fatality rate per thousand vehicles that was 25% lower than the other states. Today it is often among the highest. Given the pre-eminence of Adelaide as the State's major population centre, the absence of freeways would seem to be a factor.

The high proportion of serious accidents on local streets that is revealed by a close analysis of the speed/accident relationship data upon which Australia's urban speed management is being based indicates that rat-running is endemic in the absence of freeways. Despite that, data gathered in Adelaide, *a totally unrepresentative source,* is being used throughout Australia to support what is close to a zero-tolerance approach to the enforcement of urban speed limits, a topic upon which there is much more to be said before I am finished.

Before and after the move to Canberra, the ORS also played a significant part in the adoption of LATM practices throughout Australia.

The reports of the Expert Group in 1972 and 1975 both drew attention to the role that road and traffic control improvements could make in reducing the toll of death and injury on urban roads and streets. Among the many other recommendations for action or further research the Expert Group's second report recommended the development of a set of road safety guidelines that could be applied in existing urban environments and in the planning of new urban developments.

The ORS took up the recommendation from EGORS and the consulting firm of Loder and Bayly was commissioned to provide the first draft document. Much of the content of the document was derived from their literature review *Town Planning in Relation to Road Safety*, one of the twenty-four reviews undertaken for the Expert Group. Relevant State and Territory authorities also contributed information that would be incorporated into the guidelines document. Our principal contact with Loder and Bayly was Ray Brindle who would later become a recognised academic in the field of town planning at the Australian Road Research Board where his work earned him a Doctor of Engineering degree in 1995.

In 1978 the ORS published *Town Planning Guidelines for Road Safety*. The document set out a total of thirty-one guidelines. Wherever possible they were illustrated with examples from various locations around the country. The document was basically divided into four sections plus a case history from the City of Woodville and an appendix relating specifically to intersection treatments. Copies were sent to every municipal council in Australia.

Work on town planning in relation to road safety did not stop with the production of the guidelines. It was decided that what was needed was a comprehensive field trial putting into practice many of the LATM techniques as had been identified by that time. This was, however, not just a demonstration project, valuable though that would be. It was also to be a research project by which the identified measures could be refined and standards established for them.

By a remarkable coincidence, the head of Public Education in the ORS, Graeme Evans, had also been the mayor of one of the municipalities in the bayside area of Melbourne, the City of Sandringham. The area proved to be an ideal test bed for LATM practices.

The older part of the municipality had been developed in the first half of the twentieth century, growing outwards from the suburban railway stations of Hampton and Sandringham, where the line terminated. As a result much of this area had a grid pattern of streets. In Hampton many of the streets running inland from the railway line, and carrying significant volumes of traffic, were surprisingly narrow and indeed unsuited to their function as distributor streets.

The southern part of the municipality, aside from the area close to Port Phillip Bay that had been settled much earlier, offered a remarkable contrast of urban style. By the time the newer parts were being developed in the 1950s and 1960s - the suburb of Beaumaris - the native ti-tree scrub that in earlier years would have been cleared had come to be highly valued. Streetscapes were much more informal and there was a notable local controversy over council plans to pave one particular street, Point Avenue, then a sandy track. (It is, however, not quite correct to describe Beaumaris as a 'new' area as an unsuccessful attempt was made in the early years of the century to develop the area for housing. An electric tramway was pushed through the ti-tree bushland in 1926, extending the line that had been built from Sandringham to Black Rock that opened in 1919. The extension was closed in 1931, during the Great Depression, and the earlier section in 1956. Tramway Parade in Beaumaris provides a reminder of that time.)

With this background in mind, two demonstration projects were designed, one centred on Thomas Street in Hampton and the other on Anita Street in Beaumaris. The whole project went by the name Sandringham Local Area Traffic Management and Safety Study, leading to the rather catchy acronym SLATMASS. Extensive public consultations took place at which the ORS was represented by Graeme Evans, and Laurie Evans, a town planner, who had joined my section. Reactions in the areas concerned were mixed and one objector even took his fight to the House of Representatives, getting his local member to ask a question of the Minister for Transport about the justification for the project. We in ORS were only too happy to provide the Minister with his reply. The answer failed to mollify the objector who even contended that the entire project was a benefit for the consultants.

Important findings came out of the study, the most notable of which arose out of the study in Thomas Street. This was that 'slow points' such as speed humps, narrowings and chicanes need to be placed about every 150 metres otherwise the effect on speed is lost and acceleration noise becomes a problem. LATM devices remain in place along Thomas Street. Film Australia was also involved and produced two films. *Streets are for Sharing* illustrated the wide variety of measures that can be taken to produce safer, more attractive, urban environments and *Local Traffic: A Suburban Dilemma* showed how one community dealt with the traffic problem on its local roads. The concept of sharing the road now finds direct expression in the creation of 'Shared Zones' in areas of low vehicle movement where priority is given to pedestrians, but on the condition of not unnecessarily impeding traffic movement.

The field of LATM moved quickly and not long after ORS moved to Canberra it was decided that a second edition of the guidelines should be developed. This would build on the SLATMASS findings but also on knowledge derived from work elsewhere in Australia, and also take account of the need to reduce roadside hazards. I was put in charge of the process.

In the time since the first guidelines document was produced a number of new concepts had been formulated. Most significant of these was the distinction between the *traffic movement* function of roads and the *access* function. A basic objective of the guidelines was therefore seen to be balancing the two functions - meaning that roads having high traffic movement should have low access and vice versa - so as to minimise the number and severity of accidents whenever conflicting situations might occur.

In regard to the reduction of conflict, it is significant that in the time since the first edition of the guidelines was produced Australia had moved from reliance on an over-arching give-way-to-the-right rule of precedence at intersections to a major/minor system based on the use of Stop Signs, Give Way signs and the T-junction rule, introduced Australia-wide on 1 March 1981. Priority control at local street intersections was therefore added to the list of measures available for the management of traffic movement. Land use planning with safety in mind had also taken on a new importance in the light of these developments and was increasingly being linked with transport planning.

Accordingly, I decided that the structure of the new edition should be different from the first edition and clearly reflect these new developments.

The guidelines commenced with an introduction outlining the issues and then dealt with road hierarchy, land use planning, designing the environment, intersections and junctions, the role of public transport, parking, catering for pedestrians and cyclists and concluding with facilitation of public participation. Many of the guidelines would, of course, cross-reference others.

Producing the guidelines was a team effort between me, Laurie Evans, Cathy Parsons, who also had qualifications in town planning, and traffic engineer Dick Stott. Cathy was later selected for the Executive Development Scheme and would go on to higher posts in the planning and transport areas of the Department of the Capital Territory, so much so that not long before I retired I found myself being interviewed by her for a position in the branch she then headed!

On another personal note, the illustration with the caption 'Priority control in the local street system' shows the white Valiant sedan I was driving at the time of the Jugiong accident that is referred to in the chapter relating to the Hume Highway.

The ORS was glad to have been able to have the draft of the new guidelines reviewed by Professor Hans Westerman, who had not long retired from the position of Chief Planner of the National Capital Development Commission. By then he was Head of the School of Town Planning with the University of New South Wales. The planning and engineering consultancy, Loder and Bayly also contributed to the guidelines providing evidence relating to the effectiveness of the various measures included in the compendium for action that is included in the guidelines publication.

The new edition of the guidelines was published in 1984 under the title *Planning for Road Safety*. Again, copies of the booklet were distributed to every municipal council in Australia.

The booklet focussed on a series of guidelines that would lead to the creation of a safer system for all road users, including cyclists and pedestrians. Its purpose was to encourage informed discussion between those who plan and design urban facilities and those in the decision area who adjudicate between alternatives. No attempt was made to jointly cater for professionals working in the area by providing detailed technical information.

In line with the policy developed by my colleague and now friend, Graeme Evans, an eight-page pamphlet was also produced by the ORS as part of a series designed to acquaint the general public with the principles behind road safety actions. The pamphlet, as well as the guidelines, used attractive photographs of typical treatments. Appropriately, the cover of the pamphlet shows one of the original diagonal closures at what had formerly been a cross-intersection in the City of Woodville.

There have now been LATM projects all over Australia and most of these have benefitted visual amenity as well as safety. I would suspect that this has assisted their acceptance. The small roundabout in particular has become a ubiquitous feature of the local streetscapes in most urban areas of Australia. The success of roundabouts in general, especially in reducing the severity as well as the incidence of accidents, has also seen them coming into widespread use on urban main roads and in rural settings.

I am astounded, however, that the contribution made by LATM to reducing serious accidents in the local street system rarely receives a mention in public discourse about road safety today, yet the results are measurable and spectacular. Indeed, while there are constant references to so-called 'traffic calming' measures in European cities, Australia's place in the forefront of LATM worldwide is simply ignored.

The success of LATM goes to confirm the truth of the advice given by the legendary former Assistant Commissioner of Police at Scotland Yard, Sir Alker Tripp, in his 1942 book *Town Planning and Road Traffic* that,

> Nothing should be done by means of legal restrictions which is practical to effect by layout; this principle must be regarded as an axiom of traffic science. To restrict movement by law and police is likely to be both irksome and inefficient, whereas guidance by layout and mechanical equipment is efficient, and generally speaking, congenial.

There is more than one point being made in that quotation that has relevance to the Australia of 2015, as will become evident as this story unfolds.

In closing this chapter I go back to where it all began for me – living near an intersection that cars hurtled through willy-nilly. In that Oakleigh neighbourhood, the streets have been properly sealed and kerbed, trees have grown and a small roundabout is now in place at the intersection.

Chapter 23

Public Education – a New Way

I have already referred to the ineffective nature of so-called public education in the days of the Australian Road Safety Council. As long ago as 1968 the report by the South Australian Government Committee of Enquiry into Road Safety noted that,

> Many of the previous publicity campaigns have been directed at drivers to persuade them to change their presumed delinquent behaviour. This absolves from blame, perhaps unfairly, the many other organisations and authorities, such as vehicle manufacturers, road authorities and developers whose activities also influence road safety.
>
> In particular, posters with a general message such as *'Speed Kills'*, *'Drive carefully'*, *'The Life You Save May Be Your Own'* are ineffective.

Such messages were the stock in trade of the ARSC along with its clangers such as 'Death is so Permanent' and 'Don't Cross the Styx in 56'.

When ATAC reorganised its road safety committee structure following the demise of the ARSC, its replacement committee was given the title Publicity Advisory Committee on Education in Road Safety (PACERS).

This opened the door for a change in the way in which road safety messages might be put to the public. The key was the term 'education' and FORS enthusiastically seized the opportunity this offered.

Under the new section head of public education in the ORS, Graeme Evans, public education moved into a whole new era – to give the community information that would lay a foundation for the application of scientifically proven countermeasures. Research done for EGORS, especially by Barry Elliott and Associates, had reached the same conclusion as the South Australian committee with regard to the efficacy, or rather the lack of it, of conventional road safety propaganda. The traditional frontline was the printed word but increasing attention came to be given to advertising the road safety message on other media.

Print

While a wide array of media continued to be used, under Graeme Evans several carefully targeted eight-page colour publications were key elements.

Making Road Usage Safer

This publication set out to document the road safety revolution in lay terms. It showed how what has been found to work could be put into practice to reduce death and injury on the roads. To this end, the reader was introduced to what has become known as the *Haddon Matrix*. This was a 3x3 matrix that looked at accident events in terms of the *Human* contribution to the accident, the *Environment* (social as well as physical) in which driving, riding or walking took place, and the characteristics of the *Vehicle* involved that could make a difference to the outcome. On the other axis (across the top) are the three phases into which an accident event can be divided: *pre-crash. in-crash and post-crash.* If *anything* could have been different in any of the nine cells the accident event would not have occurred or could have been less severe.

The matrix has as its concomitant the notion of the *Causal Chain*; any intervention that prevents the accident event from moving from one phase to the next would mean that the accident would not have occurred or been less severe. The publication ends with an example incorporating all cells of the matrix to show what could have made a difference in a particular situation. A modification to the matrix as used in the publication in question was to recognise the *social* environment separately from the physical environment.

Planning for Road Safety

In an earlier chapter I have referred to the interest taken by ORS in how town planning and local area traffic management could be used to make road usage safer in urban areas. As I mentioned, copies of each edition of the guidelines documents were distributed to every local government authority in Australia, the first in 1978 and the second in 1984. Those documents were now complemented by the publication *Planning for Road Safety*. This was aimed at the general public in order to garner support for the measures proposed. As I mentioned earlier, the cover photograph is looking down on a diagonal closure at the intersection of two streets in the Adelaide suburb where such measures were first used.

The Cost of Accidents

For the best part of 50 years attempts have made to put a value on the cost of road traffic accidents in order to focus attention on the extent of the problem they represent to the community. Basically there are two lines of approach.

One method is to add up every item of expenditure that can be attributed to the accident having occurred. This approach, however, depends on a very variable variable - the total value of sums paid to victims and their families to compensate for 'pain and suffering'. It has been argued, however, that there is *no* 'economic cost of road accidents', only a series of 'transfer' payments. By this is meant that the associated expenditures have simply been redirected away from what the money would otherwise have been spent on. My take on this was that a motorist would prefer to have an air-conditioner put in the car (before they were almost standard equipment) rather than pay the panel beater's bill; the latter was an avoidable and needless expense if the accident could have been prevented or rendered less severe.

The second method, the one used today, is to determine a figure that represents in aggregate what people would be prepared to pay for accidents *not to occur*. After all the methodological arguments about costings, it is ironic that modern analytical methods have focussed on something that does not depend on the adding up of costs.

Standardised figures have generally been agreed upon for each class of accident – fatal, injury-producing or property-damage only. These values are then applied to determine whether a particular project will return more in savings than it costs – i.e. its benefit-cost ratio. By this means projects or ideas can be ranked in priority order for funding.

These were the sorts of issues canvassed in *The Cost of Accidents* in the hope of producing a more rational debate about the course road safety efforts should take based on facts, not propaganda.

This may be a good time to counter the oft-heard phrase "If it saves just one life it is worth it". If more lives could have been saved by the expenditure going to something more likely to be effective, the money spent represents a waste of resources.

Preventing the Human Collision

The idea that road safety could be enhanced by making vehicles safer was still relatively novel in the early 1980s. Hence the decision to produce a layman's guide to what goes on inside a crashing vehicle.

The intention was that if people were aware of what went on in a crash they were more likely to press for, or at least understand, the reasons why the design of vehicles had to change. People needed to know what it was in a vehicle that they would hurt themselves on if they were not wearing a seatbelt (or other restraint). They also needed to know how the vehicle itself could be designed in a way that would reduce the severity of injury. This is the concept of *passive safety*.

Back then, there were those who longed for the days when cars were built on a 'strong rigid chassis', not realising that the 'tin cans' they were now driving were designed the way they were so that the very crushing of the bodywork would reduce the forces acting on the people inside the car. It just so happened that at the time I started to drive, the UK manufacturer Nuffield had produced the Morris Oxford – a still modern-looking roomy medium-sized sedan – which had what was called 'monocoque' construction, i.e. the base panels themselves were the platform upon to which the other panels were welded. A similar construction was employed in the Holden that hit the market in 1947 as 'Australia's own car'. 'Chassis-less' construction has since become standard. It is ironic that I should be writing this at the very time that General Motors has announced its intention to withdraw from local production.

Radio

The Road Safety Branch commissioned the development of radio, and television, commercials directed at specific aspects of vehicle operation starting with the need for children to be wearing seatbelts, or better still, specifically designed child restraints. Despite winning 'Radio Commercial of the Year' one such campaign had no measurable effect on behaviour, whilst the associated television commercial had limited effect. Principles for future campaigns were, however, derived from the experience.

Key elements were that the educational material had to be directed at a specific behaviour, with the need to change being reinforced not by old-fashioned shock/horror but nevertheless by inducing a mild level of fear at the injury or worse that might occur if the desired behavioural change was not made. The role of enforcement would be to reinforce the message by punishing non-compliance

Television

The Cronin commercials – What sort of friend are you? Would you let a mate drink and drive?

It was in the medium of television that the most ambitious public education project was the undertaken by the RSB. This was to commission the development and screening of the *What sort of friend are you? Would you let a mate drink and drive?* commercials. These featured the well-loved actor Paul Cronin, most remembered for his part in the immensely popular TV series *The Sullivans.*

Road safety publicity had always suffered from the lack of a marketable product. We have seen the uselessness of *Drive safely* as a message. That is what most people do to the best of their ability. Even drivers guilty of the most dangerous acts behind the wheel rarely set out *deliberately* to harm anyone. Moreover every journey that is completed without incident reinforces the idea that whatever people have been doing it has been safe, at least as they see it.

What the Cronin campaign did, perhaps for the first time, was to sell a product – *the good feeling it would give anyone when they stopped a friend from getting behind the wheel when they had obviously had so much alcohol as to be incapable of driving safely.*

As it happened, not long before I moved to Canberra, I had seen younger members of my tennis club take a much older member home from a club function because they were fearful that he could not safely drive himself.

The possibilities shown in the commercials were to call a cab or to give the affected driver a bed for the night, each reinforced with the message "Would you let a mate drink and drive?" Although the Cronin commercials were made some thirty years ago, echoes can seen in the 2013 television commercials from New South Wales *RBT means you need a Plan B* in which one character throws a blanket over his alcohol-affected mate slumped on a couch.

Technically, the commercials made use of the advances such as the blue [now green] screen technique for superimposing characters into scenes, but it was at the conceptual level that it broke new ground.

Second wave feminism was also a factor in deciding what form the commercials would take. Many overseas products were looked at as part of the process. Some gave a shepherding role to a spouse or girlfriend. The decision was very deliberately made that females should not be expected to be the watchdogs on their male companion's behaviour or to bear responsibility for getting them home safely. That said, the Cronin commercials did have a decidedly 'blokey' flavour and I cannot help wondering whether if the same product were being put together today it would have had to be gender-neutral!

Disappointingly, given their technical acclaim, evaluation of the commercials showed that they had only limited success in changing behaviour. This was despite the intensive research that had been undertaken including reviewing the acceptability of themes and approaches from across the world and the conduct of a test-run with the co-operation of the Tasmanian authorities.

Older Pedestrians

Use was subsequently made of television after FORS moved to Canberra, notably, if less successfully, in a three–commercial campaign to encourage safe crossing behaviour amongst older pedestrians. It is to get ahead of the story, but one of my last assignments there was to be on-site during the shooting of these commercials. (By then, the ORS had been renamed the Federal Office of Road Safety [FORS].)

Each of the three commercials dealt with a major point that older pedestrians can apply when crossing roads: planning to use pedestrian crossing facilities such as traffic lights; making sure they can be seen at night, especially in the wet; and concentrating on the crossing task and using median strips or refuge islands to break the crossing into two parts.

The commercials featured people in the 60-plus age group, not actors, engaging in challenging pastimes made safe by the following simple safety rules. The same people then presented similar messages related to crossing the road. In the first, a woman aged 78, was shown preparing to abseil down a cliff and emphasising that *planning ahead* is important; she was then shown planning to use the traffic lights or a pedestrian crossing on her walk to the local shops. The second one showed a couple, both aged 68, scuba diving with the emphasis on high-visibility underwater gear: they then applied the same principle to crossing the road at night in *light-coloured clothing*. The third commercial showed a glider pilot, aged 65, in his glider, emphasising the importance of concentration and then applying that to crossing a busy street, and making use of a median strip, The common voice-over at the end of each was "crossing the road's a challenge – think about it", the double meaning intended to stress planning ahead, but also the need to concentrate and not step onto the road when one's mind is on something else.

I did become acutely aware of the difficulty of using non-professionals in acting roles. As a night shoot wore on past 11 pm we finally decided that the delivery of the line "If drivers can see you easily, you're a lot safer" in Take 39 would do. (The more familiar line to "wear something bright to show at night" might have worked better!). Nevertheless I still copped flak from my superiors because in this last take the bumper of the car involved was just over the pedestrian crossing marking. I recall, too, the producer saying that their job was to 'create reality'. The commercial filmed at night simulated a wet road using a borrowed garden hose.

Things, however, did not always work out as planned. Indeed, the impact of the whole campaign commercials was in part lost because of one unfortunate piece of happenstance. A site in the Brisbane CBD was found for what was expected to be the easiest of the three commercials to shoot. The subject simply had to say the words 'Concentration's the secret' and then cross the road. At the very moment he stepped out, a bus passed by on an adjoining *but quite separate* road and was caught in the shot. This was not discovered until the rushes were being looked at, by which time it was too late to do anything about it. I suspect that today's technology would have got rid of the bus. In the event, the bus was the only thing people remembered about the campaign.

Other campaigns

Other television commercials made after FORS moved to Canberra included one directed at young pedal cyclists that featured then state-of-the-art space-themed special effects and another directed to motorcyclists that featured champion rider Wayne Gardner.

Campaigns or Construction

My experience in the field has convinced me that governments often take the view that if you don't want to spend money to design out the problem, you run a campaign. I leave my readers to guess what today's most evident advertising message (apart from drink-driving) is directed at, in the absence of a real commitment to build the roads that are still lacking in one of the three or four most motorised nations on Earth. It must be said, however, that recent announcements by the federal Coalition government indicate that the deficiencies in the road network in the cities appear to be finally getting the attention they deserve, although the full benefits, especially to safety and urban amenity, will not be realised if drivers have to pay tolls to use the new roads.

Chapter 24

Priority Control at Intersections and the T-Junction Rule

Three crash locations in Victoria featured regularly in the news in the 1960s as locations where fatalities had taken place. These were the intersections along Stumpy Gully Road on the Mornington Peninsula, at Waurn Ponds just west of Geelong and on Deakin Avenue in Mildura. Each of the locations had features that made them especially hazardous in the days before the give-way-to-the-right rule was replaced by the system of priority control by signs, signals and roundabouts that has helped make driving so much safer than it was in the 1950s and 1960s.

Stumpy Gully Road is a north-south road on the Mornington Peninsula, roughly bisecting it. Along it, about 1.6 km apart, were numerous cross intersections. Far too many drivers failed to slow down at the crossroads, tearing across, with fatal accidents being the inevitable result far too often. Priority control and roundabouts have now reduced the dangers at such rural crossroads.

Waurn Ponds is the name of the locality near Geelong where the road to Anglesea, a resort town on what is now known as the Surf Coast, used to meet the Princes Highway West at an angle just after crossing a small bridge and intersecting with another side road. The location was especially hazardous at night with serious collisions occurring between vehicles returning from the beaches and traffic travelling at speed along the highway. There is now a roundabout at the location and the highway has been duplicated.

Deakin Avenue is the impressive tree-lined entry into Mildura with a wide central median that puts one very much in mind of Canberra's Northbourne Avenue. The city is laid out on a grid pattern and so Deakin Avenue is intersected at regular intervals by streets that are named numerically out from the city centre (a nod to the American origins of the pioneer Chaffey brothers around whose citrus orchards Mildura developed). These uncontrolled cross-intersections exposed the greatest weakness of the then total reliance on the give-way-to-the-right rule. If the vehicle in the median was coming straight across, drivers on Deakin Avenue would have to give way, but if the vehicle was completing a right-turn its driver would have to give way; the problem was that there was no way of telling one from the other. Fatal accidents were the regular and inevitable result. It should be noted that a give-way-to-the-*left* rule when *driving on the left* - which is the equivalent of the giving way to the right when driving on the right - would not have produced the same confusion. A driver coming through the median would have to give way whether turning through the median or going across.

Perhaps the most destructive decision ever taken under the aegis of ATAC was the decision in 1964 to make the give-way-to-the-right rule absolute across the whole of Australia. It is hardly an exaggeration to say that this was the beginning of the end for South Australia's spectacularly lower rate of road traffic accident fatalities which dates from 1964 when its government agreed to accept the ATAC'S decision and abandon the 'stop and give way' meaning for the Stop sign mainland, so putting Australia at variance with the rest of the world. In Adelaide with its predominantly grid pattern of streets the situation was even more devastating. In fact, on my first visit to Adelaide in 1953 I had noticed a certain determination to drive strictly in accordance with what the book said. (Bear in mind, though, that if Victorian drivers had adopted an approach of strictly observing the state's idiotic rules, Melbourne's roads would have ceased to function.) On a visit to Tasmania in 1970 I was astounded to find out that the Stop sign still meant what it did in the rest of the world, and indeed continued to do so until the rest of Australia caught up by changing the meaning.

On the mainland, worse was to come when Victorian courts began rigorously applying the give-way-to-the-right rule. There, the Winneke judgement of 1966 in Payne vs. West (VR 489) marked the low point in traffic law enforcement in Australia. The results were tragic and predictable in the light of the finding that the approach at a high speed by the driver on the right only heightened the other driver's obligation to give way!

It is hard to imagine how a situation could have been countenanced across a nation where one driver was under an obligation to give way to another who had driven past a Stop sign, run a red light, or approached from the right at such a speed as to make evasive action on the part of the driver on the left impossible. Indeed, the notorious Winneke judgement in a Victorian case cemented the absolute nature of the obligation.

South Australia, however, acted to mitigate the situation that would otherwise have flowed from such a decision and included a 'saving clause' in its traffic rules; this meant that 'it shall be a defence to a charge of failing to give way that the driver could not by the exercise of reasonable care have become aware of the approach of the other vehicle'. I was able to get this incorporated into the National Road Traffic Code when the ORS took over the servicing of ACRUPTC.

I have made mention before of my good fortune to be in the right place at the right time as the road safety revolution got under way. I was doubly fortunate to have had time left over to delve into areas that were of special interest to me. Provided that I kept up the flow of elementary statistics to the Australian Road Safety Council and of written material that described the situation, while doing nothing to remedy it, I was pretty much left alone.

The result of my being left alone was a paper that was presented to the Australian Road Traffic Code Committee in August 1968 on the suggestion of its Executive Officer and colleague, Bob Hancock, and its chairman, John Pitt, entitled *Giving Way at Intersections*. This paper foreshadowed the introduction of the T-Junction Rule and the adoption of the meaning of Stop sign bringing Australia into line with the rest of world – namely stop and give way.

During my first year with DST I also became aware of another peculiarity of Australian traffic law, namely the use of the expression 'to give way' rather than 'to give right of way'. That particular matter came to my attention when DST was providing the Australian representation to the meeting in The Hague to thrash out a new Convention on Road Traffic. On this, Australia got its way with the expression 'to give way' being used rather than 'to yield the right of way'. In the light of what was to follow, there was something Orwellian about ending up in Australia with an absolute right of way dressed up as an obligation to give way.

In the time I was travelling to and from Oakleigh to Wesley College in Prahran by train and tram I had become aware that the majority of intersections along High Street were not crossroads but T-junctions. It was as though the suburban developers wished to see that their subdivisions were entities separate and distinct from each other. This arrangement also contrasted with the generally grid layout of the main roads. In this there was the genesis of some sort of hierarchy even if the traffic code ignored it, at that time giving the smallest side street (or lane) equal status with the busiest roads for the purpose of who should give way to whom.

My arrival at DST coincided with the publication of the first Melway [brand] street directories that colour-coded roads into what we would today refer to as local streets (brown), distributor roads (red) and main roads (black). I knew I was onto something and fell on the Melway with gusto. As I said before, I had plenty of spare time. The Melway had an overall grid spacing within each map and I was able to use this as the basis for taking a structured sample of squares and cross-classifying intersections within them according to the class of road and type of intersection. Over the Melbourne metropolitan area intersections between local streets and main roads were overwhelmingly T-junctions. My thought was that this could provide the basis for the adoption of a system of priority control without the need for so many Give Way signs or Stop signs (if they meant stop and give way). Much the same could be said to apply in the local street system where local streets met those of higher classification.

Among the papers that crossed my desk was the one by Brian Harper (who later became Chief Engineer with Victoria's Road Safety and Traffic Authority) entitled 'Design of the Local Street System' that I have already referred to in the context of local area traffic management. He had come to the conclusion that under the give-way-to-the-right rule there would be one collision for every 9000 passes through a particular cross-intersection. Given that a local street can often carry more than a thousand vehicles a day, the mathematics speak for themselves in terms of accident potential, bearing in mind that at the time there was nothing to moderate the approach speeds.

In the paper by Howard Marks that I also mentioned earlier, he attributed the lower rate of accidents in subdivisions where T-junctions predominated to the need for the emerging driver to slow down merely to turn. This reduced the approach speed to a level nearer to the safe approach speed and there were also fewer conflict points within the intersection itself.

I have already referred to the way in which my time at the Australian Broadcasting Control Board gave me local knowledge of Sydney. Part of my duties at the board was to make myself familiar with as many of the programs then being shown on the then four television channels. It may perhaps come as a surprise that a drama series could give me an insight into traffic control in the United States. The one program that stood out for me was *The Fugitive*. (The selfless actions of the hero in helping other people, even though he was on the run, and the trust he put in them, were all but missed in the spin-off film.) What I noticed in every episode, many of which were in set in rural areas, was that there was a Stop sign or Yield (Give Way) sign at *every* intersection. Then, too, there was the single traffic light swaying suspended *above the middle* of intersections in many of the small towns, bringing order to traffic at minimal cost. In other American television programs, too, the reference to traffic lights was most often in the singular form, as in "we need a traffic light there".

The idea of a T-junction rule was mentioned favourably in the South Australian road safety report of 1968 and was included in both EGORS reports, the latter suggesting that the give-way-to-the-right rule remain in place only until there was priority control by means of signs and signals at cross-intersections. During a meeting of the Research Committee of EGORS there had been some discussion about recommending a change in the meaning of the Stop sign. I seized the opportunity and said that it would be a help if it meant something (i.e. to stop and give way). The committee agreed and recommended the change.

The first steps towards priority control by signs and signals took the form of priority road projects. The first of these was in Canberra and their success led to trials in Perth and Sydney both of which I was able to observe, whilst Victoria made selective use of Stop signs and Give Way signs.

In Perth, as was usual with meetings of ACRUPTC, a tour was arranged to show off the latest innovations. As we were crossing the Narrows Bridge on the way back to our accommodation, having observed the effect of raised pavement markers as an alternative to painted lane markings, discussion turned to what was then a ubiquitous concern with intersection rules. A study had shown a dramatic reduction in accidents following the introduction of priority control along Shepperton Road, a major, undivided, traffic route on the way to Fremantle to the east of Swan River. I had been aware that it was a narrow road with a strip shopping centre and a succession of blind corners. I therefore suggested that we should take a look. I think I can say that the experience of seeing what priority control could achieve convinced at least one state representative of its virtue.

Full priority control happened first in Victoria. In 1972, the Transportation and Highways Branch of the Victorian Division of the Institution of Engineers had made a dramatic case for it on a benefit/cost basis. In a remarkable turn-around, following a visit to the United Kingdom in 1974 by the esteemed premier Dick (later Sir Rupert) Hamer, the decision was made to introduce full priority control of all intersections in Victoria.

In 1975, the Victorian government rolled out, first, METCON bringing priority control to every intersection in the Melbourne metropolitan area and, shortly after, STATCON covering the rest of the State. Victoria also pioneered the extensive use of roundabouts that reduce crashes at intersections or reduce their severity, but also reduce speeds on the local street system. The now ubiquitous roundabout give way sign that indicates when an intersection is operating as a roundabout originated in Victoria at that time.

The coming of METCON also provided the idea for a board game of the same name developed by a former Shell Company executive, Tim Webb, who sought my advice on the technical details of the rules.

A degree of controversy has recently erupted with regard to the signalling requirements when exiting or passing through a roundabout. The FORS attitude was always that there was no need to signal left when exiting a roundabout to the right to complete a turn to the right nor when going straight ahead. I found it unfortunate that the original Australian Road Rules required it when turning right "if practicable" and spoke strongly against it at the time. Even more disturbing is the fact that some jurisdictions are enforcing it as a requirement. The question must be asked: "For whose benefit is the indication required"? Anyone approaching the right-turning vehicle from the opposite direction must give way and so must anyone approaching the roundabout from the street that is being turned into, and also if the driver turning right on the roundabout is going to continue around it to make a U-turn, which is a legitimate use of a roundabout. To arbitrarily impose an unnecessary requirement looks ominously like a return to the bad old days of 'black letter law' (by which is mean that laws are administered without regard to their context or intent).

Getting the idea accepted that priority at intersections should determined by something other than in the increasingly inappropriate give-way-to-the right rule, a phenomenon unique to Australia, was a long and tortuous process but I was in it for the long haul. More than twelve years elapsed from the time my first paper on the subject was presented to ACRPUTC at the end of 1968 and the adoption of the T-junction rule across Australia on 1 March 1981. The rule had already been in force in Western Australia since 1975. At the end, however, things moved remarkably quickly from ATAC's endorsement in the second half of 1980 to its introduction. The introduction of the rule was also accompanied by the wide distribution of a three-fold A4 pamphlet and a television commercial with the message '*That's it to a T*'.

In the interim, however, a lot had gone on, in particular what to do about 'anomalous intersections', those where priority under the T-junction rule might not be immediately apparent. An example is where a main road curves away, but there is a side road that goes straight ahead; in such cases, a Give Way sign on the side road approach to the intersection makes the situation clear. The resolution of such situations has proved to be one of the major benefits of the rule. Achieving this result involved much liaison on the part of the ACRUPTC representatives and their state and territory road authorities.

Further information about priority rules can be found in my monograph *Rules on Precedence at Intersections; An Examination of Alternatives for Australia* published as OR1 by the Office of Road Safety in February 1979.

Relocation

Along the Road to Gundagai

The House of Representatives

Standing Committee on Road Safety

Driver Training and Licensing

Four Principles for Road Infrastructure

The Lost Cause

Marginalisation

Chapter 25

Along the Road to Gundagai

Little did I think that the Hume Highway, which I first encountered during my University days, and then only as far as Broadford, 75 km north of Melbourne, and for its entire length only in 1959, would play such an important role in my life.

Even then, everyone was aware of the road's notorious accident potential, narrow - just wide enough for two vehicles to pass – and almost totally lacking in dedicated opportunities for safe overtaking Nowhere was its accident potential better expressed than in Russell Matthews's 1967 book *Public Investment in Australia* in which the author called for its conversion to a four-lane closed access expressway, something that was only achieved more than forty years later, on 23 June 2013,

> It is not very much of an exaggeration to suggest that a person setting out to drive an appreciable distance along the Hume Highway has about the same statistical chance of being killed or injured as an infantry soldier setting out on a jungle patrol in enemy territory.

Nor did Matthews leave his analogy there, adding that this was only one example of,

Australia's failure to fight her way out of an enveloping car infested jungle.

At that time the States set priorities for road construction, although the Commonwealth had used its powers under Section 51 of the Constitution to make grants to the States for road construction since 1923. I was fortunate enough to be around just after the federal government had established the Commonwealth Bureau of Roads, with its offices in the Reserve Bank Building in Melbourne. Its first report was published in 1969 and recommended a classification system for roads funding for the very first time. Until then the only stipulation that the Commonwealth had made was that 40 per cent of its funding was to be used on rural local roads, no doubt reflecting the Country (later National) Party influence on transport policy.

The way priorities were set, even on the Hume Highway, was only too evident once you got into New South Wales: the further one was from Sydney (or closer to Victoria!) the poorer the standard of the road, despite it being the main road link between the nation's two largest cities. The indifference of the NSW state government to the needs of interstate road travel was graphically illustrated by the fact that it took a grant under one of the Whitlam ALP government's initiatives to ensure that there was a flood-free route through Albury!

Once funding priorities had been changed, overtaking lanes were provided in the hilly country of southern New South Wales, but now it was in Victoria that driving became incredibly hazardous. Duplication spread northwards from Melbourne but even then the only other safe overtaking opportunities were within urban areas such as Wangaratta and Benalla. But that is to get ahead of the story.

One of my first tasks when I joined the DST was to analyse the fatal accident reports that were routinely, but rather uselessly, received from the Victoria Police, only on the condition that *nothing derived from them was to be made public*. The ones relating to the Hume Highway were of immediate interest and when a university vacation student was assigned to work with me I immediately set him loose on them. The full horror of what was going on was soon apparent. In 1969 a total of 35 people died in accidents along the Hume Highway, 21 in multi-vehicle accidents, mainly as a result of overtaking gone wrong, and 14 in single-vehicle accidents.

When the duplication of the Hume Highway in Victoria finally got underway it proceeded from the outskirts of Melbourne and the first bottleneck to be eliminated was Pretty Sally, the long steep hill south of Kilmore. The new freeway bypassed a string of small towns and ran through open undulating country well to the east of the old highway. One of the features of the new section was that its designers were able, by the use of the developing computer technology, to see the road they were planning against the background that drivers would see when travelling along it. Curves, for example, were placed in such a way as to maintain visual interest. This makes the northbound journey through the open country south of Tallarook quite a pleasant experience. Along this section overpasses carry side roads over the freeway and the freeway itself over the main Melbourne-Sydney railway, further reducing accident potential.

Nevertheless, in the 1970s there was still a powerful incentive in terms of time and accident potential to avoid using the yet-to-be-duplicated highway north of Tallarook for as far as one could. My approach was to travel across town to the Maroondah Highway passing through Yarra Glen, turning north through Flowerdale and Yea and on to Benalla via the Midland Highway. The Maroondah Highway crossed Lake Eildon at Bonnie Doon, the "serenity" of which would be made famous in the classic Australian movie *The Castle*.

Even when the duplication of the highway had reached Benalla, the problem of actually getting onto the Hume Freeway from the other side of Melbourne remained. The strategies adopted aimed to make the journey across town as easy as possible, despite innumerable turns at strategic traffic lights. As a result, my family and I became familiar with suburbs that we would rarely have seen otherwise. Going this way, we joined the highway at Campbellfield near where the duplication began.

To follow the cross-town route that I took to get onto the highway gives an indication of the potential for high-standard road facilities to encourage drivers to choose the safest and most convenient route for their journeys. Such roads take through-traffic off the surface street system and away from the places where vulnerable road users would be encountered, and away from the innumerable interactions with other drivers, many of which have the potential to end in tragedy. This should be a powerful incentive for governments to build freeways *without tolls* so as to encourage their use in preference to the surface street system. As it is, even the three-fold safety advantage of an urban freeway over even the best designed sixty metre wide divided arterial roads (complete with service roads on each side for local traffic and with right turns restricted to signalised intersections) rarely if ever gets a mention in the freeways/public transport debate.

The main reason to meander across Melbourne in this way was, of course, to avoid the notorious bottleneck of Sydney Road that used to be Melbourne's main outlet to the north. This is a busy ribbon shopping centre, four km long choked with cars, trucks and the inevitable trams. It is, in fact, just one of a number of such bottlenecks in the inner ring of suburbs that lay or, in some places, still lie, at the end of the generous boulevards, sixty metres wide, complete with service roads separated from the broad main carriageway, that were a part of Hoddle's original plan for Melbourne.

Yet even Sydney Road held one attraction at the end of a long monotonous journey south down the Hume Highway. Halfway along lay Franco Cozzo's. This was a furniture store featuring the most over-the-top bedroom settings imaginable. Sometimes the traffic lights on the corner would be red and one could gaze at oversized white enamelled and fibreglass beds and wardrobes all curves and swirls or their counterparts in burr walnut.

All this cross-town meandering across Melbourne was, however, only a symptom of a similar malaise in all of Australia's cities. Somehow governments, federal, state and local, laboured under the delusion that Australia, the fourth most motorised nation on earth and the most urbanised, could get away with having *no* grade-separated, controlled access roads (i.e. freeways) to take cross-suburban and regional traffic off the surface street system. To this day, Adelaide still has no freeways penetrating the urban fabric, let alone a city bypass, and is paying the price, with the State now having one of the highest road accident fatality rates in the nation.

Back on the Hume and travelling north from Benalla, it was too bad if you found yourself behind a semi-trailer or any other sort of heavy vehicle as the stream of traffic coming in the opposite direction was often constant. At the time, heavy vehicles were subject to an 80 km/h speed limit whereas other vehicles could travel at 100 km/h. The dangers inherent in such a speed differential finally led to the adoption of a common limit of 100 km/h.

If one had the patience you just plodded along behind until you had covered the next 45 km until you reached Wangaratta where the highway was also the main street with a median strip. Even so this was no guarantee that you would be able to pass the truck or whatever was holding you up unless you both happened to get stopped at one of the two or three sets of traffic lights in Wangaratta. We rarely stopped in Wangaratta although we were impressed that the shopping centre was not confined to the main street. Rather we would often have taken a break in the pretty little park alongside the Broken River in Benalla where there is a statue of 'Weary' (Sir Edward) Dunlop, the prisoner-of-war hero surgeon who is also commemorated in the name of an outer Canberra suburb. The splendid Art Gallery, also by the river, should not be missed.

Just beyond the bridge over the Ovens River on the edge of Wangaratta, however, there were a series of S-bends on the highway, one of which would be the scene of one of the worst crashes on the Victorian side of the border. Nine passengers died when a truck ripped out the side of a long-distance coach. The elimination of this hazard and others that existed until the Wangaratta Bypass was opened in 1994 tends to be ignored when the authorities speak about what led to the general reduction in road traffic accident fatalities in Victoria in the 1990s. This they attribute to a crackdown on speed, ignoring the effects of the economic recession. Indeed, according to an independent report by the Bureau of Transport and Communication Economics (BTCE), road improvements and economic conditions accounted for *two-thirds* of the accident reduction.

As one headed out along on to the seemingly never-ending straight road one would pass the sign indicating that 'This is the site of the Wangaratta Bypass'. The preliminary roadworks always looked to be at right angles to the old road, but were in fact the site of the overpasses on to which one would diverge if one were not going straight through. On through Chiltern, where one never stopped, lay the next of the accident black spots along the highway – the curves adjacent to Black Dog Creek, just beyond which one encountered yet another of the Victoria's road curiosities.

Here was this newish stretch of two-way two-lane road dating from the 1970s, carrying the announcement, on the familiar type of white-on-green sign, saying that certain types of vehicle were not permitted on the *freeway* (!). A lot of advance planting of trees had taken place and admittedly the road was well engineered, but there was no indication that a second carriageway would be built at any time in the near future. One must ponder what the responsible authorities were thinking of by tantalising the long-suffering travellers in this way. In fact, this section of the highway was one of the last to be duplicated despite the regular fatal accidents at nearby Black Dog Creek.

Looking back, however, one should not have been surprised given that even today the authorities still act as though they do not know or acknowledge that what distinguishes a freeway from any other divided roads is the elimination of at-grade intersections. I say this because to this day the classification of roads for the purpose of setting speed limits makes no distinction between grade-separated rural freeways and other divided rural roads. This makes a total mockery of the notion of encouraging drivers to drive according to the conditions!

Not long after the end of the so-called freeway and around another sweeping right-hand bend there would come into view in the distance and slightly downhill the first indication that the boredom of driving on the Hume Highway in northeast Victoria was coming to an end. In the distance lay Wodonga and its sister city on the other side of the Murray River, Albury. One piece of music will always be associated in my mind with the opening up of that view – *Taps for the Fallen Brave;* this was playing on a '101 Strings' cassette I had on as I rounded that bend late one afternoon. The impression was so great that I have asked that it be played at my funeral.

On the run into Wodonga one passes by what was to have been the site of the Road Safety and Standards Authority, not far from what is now the interchange between the Hume Freeway and the Murray Valley Highway that also eliminated a level crossing over the main Sydney-Melbourne railway. The last big change on the Victorian side of the border was the opening of the Wodonga Bypass. Initially the freeway ended at a set of traffic lights where it met the old highway. Before that the highway was the main street of Wodonga. The freeway that now links to the Albury Bypass on a new river crossing also eliminated the need for highway traffic to use the busy level crossing on the edge of town.

The opening of the Albury Bypass, running next to the railway line to the east of the CBD, in 2007 gave a clear run past both centres. Until then interstate traffic had encountered a series of right-angle turns, two at the southern end of the city and two at the leafy northern end of town leading on to the commercial and industrial strip of North Albury.

Once freeways and bypasses made the journey much less tiring, we could drive straight through, but before that we used to break our journey somewhere in Albury or more recently at Lavington, now a northern suburb. Even when we drove straight through a favourite stop was the place adjacent to the Myer Centre on Dean Street that sold delicious savoury potatoes. (We always found it intriguing that although the department store chain badged its other New South Wales stores as Grace Brothers, their store in Albury had the Victorian name, Myer.)

The apocryphal story is that at the time of the separation of the colony of Victoria from New South Wales a clerk in the Colonial Office mistook 'Murray' for 'Murrumbidgee' and made it the border whereas the intention had been for what is now the Riverina to have been part of Victoria. The sporting culture of the area certainly attests to the southern influence with goal posts outnumbering uprights and cross bars in the playing fields of the area.

On our first visit to Sydney in 1959 my wife and I decided that it would be more interesting to see part of the Riverina and then head east over the Blue Mountains. The road through North Albury took the name Hume Highway, but when the bypass was opened it reverted to its original name, Wagga Road.

The road we travelled on to Wagga Wagga had been newly named the Olympic Way, this being only three years after the 1956 Melbourne Olympics. It has since been renamed the Olympic Highway. On our return journey we did in fact follow the conventional route of the Hume Highway and it is one of my standing regrets that I did not turn off at Goulburn and so see Canberra as it was before Lake Burley Griffin transformed it.

It would be another six years before we would travel the Hume Highway in the northerly direction, this time in 1965 to stay with friends who had just 'moved up' from Melbourne. Once on the highway north of Albury one was immediately struck by the change in the nature of the country. The hills are much closer, trees no longer lined the road and the road itself was no longer a seemingly endless straight one, but curved this way and that. Before long, however, the hills closed in and the first opportunities to safely overtake slower vehicles presented themselves.

The presence of overtaking lanes as one entered the hilly country east of Albury always represented a welcome change from the tedium of following the heavy vehicles that characterised the trip north from Melbourne to Wodonga. Nevertheless, back in 1981, I would get my sons to note the distance from Albury of each overtaking lane. This enabled me to time my move on any heavy vehicle so as to be travelling fast enough to complete the manoeuvre in good time. Indeed, as a matter of principle, when a heavy vehicle came into sight, even well ahead, I would ease up, follow at a safe distance, and then make my move. Given that I generally find myself under-aroused by the driving task, rather than overloaded, this gave me something to do that kept me alert and alleviated what was inevitably a boring trip. It always bothered me that my wife had no such strategy and as a result the overtaking lane could be ending with her manoeuvre still not completed.

A feature of later trips along the flat sections of the road before the hills were encountered was that the NSW Department of Main Roads had picked up on the idea of the 'two and a half lane rural road'. This was the term used by Chris Hoban, a researcher with ARRB, in the 1980s. The highway was selectively widened and a 2+1 lane marking put in place. This allowed overtaking in one direction and then in the other, each section lasting a few kilometres. Once in the hills we noticed that the signs announcing that an overtaking lane was coming up would read 'Overtaking lane 3 km ahead', not 1 km or 5 km, but 3 km, as if to recognise that with a safe overtaking opportunity so close drivers would be encouraged to show patience and not engage in risky overtaking. To me this was an example of how we should be *actively* encouraging good behaviour.

One might well ask how many more such opportunities for safe overtaking could be provided for the cost of expensive duplications. The argument has, however, been put that where a 2+1 treatment is warranted the road itself may be reaching the end of its life, making full replacement, often on a new alignment, a better proposition. Nevertheless, it would seem that there are situations where duplication is unlikely to be an option on the basis of traffic volume alone, but where a high accident rate could make the 2+1 highway a viable proposition. Indeed, recent Swedish experience would indicate that such 2+1 roads can produce a level of safety matching that of a full freeway if they include a crash barrier separating the opposing traffic streams.

Sections of the highway and the villages along the way are recalled differently depending on the direction of travel. In one direction Woomargama, Mullengandra and Bowna can pass without notice yet travelling south around midday the last-named was a place with a rest area where we would pull off the road and relax for a few minutes in the shade of the trees. The first of the villages achieved some prominence when the late Diana, Princess of Wales, stayed at a nearby property. After that, at least people knew that it was pronounced W'mar-gh-mh.

Always welcome was the sight of the 'divided road 3 km ahead' as one came out of the first line of hills approaching Holbrook. It is significant that in New South Wales, and perhaps elsewhere, sections of highway on the flat were often the first to be duplicated. The stretch of divided highway immediately south of Holbrook thus provided the opportunity to get past as many heavy vehicles as possible. Somewhat surprisingly, the Holbrook Bypass would be the last part of the duplication to be completed.

It is only if one stops and has a look at the replica submarine in the park at the northern end of the long main street that one realises that the name of the town, Holbrook, commemorates the skill and daring of a British submarine commander of World War I who earned the Victoria Cross for sinking a Turkish warship, having negotiated a minefield in order to do so. Until the First World War the name had been Germantown.

For anyone with a sense of history, the next section of highway leading into Tarcutta stands out as the most glaring example of the neglect of Australia's roads in the years following World War II, and also of the parochialism that I have already commented upon. This section has a special significance in the history of road financing in Australia. It highlights, like no other, the contempt with which earlier governments treated the need to improve Australia's main roads. At the time I joined DST I learned that serious consideration had been given to the proposition that that particular section of the Hume Highway *be maintained as a gravel road.* As if to underscore its significance in the scheme of things this section, which has now been duplicated, was the second-last section of the entire highway to be upgraded to four-lane status.

The village of Tarcutta is better known today as the location of a memorial to the countless long-distance truck drivers who have died in the course of driving their rigs along the highway. There could hardly be a more touchingly appropriate location. In these more enlightened times the town has become the site of one of the first large purpose-built, well-lit and serviced, truck stops where truckies can break their long lonely journeys instead of ploughing on through the night. On a more mundane note the local council deserves credit for the high standard of the toilet facilities block located in the central median and for the conveniently located parking.

At this point I would like to place on record my appreciation of the courtesy displayed by the drivers of semi-trailers and pantechnicons in assisting drivers like myself to overtake them at night. The technique by which they achieved this was by flashing their right-turn indicator to signal that the road ahead was clear to overtake. The practice of doing so has been illegal for quite some years and I have no intention of venturing forth at night to find out if the practice still continues on other roads. Indeed, I have to say that the only times I have been aware of heavy vehicle drivers doing the wrong thing were in the daylight hours.

It was also in Tarcutta, while I was filling up at the service station, I saw close to the nadir of vehicle condition and safety when a woman drove up, sans seatbelt, in a faded early model Holden sedan with all four tyres worn down to the canvas! Perhaps she was a local who had more pressing priorities and so escaped the attention of the highway patrol. A sidelight to that is that newcomers to Canberra would be warned by their fellows to scrupulously observe the 60 sign located on the very outskirts of the town because of the likely police presence.

From Tarcutta onwards towards Canberra the reconstructed Hume Highway often runs well away from the original alignment but at one point not one but two pieces of the former road used to be visible. In time these will become overgrown as the road authorities tear up the old pavements lest they become drag strips. One must ask what else is there for young people outside the major centres of population to fill their leisure time but to hoon around in cars.

On the road again and heading towards Gundagai are two examples of the sort of road improvements that have really made the difference in reducing the toll of death and injury on Australia's roads. The first of these, heading north, is the grade-separated and brightly lit intersection of the Hume Highway and the major westward link for much of southwestern New South Wales, the Sturt Highway. More significant from an operational standpoint was the elimination of the long climb over Sylvia's Gap. The new route was completed in 1983 and links to the Tumblong deviation. It takes the divided highway on a completely new alignment. Formerly if one got stuck behind a truck grinding up the hill it could take the best part of 25 minutes to accomplish what now takes five. This new section also included grade-separating the intersection with the Snowy Mountains Highway.

From an historical perspective, however, the bypassing of Sylvia's Gap provides a spectacular demonstration of the changes to the provision of road infrastructure compared with the relatively recent past. The old Hume Highway crossed Hillas Creek on a 34m long narrow reinforced concrete arch 'bow-string' bridge that is clearly visible way down below the new road. The bridge dates from 1938 and is one of only two such bridges in New South Wales and has been listed on the Register of Australian Historic Bridges for the pioneering nature of its construction. Locally it was known as 'The Little Sydney Harbour Bridge'. The works in the area were ultimately prompted by a series of accidents including one that involved a spill of diesel oil.

Elements of a road that might otherwise pass unnoticed can assume significance if one is aware of how problems are tackled elsewhere. The very depth of some cuttings on the Hume Highway in NSW is a dramatic example of the contrast with European road building practice, notably in Italy, where smaller hills are pierced by tunnels, so enabling truck drivers to maintain a constant speed and so save on fuel.

For all its legendary fame the township of Gundagai is now by-passed and dual bridges take the highway over the flood plain from which the original township was all but washed away in the flood of 1852. Before the building of the first of the twin bridges on the bypass, a timber bridge, the longest in NSW, carried the highway across the flood plain. I drove over the bridge at night on the 1965 trip. On entering the main street there it was: one of the legendary eateries along Australia's roads – the Niagara - all chrome and mirrors, its fame heightened by its association with former Labor great, Ben Chifley, who once dined there with colleagues during World War II.

The new highway bypasses the famous Dog on the Tuckerbox, but another work by its creator is on display (for a modest fee) in the Tourist Information Centre; this is Frank Rusconi's 'Marble Masterpiece' an exquisite 1.5m square and 1.2m high visualisation of an imaginary Baroque Italian palace made from 20,948 individually crafted pieces.

Gundagai would figure again in my driving past but for a very different reason. The ORS had not long moved up to Canberra when news came through of a long-distance coach having been involved in a collision with a semi-trailer resulting in multiple fatalities on the Hume Highway on the Sydney side of Gundagai.

At that time a great deal of concern was starting to be expressed about the problem of bus and coach safety especially with regard to the strength or otherwise of seat anchorages. Indeed, the ORS had commissioned a study of that subject with the Mechanical Engineering Department of the University of Melbourne and I had been the point of contact between the ORS and the investigators. The university already had a high profile in areas related to vehicle safety and Professor Peter Joubert was one of the movers and shakers behind the compulsory seatbelt legislation that came into effect in Victoria just before Christmas 1971.

Not surprisingly, therefore, when the ORS sent a team to investigate the Gundagai crash I was included, along with the engineers from the Vehicle Structures Safety Branch, and hopefully not just to do the driving. By the time we arrived at the scene the semi had been removed but the bus that had been travelling south was still where it ended up on the outer edge of a right-hand bend having been hit head-on. The victims had long been removed and only a few traces remained of the carnage that had occurred inside. Apart from the general disarray of the seats, many of which had been torn from the floor, the most notable feature of the scene was being ankle-deep in the savoury biscuits that the semi had been carrying. The bend on which the accident occurred is no longer recognisable on the duplicated road that follows much the same alignment. This is another reminder of the way in which the role of road and traffic control improvements in reducing the toll of death and injury on the roads can be overshadowed by the rhetoric that puts it all down to speed.

As a sidelight to this issue, when the National Highway standards were being formulated a decision had to be made as to whether median barriers should be provided on divided sections or whether a wide median would suffice given that there was plenty of land. Because of the sparsely populated nature of many areas where this would be an issue, the latter course was adopted. Even so, in western Europe, as we shall see, median *and* side barriers are standard on rural motorways.

In terms of my driving past, Jugiong has a particular significance. On 30 June 1981, I was involved as the innocent party in the only serious accident in my entire driving career. Strangely enough, my wife said that she felt a sense of reluctance on my part as I set out. She had stayed in Melbourne in 1981 so that my youngest daughter could finish high school there.

Coming down the steep hill into Jugiong from the south at about 4.30 on a sunny afternoon I saw a car waiting to turn right into the Cootamundra Road and another coming up behind it. Suddenly the second car went around the other on the outside and straight into my path. Had I swung left I could have overturned into the deep roadside drain. I remember thinking "I hope the bonnet holds ....[and].... what will Jennie think"? The driver of the other car moved away slightly and his car hit mine near the driver's side headlamp. My car was still steerable and I stopped just up from the hotel on the corner from which people had rushed out. Mercifully, neither of my sons suffered any injury. I bruised my forehead on the A-pillar, whilst the other driver was also able to walk around and talk about what happened. He said he knew he could not stop in time to avoid hitting the stationary vehicle and went around the outside hoping I would swerve out of the way. My elder son who was sitting alongside me says I froze. Police breath tests showed that alcohol was not involved.

There was, in fact, a deep irony for me in the Jugiong accident. Earlier that day I had stopped for petrol on the outskirts of yet-to-be-bypassed Seymour, some 120 km north of Melbourne. Turning out of the service station onto the divided road I moved off as usual and was astonished to be signalled to pull over by a police traffic patrol officer and told I was being booked for travelling at 71km/h in a 60 zone. Less than 200m up the road from the point where I was apprehended was a '75' sign. Explaining that I just turned out of the service station *and* that this was the first time in 30 years of driving that I had ever come to the attention of the law did no good. I was unaware at that stage that I could have applied to have the traffic infringement notice withdrawn and so I just paid up. Within three months, the section of road where the offence took place became a 75 km/h zone!

The date, 30 June 1981, was also Census night so that the operator of the motel where we spent the night had to include my sons and me in the special category for those people away from their usual address on census night. The next day my dear friend Kevin drove to Jugiong and picked us up. Arrangements were made for the car to be brought back to Canberra for repair and during the period it was out of action I became, and then remained, a regular user of Canberra's ACTION buses (the acronym standing for Australian Capital Territory Internal Omnibus Network).

In a way, the accident was fortuitous as it led me to become aware of the excellence of the Canberra bus system *as it operated prior to self-government* and to use it as an exemplar in the second edition of the FORS guidelines for town planning that I would be in charge of producing a year later. Indeed, the Belconnen Interchange figured prominently as an example of how convenient public transport could reduce the need for car travel. Regrettably, the interchange was demolished in 2010 as part of a remodelling of the town centre to coincide with the enlargement of the Westfield Belconnen shopping mall, whilst Australia's first busway, that led away from the interchange, became part of an underground car park.

Jugiong was bypassed in 1995, the new road providing a spectacular view over the Murrumbidgee far below and on to the mountains to the southeast. The view, one of the few picturesque aspects of the drive along the highway, is especially so in Spring when Patterson's Curse (or Salvation Jane if you are a South Australian) covers the hills with its lilac-coloured blooms. Before the bypass was built I was pleased to see that a painted median with a right-turn lane was put in place not long after my accident at the intersection of the highway and Cootamundra Road. Such turning lanes have become a feature on many highways and other roads in rural areas greatly reducing the risk of accidents at these locations.

Although there are places in either direction where there is a long view that tells you that, there in front of you, are the open spaces of another state, the boredom of the Hume Highway has drawn the response from one Canberra wit that it is as though someone stuck in another 100 km when no one was looking. Even so, there used to be minor diversions such as in the village with the eponymous name of Bookham, now bypassed, where the main point of interest is, or was, the vast scrap yard of agricultural equipment at the end furthest from Canberra.

When I moved up to Canberra the Hume Highway still passed through Yass and it was always a relief after a long day to see through the twilight the lights of what my eldest son dubbed 'the metropolis of Yass' come into view below us, knowing that the tedium would soon be at an end. On the outskirts of town one still passed over the defunct railway crossing replete with crossbuck signs saying 'railway crossing' although trains had long since ceased to use the line. The line used to connect Yass Town to the main line at Yass Junction where the impressive bluestone station still operates surrounded by bare paddocks. This is yet another of those remarkable phenomena where the railway passed some distance from town; an even more remarkable case in point is the provincial city of Wagga Wagga where the railway station stands at one end of the Bayliss Street shopping strip, more than a kilometre away from the colonial city centre that lies beside the Murrumbidgee River.

It is hard to believe that well into the 1980s the junction of the Hume Highway and the then unduplicated Barton Highway was unlit. Although a large direction sign told you that the turnoff was coming up one was always glad when the manoeuvre was completed safely. Today the old highway goes by the name Yass Valley Way and passes under the Yass Bypass that is the new Hume Highway. Nevertheless, direction signing is counter-intuitive for people heading away from Canberra; one travels straight ahead for Melbourne but moves to the left, in the direction of Melbourne, in order to go towards Sydney.

There can be few more terrifying prospects for any driver than to be confronted by a vehicle being on the wrong side of a divided highway. Given the predilection of Australian road authorities for highway service facilities to be built alongside rather than above rural freeways, special care needs to be taken to ensure that drivers will re-enter the highway going the right way. (The then Country Roads Board in Victoria recognised the potential for similar wrong-way accidents many years ago and reconstructed numerous at-grade intersections on the duplicated Hume Highway so as to force drivers crossing the median to turn in the direction of the traffic stream they were entering.)

Given the already massive investment in duplicating rural highways, there seems to be no reason why service facilities should not be built straddling the highway, as they are in Europe rather than alongside. The possibility of finding a restaurant or a higher class of café on the first floor level overlooking the highway and the surrounding countryside could provide a real incentive to 'stop, revive, survive'.

On the run into Canberra down the Barton Highway one still passes through the village of Murrumbateman, yet to be bypassed even in 2014 because of a long-running dispute as to whether the new road should pass to the east or the west. Until that issue is resolved the sweeping bend on the southern side of the village will continue to be an accident black spot, and the site of numerous fatal accidents. The Barton Highway would be an ideal place for the Swedish 'two plus one' alternative to full duplication with opposing traffic streams separated by a wire-rope barrier giving priority in one direction or the other, alternating every few kilometres. This measure is in place along stretches of the Pacific Highway; in fact wire rope barriers are being used on sections of 20km or more to separate the opposing traffic streams on *two-way/two lane* sections, but with a wider paved shoulder.

In the ACT, things were decided rather more quickly and the village of Hall fared better with the Barton Highway now skirting around the western side and offering a first, splendid, view of the Brindabellas. Just before Hall, as one approaches from Yass, comes the first sight of Canberra in the form of the Black Mountain telecommunications tower. I well remember radio reception suddenly improving just in time to hear St Kilda, yet to win a VFL (now AFL) premiership until the next year, go down by a point to Essendon in the 1965 Grand Final.

The route into Canberra itself was also different in those days. Rather than continuing on to meet Northbourne Avenue (the Canberra end of the Federal Highway) the Barton Highway led into what is now Ellenborough Street and then into Mouat Street to the intersection with Northbourne Avenue. As is often the case in rural centres the buildings on the city side of the corner, both since demolished, were a hotel on the south and a motel on the north.

The hosts on my family's first visit to Canberra had only recently moved to the raw and new edge of the now leafy suburb of Ainslie; indeed their street was the start of a fire trial. This was reassuring given that there was a bushfire on Mt Ainslie when we arrived that was allowed to burn itself out that night on the back boundary of the block that backed onto the still extant Monash Drive reservation. "We (the locals collectively) will never allow it to be built" my friend said, and that is still the case almost fifty years later.

This leads me to a final point about the Road to Gundagai. The Hume Highway bypasses every city, town and village on the way between the national capital and both Sydney and Melbourne. Despite this, semi-trailers still thunder through the commercial heart of Canberra, Civic, dividing it in a way that should be unthinkable in the developed world in the year 2015. Later I shall refer to the underpasses that carry intersecting streets under arterial roads in places as diverse as Downtown Washington and along the Seine in Paris. The centre of Canberra will never be integrated into a functioning, coherent and lively whole while Northbourne Avenue continues to divide it, with pedestrians needing to wait at traffic lights to cross it and being unable to safely reach City Hill.

The need to place Northbourne Avenue underground from somewhere near its intersection with Cooyong Street to the far side of City Hill is blindingly obvious. It would have been be a fitting present for Canberra's centenary in 2013 for the Commonwealth to have stumped up the money. It would seem, however, that the civic heart of the nation's capital will stand as a potent symbol of Australia's failure to provide adequately for the level of motorisation that exists in the 21st century.

Chapter 26

The House of Representatives Standing Committee on Road Safety

One of the most satisfying parts of the early time with the ORS in Canberra was my involvement with the House of Representatives Standing Committee on Road Safety (HORSCORS) as one of two advisors to its Inquiry into the Training and Licensing of Drivers including the Needs of Disabled Drivers. The other advisor was Dr David Saffron, a behavioural scientist with the then Traffic Accident Research Unit of the New South Wales Department of Motor Transport.

HORSCORS had been established, initially as a select committee, largely as a result of the efforts of the then member for the New South Wales seat of Robertson, Barry Cohen. The electorate on the central coast of New South Wales was notorious as a location of accident black spots, or so it would have appeared from the number of representations received from people in the area. The area had, however, also included the seat of the long-serving state Minister for Transport, Milton Morris. The seat of the Minster for Transport in the Whitlam Government, Charlie Jones, member for Shortland, also lay close by. Indeed, one local medical practitioner became so concerned about the number of accidents on the Central Coast that he set up the Tea Gardens Clinic to research the nature of the problem.

Before proceeding, it may be worthwhile to reflect that in 1959, well ahead of its time, the Senate had appointed a Select Committee on Road Safety to conduct a general inquiry into road safety in Australia. Had the recommendations made in the committee's report presented in September of 1960 been acted upon, effective countermeasures could have been put in place much sooner.

In particular, the Senate Committee's report noted that a case could be made for a change to the rules of precedence at intersections that would have seen priority given to the left not the right; this is, of course, the equivalent of what applies in those countries that drive on the right and give way to the right, although most now drive to a major/minor system. The study recommended by the Select Committee would have exposed the weakness of the general give-way-to-the-right rule much sooner and could have led to the saving of thousands of lives over the next twenty years. The government's general response at the time makes extremely disappointing, if not unexpected, reading, given the baleful influence of the ARSC and its secretariat in DST.

One other paragraph (# 44) from the1960 report, however, fairly leaps from the page with its relevance more than half a century on and I therefore quote it in full despite its length,

> On the subject of enforcement of the traffic laws as they now exist, there is controversy as to the suitability of traffic control as a subject for strictly enforced legislation. While the necessity for enforcement in not denied, self-enforcement by the driver, or pedestrian, based on thorough education and acceptance of restrictions for the sake of safety, is the ideal for which the authorities should strive. Traffic rules, as at present enforced, tend to be confused with the criminal code. They bring a large section of the otherwise law-abiding public into conflict with the law, and on the other hand, bring the police into conflict with the general public, with who they should be in the closest accord. The police have the unenviable task of enforcing traffic laws and maintaining the co-operation of the public, making decisions on the spot to

distinguish intent from inattention and negligence from honest human error.

Within that one paragraph the Senate Committee's report highlights no less than four key aspects relating to how traffic law is perceived and enforced. I shall be returning to discuss them further in the second part of this work.

In its first iteration HORSCORS was a Select Committee. Later, with recognition of the need for the Commonwealth government take a more productive role in road safety, the committee's status would be upgraded to that of a Standing Committee.

It was, however, as a select committee, in April 1973, in the first year of the Whitlam Government, that the committee was reappointed to inquire and report on,

(a)   the main causes of the present high level of the road toll in Australia;

(b)   the most effective means of achieving greater road safety in Australia;

(c)   the particular aspects of the problem to which those concerned with road safety could most advantageously direct their efforts;

(d)   the economic cost to the community or road accidents in Australia in terms of
      (i)   material damage
      (ii)   loss of man-hours and earning capacity
      (iii) cost of treatment of accident victims,

Along with the first report of the Expert Group, the HORSCORS report had a significant influence on the direction of government policy in regard to road safety. The report's title neatly drew attention to critical areas where action could be taken. Its title was *Road Safety - A National Authority: the Constitutional Position; Statistical Needs.* The report was presented in September of 1973 with the committee having heard from 70 witnesses and taken 2300 pages of evidence.

The committee's 1973 report not only recommended the establishment of a national body to take a leading role in tackling the problem of death and injury on the roads, but it also set out in detail what its functions should be. This would form the basis for the legislation that would soon establish the Road Safety and Standards Authority. Notable among the other recommendations was the emphasis placed on the importance of collecting accident information on a uniform basis throughout Australia. To this day that has proved all but impossible. Indeed, reading the committee's next report it would seem that this recommendation was simply put in the 'too hard' basket.

By the time of the department's move to Canberra the committee had already produced another report. This had been presented in May 1980 and dealt with the topic *Alcohol, Drugs and Road Safety* highlighting many of the issues, such as the desirability of random breath testing and well-targeted public education campaigns. These would soon become a standard and highly influential part of the road safety effort.

With a coalition government now in power, the chairmanship of the committee had passed to another committee member, the Hon. Bob Katter Snr, the long-serving National Party member for the large north Queensland seat of Kennedy, a seat now represented by his influential son of same name, sitting as an Independent.

The move of the ORS to Canberra occurred before the government of the day took the decision to build the new Parliament House on Capital Hill. The shortage of accommodation at the then Parliament House (which had to be seen to be believed) meant that a number of other buildings in the Parliamentary Triangle were pressed into service. These included the historic Hotel Canberra that had ceased to function as a hotel some years before. It had, however, been functioning as a high-class hotel in 1972, the time of the first National Road Safety Seminar, and the Road Accident Information Seminar in 1974, providing accommodation for delegates. It was therefore a shock to walk into the building and see how it had been unceremoniously turned into office space, notably the veranda rooms where the HORSCORS staff worked.

The proposed terms of reference for HORSCORS inquiries were routinely referred to the department for comment. I am glad to say that I was able to convince the powers that be that the opportunity should be taken for the committee to look at training and licensing issues as they affected people with disabilities. I had been influenced by the strong advocacy of this issue by the first chairman of the Expert Group, Mr Justice Meares. The judge had played a leading role in drawing the needs of people with disabilities to the attention of the New South Wales government through his work with the Australian Council for the Rehabilitation of the Disabled (ACROD). My wife Jennie, who was by then a special needs teacher in the ACT, had also sharpened my sensitivity.

I might mention in passing that the early 1980s were the dawn of the era of political correctness and it was no longer acceptable to refer to 'disabled people', but rather to use the expression 'people with disabilities'. Mercifully, the fashion for excesses such as 'differently-abled people' soon passed.

The member of the committee whom I most remember was a colourful member from Western Australia. I remember him fondly for one notable contribution to the committee. This related to pre-licence training. At the time the idea of advanced driver training at specially constructed ranges was a popular one, especially in rural areas where out-of-control accidents involving young drivers were all too common. Such training appealed to a number of committee members. Study after study from the United States, however, had shown a complete lack of effectiveness as an accident reduction measure. As advisors, New South Wales researcher David Saffron and I were present when the relevant section of the secretariat's draft report came up and were asked what we thought. We reiterated our opinion that range training was a waste of time and money. (Unlike the practice with Senate committees of the time, advisors to House of Representatives committees could contribute to discussions.) The committee was equivocating about the matter when the member in question ended the discussion by saying that he had thought range training was a good idea too, but having had the experts tell us it was waste of time, the committee should move on. The committee agreed.

There can be little doubt that the opportunity offered for the making of submissions by people with disabilities, and those representing them, was welcomed and the recommendations in the HORSCORS report would certainly have helped the acceptance of the fact that people with a disability were able to safely drive suitably modified vehicles.

Today, however, forty years on from the 1973 HORSCORS report that drew attention to the importance of having uniform data available, one must ask whether the current approaches to the accident problem are so ingrained that the need for objective evidence has been ignored! Nowhere is this more evident than in the matter of driver licence records, a subject was to sorely exercised the minds of the committee that when it produced its 1982 report on the *Education, Training and Licensing of Drivers.* It was particularly scathing about the failure to integrate the different records relating to drivers saying, at para 276 that,

> The committee cannot accept that it is possible to link traffic violations to a driver, but not accidents.

The committee went even further making the disturbing finding, totally ignored, that,

> Convictions, although raising significant revenue, do not relate well with accidents.

Accordingly, the committee then went on to recommend, in para 279 that,

> Records should contain at least the following basic information:
> * licence application information, including name, address, age, sex and licence test reports;
> * involvement in reportable traffic crashes;
> * conviction for traffic violations;
> * licence sanctions taken whether by court, or licensing authority; and
> * all vehicles registered in the name of the licensee.

The committee added a further recommendation, at para 280, that,

> The design and implementation of driver record systems must ensure that there is a database from which to carry out evaluative studies of driver licensing and improvement programs.

The committee then addressed misgivings about such systems representing a possible infringement of civil liberties, saying significantly, at para 281, that,

> The public should understand that such a system would be implemented in order to assist drivers not to harass them.

The committee was also at pains to point out that,

> Each driver would have the right to inspect or question his own record to verify or dispute its accuracy.

It is almost inconceivable that in the thirty years since such strong recommendations were made and despite the rollout of ever more elaborate networks of automated enforcement devices, *not one* of the committee's recommendations with regard to driver licence records has been acted upon, Queensland being an honourable exception.

Data matching of the type envisaged by the Standing Committee, which would enable better targeting of enforcement activity, has been routine for more three decades in the most motorised place on earth – California, yet it is still only in Queensland that it is possible to match accident involvement and traffic infringement data. Worst of all there seems no will to remedy the situation. One must ask why.

It is small wonder that the law-abiding individuals who have driven for a lifetime without ever being involved in an accident should express cynicism at the cavalier way in which their driving records are tarnished by having convictions recorded against them, given that there is no way of determining whether those being targeted by the system are in fact the ones having accidents. With the system so comprehensively stacked against them, what's the use, they say, and so the sausage-machine-justice machine grinds on, all the while failing to deter the miscreant minority. I shall have more to say on that matter in a later chapter.

Chapter 27

Driver Training
and Licensing

As it was

Driver licensing has always had a central place as a means of reducing the risk of accident. Not long before I joined DST the Committee on Driver Improvement had prepared a report for ATAC. Reading it gave me no joy. The only new idea in the report seemed to be a recommendation that Australia adopt the idea of the now-familiar *points demerit* schemes that were just starting to be used in the United States. Indeed the report seemed to belie its title. In the light of its emphasis on enforcement and punishment, I thought of it, under my breath, as the committee on driver bashing.

Not surprisingly, driver training and driver licensing were dealt with as part of the EGORS National Review process. I had been given the task of drafting the chapter setting out what it had come up with. Reviewing the consultant's report only reinforced my feelings about the licensing process as carried out in Australia. Indeed, what came to mind were the well-known words of the 'General Confession' from the Anglican *Book of Common Prayer* – "We have left undone those things that we ought to have done. And we have done those things that we ought not have done". I could not resist the temptation to use the same words as the conclusion to be drawn from the review and accordingly referenced the prayer book. It was one of the highlights of my career to see my boss at the time, Bob Ungers, collapse into laughter as he turned to the bibliography, saw the citation and decided that the members of the EGORS Research Committee at least should share the joke.

Guidelines for Driver Licensing and Driver Improvement Programs

In line with the thrust of the recommendations from the Expert Group's second report, the ORS engaged Ronald S Coppin, head of licensing research with the California Department of Motor Vehicles, and the co-author of many influential papers on driver training and licensing, to conduct a review of Australian practices. It was he who introduced us at the ORS to the expression 'doing things *for* people, not *to* people'.

The most prominent outcome of the Coppin review was the publication in 1980 of the *Guidelines for Driver Licensing and Driver Improvement Programs in Australia* that was prepared by ACRUPTC for ATAC. The guidelines were considered and endorsed in principle by ATAC in July of 1980. Some of the recommendations for action to be taken on a uniform basis may seem to be simple matters of commonsense bearing in mind that Australia is a federation. There have, however, been times when many of us felt that the European nations, who had not that long before been at war with each other, were able to harmonise transport-related matters more easily than the Australian states.

Recommendations in the guidelines document covered such matters as a uniform licence system including an end to multiple licences (for each type or class of vehicle and for reciprocal recognition of learners' permits. Driver improvement programs received systematic coverage with measures such as warning letters, individual counselling, group education meetings, rehabilitation programs for drink-driving offenders and referral to training and instruction programs all being canvassed.

Provisional or probationary licence schemes that placed restrictions on what a novice licence holder may or may not do were commonplace by the 1970s, creating new a class of driver, the P-plater. Some of the restrictions such a lower or zero BAC limit made sense, others less so, notably those that punished new drivers more harshly than other drivers for the same offence at a time when there were no driver improvement programs in place. Indeed, the punishment of a now readily identified group seemed to be the central focus of the first generation of P-plate schemes.

Graduated Licensing Schemes

Graduated Licensing schemes have been adopted across Australia though not on a uniform basis. The concept of graduated licensing as initially proposed by US researcher Patricia Waller from the Highway Safety Research Centre in North Carolina had always held much appeal for me since I read about it in the early 1970s. I had seen this as going some way towards breaking down the Victorian determination to hold to a minimum licensing age of 18 years despite its coinciding with the minimum age for the service of alcohol, and being higher than elsewhere in Australia, New Zealand and the USA.

I had always been intrigued by the fact that the USA in particular, but also New Zealand, granted young people their driving licences some years before any Australian state or territory. The common factor seemed to be a greater extent of the small farming lifestyle, meaning that more young people would become familiar with the operation of motorised vehicles at a much earlier age. Leaving aside its cities with huge populations, the USA is a nation of small cities, as is New Zealand, possibly offering a less frenetic, but nevertheless controlled, learning environment to a larger proportion of the population. Attitudes in Australia, a nation of large cities and small towns, may still reflect the inherent dangers arising from the reliance at the time on the absolute give-way-to-the right rule. The wish to delay granting the driving privilege was not all that surprising, but could be open to change today, given the now controlled driving environment.

The downside of delaying the granting of the driving privilege, however, is that young people lose the opportunity to develop a sense of responsibility while still under parental guidance. Ron Coppin's teenage children expressed surprise at the lack of maturity in their Australian classmates in the year they spent in Melbourne while he was conducting his 1977 review of driver licensing practices in Australia.

Graduated licensing as practised in Australia sets more restrictive limits on permissible blood alcohol concentration than apply to other drivers of light vehicles and has also picked up on the idea of setting limits on the number of passengers that may be carried in a vehicle driven by a novice driver, whilst some now include curfews (that also put a driving burden on parents). Schemes such as the ACT's 'Road Ready' Year 10 classroom program, provides learners with useful knowledge before they venture onto the roads. Keith Wheatley, whom I knew from FORS days, developed the Road Ready program. The requirement for learner drivers to have a certain number of hours of supervised driving is the latest measure impacting young drivers and their parents, guardians or older mentors. The fact that Victoria requires 120 hours of supervised driving, which is the highest in Australia, should come as no surprise. Indeed, it could, along with the higher minimum licensing age, be seen as a legal means of keeping a cohort of young drivers off the road for as long as is deemed possible. Ron Coppin, however, pointed out that it is inequitable to deny licences to *all* young people on the grounds that *some* of their number will have accidents.

Demerits – What's the Point?

By the time the ORS had moved to Canberra, points demerit schemes were operating in all states and territories, but their effectiveness was open to question. Among the staff who joined ORS at the time was Maureen Kingshott, a criminologist. Who better than a criminologist to investigate the worth of points demerit systems and more particularly the weightings that were an integral part of their operation?

The idea of assigning demerit points to various driving offences had been picked up from the United States in the report of the [so-called] Committee on Driver Improvement that had reported under the aegis of ACRUPTC in 1964.

Points demerit schemes as they operated in the states and territories varied widely in the weightings they gave to various offences. What more apt task for us at this time could there be but to see what relationship there was between various offence weightings and accident involvement. There was just one problem. Despite the clear need for that sort of research, the necessary data is not readily available even for research purposes in Australia although it is routinely available in California, the most motorised place on Earth. With the co-operation of the ACT administration, we were, however, able to get access to the relevant data on a confidential basis.

We in the ORS thought that weightings might hopefully bear some relationship to the *threat to life* that a particular offence represented, so that was one of the weightings we used. Then there was the scale to be used in the ACT. There was, however, a third possibility: that *a simple count* of the offences might work as well as any weighting regime.

The result was perhaps surprising. Neither of the weightings predicted subsequent accident involvement any better than the simple unweighted count. Surprisingly, including parking offences slightly improved the result. One confounding factor, however, was that the offence records for young drivers tended to be skewed towards non-traffic offences such as driving an unregistered or un-roadworthy vehicle or driving while disqualified. More worrying, however, was the smallness of the overlap between drivers who had both traffic offences and accidents. All accidents, however minor, have to be reported in the ACT.

The report of the study was never published but the title Maureen gave it said it all: *Demerits – What's the Point?*

The Barbecue Paper

A paper prepared by Bob Budd, Carol Boughton and I for a seminar 'Steering a course for the future' [in terms of driver licensing] sponsored by the Transport Regulation Board, Victoria, in early 1982 summed up what we had discerned up to that time about driver training and licensing, but there was more. The chill winds of managerism were already starting to be felt in FORS around that time and there was a feeling that frank and fearless advice may have had its day. We were only too well aware that some sensibilities might be offended by what we had to say. Indeed, we felt that we might as well go out in a blaze of glory and so we pointedly chose the ordering of our names: to this day Bob and I still refer to it as 'the barbecue paper'.

I had met Bob years before I joined DST and it was pleasure to hear that I would be working under him in FORS in his position as the new head of RSB. Bob was naturally attuned to the philosophy at the heart of 'the cause' that was looking to do things for people not to them. Bob of course took over chairmanship of ACRUPTC and had been immediately accepted. He could always see the funny side of things and this was particularly useful when we were dealing with what he dubbed the 'stands to reason club', people who held a position on how to handle a situation that was the exact opposite of what had been found to work.

One such area was the issue of driver training and this was very much to the fore in the 1980s. Even today, calls are still being made for additional skills training for drivers, despite off-road training for car drivers having been comprehensively shown to be ineffective in reducing accident involvement, as opposed to that for heavy vehicle drivers and novice motorcyclists. In one state a large proportion of would-be motorcyclists in fact gave up on the idea after trying it out.

In the barbecue paper, we also noted that some offset from increased exposure from an earlier driver licensing age would occur in terms of parental chauffeuring (often twice in each direction). There would, however, be a reduction in passenger deaths amongst young females currently dependent for transportation on slightly older licensed males. Indeed, were it not for a perverse consequence of anti-discrimination legislation, provisional licenses with fewer restrictions could be granted to young women at an earlier age or stage in driving than for young men.

For me, however, one recommendation for change had particular significance yet has still to be implemented, namely, integration of accident involvement into an individual driver's record. The Guidelines document referred to earlier was only one of a number of places where this has been recommended, but only in Queensland does this occur. It seems odd that to this day, no research seems to have been undertaken to determine the relationship or otherwise between traffic infringements and accident involvement. 'Don't confuse me with facts, my mind's made up' seems to be the prevailing attitude.

Medical guidelines for determining fitness for drive

The formulation of uniform national guidelines for determining medical fitness to drive on behalf of ATAC was a task undertaken by ACRPUTC during the time I was associated with it as convenor of its Driver Licensing Committee. We were fortunate to be able to use, as a basis for our deliberations, a booklet prepared by the Queensland Branch of the Australian Medical Association on behalf of the Queensland Department of Transport. Other organisations representing the various medical disciplines were also involved whilst Associate Professor B A Smethurst assisted with co-ordination and editing. The full title of the document, which was published by FORS, was *National Guidelines for Medical Practitioners in Determining Fitness to Drive a Motor Vehicle.*

The final chapter of the guidelines document was devoted specifically to the older driver. Issues that were dealt with were: the role of ageing in driving (mentioning how the physiological changes might be compensated for by long experience and voluntary limitation of driving); mental deterioration; multiple physical defects; evaluation of the older driver; and restricted licence privileges. The chapter ended with a statement under heading 'Flexibility' that is worth repeating today,

> Any licensing standards applied to the elderly should not discriminate against the elderly on the basis of chronological age alone.

Whilst the rise in accident rates for elderly drivers puts them nowhere near the accident rate of the youngest drivers, increasing frailty make the injury consequences more severe, especially if they are in older cars.

Our position at FORS was always that taking away anyone's licence to drive should only happen as a last resort, not as a routine procedure. In particular we were concerned at practical driving tests being used 'to get old people off the road'. We were very much aware of the consequences for a driver's self-esteem and the additional burden placed on family and friends.

Chapter 28

Four Principles for Road Infrastructure

One of the joys of the early years with the ORS in Canberra was the complete acceptance of the notion that the road system had to conform to the expectations of road users rather than the other way around. We were encouraged in this by the fact that the head of the ORS, the much-admired Frank E Yeend (as he always signed himself), had previously been the head of air safety investigation with the former Department of Civil Aviation, which made what was follow so hard to take. Bob Budd, who I mentioned earlier, had come to the position of head of the Road Safety Branch when FORS moved to Canberra and become an enthusiastic advocate of 'The Cause'.

The nature of the road system significantly influences road user behaviour. Whether this influence is a positive or negative one depends in large measure on the extent to which human capabilities and limitations have been taken into account as an integral part of the design process. The parallels with aviation have already been noted. We have also seen how deficiencies at specific places in the road system can be eliminated through black spot improvement programs and by local area traffic management measures.

The road system as a whole, however, can have safety designed in and danger designed out and at FORS we reduced this to four basic principles that can be put into effect on all classes of roads. These are:

- minimising the potential for collision
- ensuring relatively consistent design standards so that drivers are not presented with unexpected situations
- providing accurate information to road users
- providing a forgiving roadside.

These principles have application not just to new construction. Measures that are highly cost-effective can also be applied to existing roads and streets, frequently avoiding expenditure on complete reconstruction, even on fairly heavily trafficked routes. One such example on the Hume Highway north of Albury prior to duplication has already been noted.

This excursion into the elements of road design is to redress what I see as a turning away from using road design to encourage desired behaviours in favour of measures that attempt to modify behaviour through the use of 'enforcement crunch'. It should never be forgotten that once a road environment has been modified or built with that end in view, the positive influence continues for the design life of the piece of infrastructure whereas punitive approaches have to be constantly reinforced. The better informed the public is the more likely it is that they will be able to encourage governments to act on their behalf.

An informed public will demand that governments act to ensure that a safe road environment is provided for them. This is why I am taking this opportunity to provide a short exposition of the technical issues behind the four principles. In this regard, it is important to remember that the provision of safe travel conditions may involve quite modest design standards and this can be very important when considering the appropriate level of technology needed for road construction.

The first pre-requisite to the design of a user-friendly road system is a realistic understanding of the nature of the driving task and the varying levels of the demands that are put on all road users. What is important is not simplification of the task to the point of boredom, but maintaining an *optimal level of arousal*. This may involve, for instance, simplifying a complex intersection by redesign so that drivers are presented with a sequence of tasks with which they can reasonably be expected to cope and, therefore, avoid conflict with other road users or damage to their own vehicle. On the other hand it may be appropriate for a driver to be expected to maintain a high level of arousal, for example, in mountainous country, but the road environment should still not present them with unexpected hazardous situations.

The aim therefore should be to provide a *consistent driving environment* appropriate to the function of the road but one that is also perceptually valid – that what the driver appears to be presented with is what they in fact encounter. Such considerations have a significant impact on the design standards adopted for particular sections of road.

Minimising the potential for conflict comes first among the principles whether it is vehicle with vehicle, vehicle with pedestrian or vehicle with roadside object etc. The most obvious means of minimising conflict are grade separation (overpasses and underpasses) on the busiest roads and the provision of separate carriageways for traffic in each direction. Overtaking can, however, be made safer on two-way two-lane roads by the clearing of roadside obstructions to view and the lowering of crests to improve sight distances. Where traffic signals are installed, the provision of separate turn phases or the construction or marking of turning lanes can improve sight distances and make turning safer. Other measures have already been referred to as part of local area traffic management.

Designing out the unexpected can be achieved by employing consistent design standards. It has been shown that isolated curves or the first curve in a series are the ones more likely to experience crashes. Modern road designs incorporate complex geometric elements that make curves safer and we have seen how low-cost improvements can make existing roads safer. This can involve realignment of short sections and it is increasingly noticeable how often curves on rural roads have been eased and in some cases heavily banked so as to make them easier to negotiate. There are numerous cases where an easily negotiable route has been established along a road that originally turned at right angles around property boundaries.

Providing guidance for drivers is perhaps the area of road design where change has been the most evident and certainly the most visible. When I started driving, a painted centre line was about all one could expect. The introduction of raised reflective pavement markers (RRPMs or 'cat's eyes') on Australia's roads is a comparatively recent innovation although they were first used in the UK in 1934. In recent years, flexible plastic markers incorporating reflective material have replaced rigid wooden guideposts to give an indication to drivers of which way a road is curving. RRPMs also provide a tactile warning if a driver has strayed off course, whilst, most recently, has come tactile paint for edge lines. Another comparatively recent innovation is the use of street lighting at major highway junctions in rural areas, an example of enhancing safety by improving the conditions under which driving takes place rather than trying to change behaviour.

Ian Johnston, a member of the original Road Safety Research Section, undertook a significant piece of research in the field of delineation when he moved to ARRB. He gave it the engaging subtitle 'Getting them round the bend'. The study was originally undertaken to reduce the risk of alcohol-affected drivers crashing on curves – another example of changing the environment in order to influence behaviour. It was, however, pivotal to the introduction of the familiar black-on-yellow chevron signs now used to indicate unusually sharp curves. Indeed, the almost universal uptake of retro-reflective devices has been a feature of road engineering in both urban and rural settings over recent decades, along with advisory speed signs, pioneered by Doug Kneebone, an Adelaide engineer.

Providing a forgiving roadside environment is the fourth element. I have already drawn attention to the elimination of roadside 'booby traps' as part of the revolution in thinking about the road accident problem. Indeed, one of the most marked changes I have seen over the last thirty years has been the shielding of solid structures close to the edge of the road by guardrail, moving signs further from the travelled way, and designing sign supports so as to give on impact.

Particular groups may also need special protection. A recent change in guardrail design has been the addition of an extra panel below the normal guardrail at locations where motorcyclists might otherwise slide under the rail should they lose control on a wet or frosty bend. An example can be found on the steep descent of the Snowy Mountains Highway down Brown Mountain towards the Bega Valley.

The situation with regard to utility poles, however, is quite different. This is disappointing having regard to the work for the ORS in 1978 by the

Mechanical Engineering department of the University of Melbourne on methods for identifying poles that were likely to be hit and on the design of poles to make them less of a danger. The same can be said of the work done for FORS in 1984 by the Faculty of Law at Monash University that made it clear that an authority responsible for erecting an inappropriate type of pole in a particular situation could be liable to an action for damages were the pole to be hit. I regard these matters as unfinished business and the issues involved are dealt with in more detail in a later chapter.

Before leaving the subject of how road design can influence driver behaviour, some other achievements over recent years deserve attention in their own right.

Signs and signals

These are now standardised with warning signs being distinguished from regulatory signs by being black on a yellow diamond. Drivers today are also provided with much improved direction signing. This is an instance of designing out uncertainty by having signs in advance of intersections, signing at the intersection and then 'reassurance signing' (to let you know whether you are on the right road or not).

The creation of the signs themselves is the subject of a rigorous process that involves testing for both comprehension and legibility. A good example is the wombat warning sign - drawing something that did not look like a pile of rocks was quite a challenge and the latest version has been reduced to an outline drawing.

Improvement of street lighting

Lighting to 'Code Standard' has played a major part in making driving at night in urban areas so much safer than it was when I started to drive. This is perhaps the prime example of changing the conditions to make the roads safer for drivers, riders and pedestrians rather than trying to change behaviour, of doing things for road users rather than to them. Prominent researchers in the field were Hal Turner and Alex Fisher from the University of New South Wales who had established by the time of first EGORS report in 1972 that lighting to Code Standard was justified once there were about 3000 vehicles per day on au urban road or street.

In the 1950s, however, street lighting on local streets was limited to one small incandescent lamp at each intersection or about every 100 metres and the situation was barely better on arterial roads, although a single sodium (yellow) or mercury (blue) vapour lamp could be seen at some major intersections. I can still remember coming out of Sydney Terminal Station onto Railway Square in the early 1960s and being astonished to see it lit only by incandescent lamps, whereas the CBD in Melbourne at least was lit by mercury vapour lamps on their ornamental dark green lampposts. The situation in provincial centres was no better than in Sydney if Ballarat was anything to go by. There was an eerie darkness as one looked down Lydiard Street as the train crossed it on the journey to Adelaide, seeing only a few small incandescent globes.

Co-ordinated traffic signal systems

Building on the pioneering work of Arthur Sims, the designer of Australia's first such system, SCATS (Sydney Coordinated Adaptive Traffic System) have now been installed across Australia. Readers will recall the finding that safety benefits alone would justify co-ordination of traffic lights was brought to attention at the first National Road Safety Symposium in 1972. The technology developed by Arthur Sims has been exported all over the world. Australia's leading role in traffic signal control deserves to be better known. Largely unseen by the road users it serves, this is truly buried treasure.

Chapter 29

The Lost Cause

Those of us who had moved up to Canberra had done so with the hope that we would be able to continue working for what we affectionately referred to as 'the cause'. The cause represented the systematic approach to making road usage safer by finding out what worked and then working with the states and territories to implement it while discarding what didn't. The notion of a 'cause' did not sit well with a Canberra management style that was more attuned to giving the sort of advice that their political masters wanted to hear. Nevertheless, in the first few years after the move to Canberra the ORS initiated numerous projects and continued work on other areas.

I have already referred to the role of the Office in promoting local area traffic management and low-cost road and traffic control improvements, nor was the human factor neglected and two projects of particular interest to the work of ACRUPTC in regard to traffic regulation and driver licensing were undertaken by my section, now renamed Road User and Traffic Standards Section.

In addition to my friend and able committee secretary, Kevin, who had moved to Canberra the year before me and greatly assisted me in settling in, my staff included engineer Bill Danaher, who with Maureen Kingshott, conducted the study of points demerit systems referred to earlier. This was the time we still fondly harboured the notion that one day there would be full integration of driver licence records, including accident involvement as well as traffic offences, that would be uniform across Australia and accessible between jurisdictions.

Another study dealt with the then contentious issue of keeping left unless overtaking. The simplistic application of the general rule requiring vehicles to be driven as near as practicable to the left-hand edge of the road was clearly unworkable on multi-lane urban roads. There were still some people on the roads that regarded overtaking on the left anywhere with suspicion. Perhaps they still thought that if the road was wide enough they could drive anywhere they liked on their side of the centre line; there were, of course, no lane lines at the time I started to drive

Research from the then West Germany had shown that beyond a certain volume of traffic drivers distributed themselves equally over each lane of two in the urban situation. The finding needed to be confirmed in an Australian setting and so Bill made an observational study on Canberra arterial roads. What the study showed was that observance of the idea of keeping to the left unless overtaking was just as much in evidence in places where there was only a warning sign reminding people to do so as where there was an absolute prohibition on driving in other than the left lane unless overtaking.

Good sense soon prevailed in the urban situation and not only was overtaking on the left permitted but also driving in any lane of a multi-lane road where the speed limit was 80 km/h or less. On the open road the situation was less clear although at the higher speeds it was desirable to limit the need to overtake on the left.

In an earlier chapter I referred to having been involved in the investigation of a fatal collision between a long-distance coach and a semi-trailer near Gundagai. Work done by the University of Melbourne had cast grave doubts on the adequacy of seat anchorages. Accordingly, data was collected relating to injury patterns and seat positions. The major lesson learned from the investigation of the crash was that there was no point in even thinking about fitting seatbelts to passenger coaches if their mountings were simply going to be wrenched from the floor; seats on the coach in question had come loose. Also evident was the high price in injuries that was paid for being able to recline the seat: in many cases the reclining mechanism snapped. There is value in seats and their anchorages being strong enough to 'pocket' passengers in between them. Where the seats had come loose, people were catapulted over the seat or seats in front. I am glad to have been able to see modern long-distance passenger coaches being fitted with seatbelts in all positions so that loss of life in tragedies of the kind I have been referring to should be a thing of the past.

I was also involved in the investigation of another crash, this one in Canberra involving an ACTION route service bus carrying forty passengers that had occurred during the morning peak. I had been heading to Belconnen along Eastern Valley Way and saw the large number of police and other emergency vehicles at the intersection with College Street. A car driver had gone through a red light and struck the left front wheel of the bus which then fish-tailed down the road, mounted the kerb and ran into a large gum tree that penetrated the front of the bus by more than a metre. Hurrying to the office I alerted the staff, and a team of engineers and other researchers were soon on the scene documenting injury patterns and seating positions.

The most seriously injured were the driver and the passenger occupying the single front seat facing the screen beside the entry steps. The driver suffered severe internal injuries and the passenger a fractured skull. Other passengers received only minor injuries, remarkable given the force of the collision. This, we would later learn, was the result of the MAN bus having a 'space-frame' chassis that absorbed much of the force of impact. Conventional buses at the time would have had a rigid frame. When news of the crash reached the manufacturers in the then West Germany a team of engineers was despatched to see how their design had worked. The other remarkable outcome was the total absence of dental injuries. The reason for this was immediately evident. ACTION had been notable for a number of innovations and one of these was the installation of energy-absorbing roll-top padding on the top of the seats rather than the conventional round chrome-plated bars.

In FORS we had always seen the Black Spot Programs as a significant part of *the cause* of doing things *for* road users rather than *to* them. We were therefore happy to see that such programs were included in the policies of the incoming Australian Labor Party (ALP) government that replaced the Coalition government led by Malcolm Fraser following the 1983 election. It was clear, however, that new ALP government led by Bob Hawke was keen to avoid being tarred with the big-spending brush that had come to be associated with the Whitlam government. One casualty was black spot funding.

The writing was on the wall. Publicity programs that cost less but were of dubious benefit were about to replace concrete action (pun intended). One such area was pedestrian safety where far and away the greatest benefit was to be obtained by the provision of median refuges that effectively divided the crossing task in two.

Symbolically, things came to a head when a divisional lunch was organised in to mark the move from our former offices in the Belconnen Town Centre to a location in Civic (the still unofficial name for the Canberra CBD).The lunch was held at a favourite picnic spot nearby, Black Mountain Peninsula. This was intended as bonding exercise, a device well known to the new managerial class. We newcomers to Canberra represented only about one-quarter of those people who had been with the Office of Road Safety in Melbourne and were clearly out-numbered in the new set-up.

Our situation became worse when a member of the managerial class whose function, we heard, was 'to bring us into line' replaced the highly regarded head of FORS, Frank Yeend. In despair, some of us turned to humour to relieve our growing frustration, finding inspiration in the tales of how the ancient Israelites had suffered at the hands of their oppressors. A number of the pieces written at that time are reproduced here, beginning with the one I wrote at the time of the Black Mountain picnic.

The Captivity

And when the wanderers from the south had taken up a new habitation nigh unto the seat of power a great feast was ordained at the Place of Many Barbecues and the fatted calf was killed that all might be filled and much wine was procured that all might make merry.

And the Great One appeared amongst the host, and his minions, who had come to share the habitation of the people from the south, moved amongst them and revealed that which had previously only been seen in a glass darkly. They had come amongst the people from the south to show by their example the greater glory of The Policy so that those who had strayed from the Word might desist finally from their delusions and cease from troubling their master with great talk of The Cause.

And thus it came to pass even as the prophets from the land of RoSTA had foretold: that their new masters had sought only to ensnare them that the scourge of The Cause might be banished from the realm of The Policy.

And a proclamation went forth that all had been accomplished. No longer would the lands beyond the realm of The Policy hear the voice of those who had so mistakenly had it in their hearts to save the lives of their fellow men and women not by condemning their folly but by understanding their frailty.

Other ways of saving the government money were also looked into, sometimes putting at risk the long-standing practices relating to the conduct of ATAC committee and sub-committee meetings. These had traditionally been held on a rotating basis among the states and territories. As well as fairly spreading the costs of travel and accommodation, this arrangement had particular relevance to the work in the fields of road signs and signals as well as traffic law. Innovations could be demonstrated and contentious issues discussed on a more practical basis. Out-of-session discussions between professionals almost invariably come back to their fields of interest, but the importance of such informal contacts tends to be lost on the managerial class. From the mid-1980s, meetings tended more and more to be conducted in the Canberra-Sydney-Melbourne 'triangle' and there was also a push for meetings to be limited to one day.

Increasingly, decisions were being be made centrally and then passed on to the states and territories. In one notable case a concord was made between FORS and the state and territory bodies about the way in which road safety matters generally would be dealt with. My branch head at the time, Noel Matthews, asked me to prepare appropriate briefing notes about the new arrangements. The idea of a concord resonated with me as having a lot in common with a supersonic aircraft of a similar name that held much promise, but was of distinctly little practical value. Accordingly, I carefully folded a copy of the brief I had prepared into the form of a paper dart and then, standing at the door of Noel's office, flew it on to his desk.

It so happened that my early years in Canberra were the years that saw the construction of the new and permanent Parliament House. I was wary of what might happen to the Australian federation when the House of Representatives and the Senate moved into their palatial new premises on Capital Hill. I remembered C Northcote Parkinson's observation about a firm's best work being done in the converted aircraft hangar and to fear for it when it moved to sparkling new premises. This unease led me to pen the following cautionary tale.

The Prophecy

And it came to pass that the Great One appointed a new governor to ensure that word of The Cause would not trouble those even higher than he. And those who had made the journey to the land of their captivity with such hope in their hearts read aloud from the Book of Haddon and called upon the Minor Prophets, but to no avail. "Folly, folly" the governor cried. "The Cause is a Folly – an affront in the realm of The Policy".

Then one amongst them told how he had had a troubled dream of the ruin to come when the great new temple was consecrated on the hill, the name of which is Capital.

Now there came from time to time to that city, emissaries from other parts to meet in high council with the governor and it had been the custom that their counsellors should also meet. And there was much joy in these meetings for they all sat as brothers to discuss their masters' business that the counsel they gave might be to the mutual good.

But even this was counted folly and the high council decreed that their business was to be done in the forenoon and the afternoon of one day that the price of lodgings might be saved. And soon they came not at all.

And the governor gathered counsellors from another part of his realm, both male and female, for the opportunity to err must be equally open to all. And the governor began to take counsel from the false prophets amongst them on how he should communicate with the lands beyond the land of The Policy. And this was their advice, that he should speak loudly of concord and consultation, but do in secret what the false prophets had advised was for the good of The Policy.

And finally my advice for anyone working on briefs in a policy department,

Policy Documents

Policy documents must be brief and to the point, encompass all exceptions and qualifications, and remain valid no matter how the circumstances change.

Chapter 30

Marginalisation

From the time back in Melbourne when the ORS took over responsibility for servicing ACRPUTC I had been its technical adviser and had attended meetings of the relevant Standards Association of Australia (SAA) committee on road signs and signals to ensure that what was contained in the Standard was consistent with the National Road Traffic Code. I also attended, as an observer, the annual meetings of Motor Vehicle Registrars so as to see that as far as practicable driver licensing procedures took best practice into account.

In 1985, a review of the ATAC committee structure was undertaken that led to new committees being set up, in which I was to play no part. I was of course disappointed but not altogether surprised. Free thinkers do not thrive in the Land of the Policy.

An indication of the scant regard for expertise was that I was immediately put in charge of the Administration and Liaison Section of FORS. The section was responsible for finance and staffing matters, as well as for ensuring that ministerial correspondence and briefings were running to schedule. What made the move more remarkable was that in all the time we had been in Canberra my devoted offsider, Kevin Larkins, had taken care of all matters relating to finance in our section.

As it happened, Kevin was headhunted by the Queensland Department of Transport to work in their driver licensing area, but sadly died only a few years later, aged 49. Christine Carseldine who filled his position in my section proved to be a very efficient committee secretary, so much so that she was co-opted to fulfil a similar role when Austroads was developing the Australian Road Rules in 1993. Sadly she too passed away soon after. I should also mention my other assistants, Helen Percy who had moved up from Melbourne in 1981 with her husband Wal, a senior technical officer with FORS, and Mike Key whose photographic skills I put to good use in a number of instances. Helen's compilation of 'significant papers for information' remains a valuable resource for me.

For all that I wished I was doing something more relevant to my skills and interests, I made a difference to A& L within a week. There had been close to an international incident when a Japanese company did not receive its copies of amendments to Australian Design Rules (ADRs) because the records showed it was not up to date with its subscription fees when in fact it was. The problem, easily fixed, was simply the time lag between receiving and recording payments.

I have mentioned earlier the issue of bus and coach safety and this would figure again as my career drew to an end, this time as a staffing matter. FORS had one engineer working in the area, but it was also one unit over its establishment [staffing] limit. An unfortunate aspect of this way of looking at things is that each staffing unit counts as one whatever the classification. At its worst, no account seems to be taken as to what areas of activity should be accorded priority. As it happened, bus and coach safety was not a traditional area of concern for the Vehicle Structures Safety Branch, but that was what the one engineer over establishment was working on. Knowing that I would only be in the A&L job for a limited time, I let it ride.

I was not alone in feeling the lack of regard for expertise. The Bureau of Transport Economics (BTE) was also ridding itself of people with specialised knowledge in areas other than economics. I was to be the beneficiary of this, however, when a senior engineer was found a place in my section, now renamed User Safety. Kay Loong had three Masters degrees in engineering and related areas and had been a lecturer at the Queensland University of Technology. In my section his work related to the appropriateness of speed limits and the role of traffic law and its enforcement, producing position papers on each.

By this time, we had lost Bob Budd who had headed the Road Safety Branch since the move to Canberra, replaced by Carol Boughton. Bob took early retirement, trained as a teacher and then taught secondary school mathematics.

Much of the new approach to road safety had in fact involved overturning the misconceptions that abounded about the way the road accident problem should be tackled. This led Bob, not long before he left, to produce a delightful piece entitled *Road Safety Folklore – Conventional Wisdom or Wishful Thinking* in which he took apart such nostrums as:

- *more rigorous licence tests* - put emphasis on roadcraft, not carcraft;
- *periodic retesting of drivers* - even those who have had their licences taken away for traffic offences have no difficulty passing a licence test;
- *more driving training* - useful for motorcyclists especially novices, but other interventions such as counselling better for repeat offenders;
- *general reduction of speed limits* - drivers respect appropriate limits
- *tougher penalties* - deterrence is the key, especially as offenders are not necessarily those having accidents;
- *tougher penalties for drink driving* - as many as 60% do not offend again, rehabilitation better for most, together with road improvements;
- *keep left rule* - requesting 'keep left unless overtaking' works as well;
- *periodic vehicle inspection* - only useful for heavy vehicles; vehicle condition is not major contributor to other crashes though inspection on resale of older vehicles may be worthwhile;
- *more road safety publicity* - 'preaching' and slogans not effective, only specific messages aimed at specific behaviours and target groups;
- *more 'blood and guts' publicity* - only effective in the very short term and may reinforce defence mechanisms against anxiety.

The conclusion to be reached is for road safety authorities to give priority to safer and more forgiving road environments, targeted education and enforcement, and the use of protective equipment such as occupant restraints and helmets.

Not long after, I also put together a compendium arguing the case for those measures that did work in the hope that it might prove instructive to those who followed me.

Someone else from my past also left the BTE around the same time as Kay. Howard Quinlan had been with the Bureau of Census and Statistics back in the 1960s. My first contact with him had been a mild skirmish over whose job it was to provide the Minister for Shipping and Transport with road accident statistics for parliamentary purposes. It was ironic, therefore, that the place found for him in FORS was in the research section looking after road accident statistics and related exposure data. Howard, with a Doctorate in Geography, had a particular interest in railways and in the measurement of the freight task more generally. He soon found work as a consultant working on his specialty. In retirement I would encounter his son as manager of road safety in the ACT Department of Territory and Municipal Services.

I was, however, given one last opportunity to do something worthwhile. This was to study the safety of older pedestrians. Perhaps it had something to do with my being close to the '60 and over' age group that was to be studied. Pedestrian safety in general had always been important to me, particularly since I had been given the opportunity to present a paper on child pedestrian accidents to a Pedestrian Safety conference back in Melbourne. Above all, that paper had shown the importance of working to prevent 'dart out' accidents some of which are easily prevented by fencing along the kerb outside schools. Witnessing a dart out accident involving a young person while I was in Melbourne had sensitised me to the consequences of such impetuous behaviour. Barrier fencing is also coming to be used more generally on main roads to restrict crossing to places where there are traffic lights. One notable example is in Sydney along the strip shopping centre on Military Road between Neutral Bay and Cremorne.

With older pedestrians, however, the problems are different and more related to declining powers of perception and agility. The report *Safety of Older Pedestrians* was published in 1986. The standout finding was that, by dividing the crossing task in two, median refuges were far and away the best and most cost-effective countermeasure that could be put in place. Another finding from the study, perhaps paradoxical, was that older pedestrians were at most risk on what are termed 'sub-arterial roads', rather than on the busier main roads where it appears that the measures to assist traffic to interact safely also benefit pedestrians.

In addition to the statistical study, bodies representing the interests of older people were invited to put forward their views on the issue of pedestrian safety. Their overwhelming concern was that the 'walk' time at traffic lights was too short. I took this matter on with enthusiasm and an appendix was included in the report for the edification of traffic engineers, a term I use advisedly. This is something I will return to later. Issues considered in the report included the devastating effect that injuries sustained in old age have on the lifestyle and independence of older people. It is perhaps a measure of the official attitudes prevailing at the time that I had to fight hard to have such a self-evident statement included in the report.

The report of the study entitled *Safety of Older Pedestrians* was widely distributed by FORS. Despite this, in the political climate of the time, recommendations that involved the federal government committing to capital works did not find favour. Instead, the decision was made to run a campaign to encourage older people to take care when crossing the road. These were the three television commercials I referred to in an earlier chapter.

By then Graeme Evans, who had moved to Canberra with FORS, had transferred to the Vehicles Branch where his task was twofold – to turn the ADRs into Plain English, but also presenting them in a new manner more appropriate to their being enforceable legal instruments. Major progress was soon made on the general task of introducing drafting standards for the ADRs, but, interestingly, an early query addressed to Graeme by a number of branch engineers led to prompt addressing of a long-standing need to clarify whether 'seat belt' was one simple word, or a hyphenated word, or two words. This matter was soon put to rest. Graeme's negotiations clarified once and for all that it was one word – and was not a hyphenated word. Progress sometimes occurs where it might have not been expected! The spelling of 'seat belts' as one word can now be found in the

Australian version of the *Concise Oxford Dictionary* and in the *Macquarie Dictionary*.

As is the way of things, Graeme's successor as section head was a psychologist, Stephen Jiggins, who had initially come to the RSB from Roads Division. I therefore found myself working for someone who had worked under me when he first came to RSB. Mercifully we had got on well. His section was seen as a convenient place to 'park' me. Steve, as he was informally known, would later do a PhD on the effectiveness of mass communications in promoting road safety around the world and play a big role in the Australasian College of Road Safety.

Then came the introduction by Management Services of 'program budgetting'. Under this regime every aspect of the work of a department had to be classified under a particular program heading. In our pursuit of 'the cause' we had, within proper constraints, been used to just getting the job done. I recall spending the best part of an afternoon with a 'know nothing' from Management Services that left us both frustrated but none the wiser.

I had intended to go on working in FORS until at least age 62, possibly part-time. At about the time I was considering what I should do, the government had embarked on a campaign of offering voluntary redundancy packages to what were then known as Second Division positions – branch heads and above. This set me thinking. Perhaps Third Division staff like me might also be offered redundancy packages. Before making my decision to take early retirement – I was 57 at the time – I contacted the union to enquire about third division redundancy packages being offered and was told that this was not to be the case. That was in April 1988.

I went out in May and I will never forget opening the *Canberra Times* in November to read that there were indeed such packages about to be offered. With 20/20 hindsight I should have just bided my time, taking six months long service leave on half-pay to get used to the idea of retirement and a lower income.

I had been in a holding pattern doing odd jobs for most of the time since the older pedestrians study. When it became necessary to find a position for me that was "organisationally appropriate", it was the nature of the position that I was offered that sealed my choice: to be put in charge of the statistical unit of FORS within the Research Section, a position that had just been vacated by none other than Howard Quinlan! That would have taken my career in road safety full circle. There, I would have spent my time grinding out statistics to justify doing nothing that was really going to make a difference – which, as they say, is where I came in.

Retirement

CONSULTANCIES AND SUBMISSIONS

GOING OVERSEAS

THE AUSTRALASIAN COLLEGE OF ROAD SAFETY

TOGETHER AGAIN

LETTING GO

Chapter 31

Consultancies and Submissions

While one may retire form the paid workforce, one does not retire from driving unless and until circumstances bring it about. A traffic engineer of my acquaintance said he had a similar experience of 'living his work' even on holiday trips. Partners, mine included, find this irksome. That people should be so involved in their work is something the managerial class find difficult to understand. One of the best things about being retired, however, is that one can speak one's mind on issues where one would otherwise be circumscribed by protocol.

Consultancies

I am pleased to be able to record that my expertise in the area of traffic regulation that had been summarily ignored in the lead-up to my retirement was recognised in 1993 when the draft of the Australian Road Rules (ARRs), which came into effect in 2000, was under consideration. I undertook two consultancies, one for Austroads, the organisation that had carriage of the project, and the other for the then New South Wales Road Traffic Authority. The first consultancy was to collate comments on the draft rules that had been made by the states and territories and to suggest how the matters raised might find expression in the final set of rules. The second was to find the places where corresponding draft rules were to be found in the three pieces of legislation then governing road traffic in New South Wales and to discuss any issues relating to them.

I could not help thinking at the time of the push made by FORS to have uniform road rules adopted to coincide with the Bicentennial of European settlement in 1988. It was also somewhat ironic that the meetings, for which my work had formed a basis for agreeing on what was in and what was out, were held not in Canberra but in Melbourne where it had all begun for me.

It was at these meetings that I was able to catch up with another former member of the Road Safety Research Section, psychologist David South, who had gone to RoSTA at the time of the Canberra transfer and who was now working with the Austroads secretariat developing the ARRs.

The final version of the ARRs came into effect in 2000, but complete uniformity has still not been achieved, notably with regard to the hours of operation of school crossings. Some jurisdictions such as the ACT enforce the 40 km/h restriction over the whole period 8am to 4pm whereas others including New South Wales restrict speed only when children are likely to be using the crossings.

In one further twist, the ARRs allow drivers to pass a stationary tram (or a public bus in a tram lane) when it is safe to do so at a speed of no more than 10 km/h. Passing a stationary tram unless signalled to do so by tram crew or a police officer was *never* allowed in Victoria where the Melbourne network survived and is now one of the biggest in the world. Passing stationary trams at no more than 5 mph (8 km/h) had always been allowed in Adelaide where all but one line, that to Glenelg, have been replaced by buses. This was allowed despite the suburban streets with trams in Adelaide being wider than they were in Melbourne, thus providing more opportunities for overtaking, and the fact that the running board on the H class trams (the famous Bay Trams) actually folded up. I also found it intriguing that the initial move to permit the practice in the ARRs came not from South Australia, but from New South Wales when trams (euphemistically called light rail vehicles) were reintroduced in Sydney.

My last consultancy was to prepare drafting instructions for the changes to the ACT Road Traffic Act to permit taxis to use designated bus lanes.

Submissions

Another foray back into the field of road safety was to make a submission on speed limits to the Social Development Committee of the Victorian Parliament. In this I was able to present a range of views that would have been unpalatable to my former departmental masters and to do so using language that would have been cut from the first draft. I was delighted to be able to say that the stiff-necked Victorian approach to any increase in speed limits, no matter how safe the road, was the same as that of the Red Queen in *Alice Through the Looking Glass* – "Sentence first, verdict later". I could have said "Don't confuse me with facts, my mind's made up", but felt that a bit of whimsy might have more impact, which in fact it did.

As it happened, at the time of the inquiry, the Minister for Transport in Victoria held the rather quaint idea that keeping the speed limit on the safest roads, of which the newly duplicated Hume Highway was one, at 100 km/h reinforced the importance of keeping speeds down generally. There was one major problem with this notion. With heavy vehicles being permitted to travel at the same speed as light vehicles, the right-hand lane was to all intents and purposes unusable. The result was soon evident - the left-hand lane of the Hume Freeway was worn out whilst the other lane was in pristine condition. This led to disruptive and premature resealing of the left-hand lane on a new road long before it should have been needed. I might point out also that this happened on a National Highway and so the federal government had to foot the bill. The committee recommended that light vehicles again be allowed to do 110 km/h on divided roads and this duly happened.

It was not long after this, and following upon my overseas trip in 1999, that I presented a paper with the provocative title *Hit by Friendly Fire – Collateral Damage in the War against Speed* to the 1999 Research, Policing and Education conference. What it said is related in a later chapter.

Since then my activities in the field, aside from representing the Australian College of Road Safety on the ACT Black Spot Consultative Committee, have been mainly attending seminars, making contributions to the various submissions from the college and, I almost forgot, writing this book!

Chapter 32

Going Overseas

In May-June 1999 I made my one and only trip to the United States and Europe, being away for five weeks. Whenever I refer to it I fear that I must sound a little like the television comedy character Uncle Arthur who was referring forever to "my overseas trip" and regaling an unwilling audience with a painfully detailed account of his experiences.

Ever since I was old enough to have contemporaries who travelled overseas I was amazed that they could come back and still accept the way in which life in Melbourne plodded on unchanged with no thought as to how things were done better overseas or for that matter over the State borders. I even got the feeling that these people knew more about Athens than they did about Adelaide. I have already referred to the seminal experience of visiting Adelaide for the first time in 1953 and realising just how backward the Melbourne of that time was but nowhere more obviously than in the areas of traffic and urban transport.

I was therefore determined to experience on the ground the things that I had previously only read about or seen on television and film. What follows is a distillation of copious notes I took on my journeys as a passenger on tour.

The United States of America

Los Angeles

Even as the plane was landing at Los Angeles International Airport I saw my first American freeway, running parallel to the runway. Despite what one hears, however, I was surprised that in the central parts of Los Angeles traffic moves mainly on the wide tree-lined roads such as the well-known Wilshire and Sunset Boulevards along which modern buses operate frequent services even at weekends. In addition, Los Angeles is also developing a suburban rail network consisting of heavy rail and light rail routes that by now stands at 150km with further extensions planned.

My tourist bus trip around Los Angeles covered Beverley Hills, the iconic Hollywood sign (actually nowhere near Hollywood the suburb, but rather a truncated reference to the earlier Hollywood Land real estate development), Farmers Market, the upmarket Rodeo Drive shopping strip and finally Venice Beach (named for a failed canal-style development) and on to Santa Monica. There I encountered the first of many four-way stop signs I would see and watched to see how drivers responded. "You just take turns [in order of arrival]" as one of our American consultants put it to a bemused Australian audience of road safety professionals in the 1970s. This was illustrative of an all-too-common failure to understand the underlying philosophy of traffic control in the USA and how it differs from the regimented Australian approach.

My journey by tourist bus from Los Angeles to San Francisco took me through the northern suburbs of Los Angeles where I noticed that the shopping centres we passed were not the gargantuan structures I had expected but rather had shops arranged around a shady square open to the road.

The coastal route north

State Highway 101 comes out to the coast just north of the fabled Malibu and on through Santa Barbara, which justifiably has been nominated as one of the most liveable cities in the United States. There I noticed the ubiquity of mopeds on the streets and the widespread use of the Christmas Bush as a street tree. Later I would see rather pathetic looking Eucalypts, a less successful import that had not done well in the harsher environment of the farms on which they had been planted.

Travelling along very close to the sandy beach one can look out to the off-shore oil rigs in the vicinity of the Channel Islands, but I recall only one or two examples of the iconic goose-neck oil rigs off the land side of the road. Beyond the army town of San Louis Obispo, and just before Ventura, the coach turned off onto a two-way two-lane road along which the State floral symbol, the orange Californian Poppy, grew wild, and from which one looked down into the Santa Ana Valley, one of the State's leading wine-producing regions.

I was rather disappointed that we had turned off the coast road before Ventura since that name had been familiar to me since childhood as the name of the bus line that ran from Box Hill to Mentone along nearby Warrigal Road. It had been founded in the late 1920s by an American who hailed from Ventura and the buses operated from a garage built in the then popular Spanish Mission style on Canterbury Road in Surrey Hills, just east of Warrigal Road.

The lunch stop was in Solvang, 'the Danish Capital of America' founded by an idealistic group of Danish educators in the early 20th century, where the clapboard architecture with windmills has been carefully maintained. North of Solvang the road climbs over the mountain range that rises to 3000 metres before the descent to the coast near San Simeon. Along this road it was surprising to see that a guardrail was only in place where the drop was greatest. The area inland from San Simeon is best known as the location of Hearst Castle, the vast amazing pleasure dome of the newspaper magnate, Randolph Hearst, on whom Orson Welles based his legendary film *Citizen Kane*. It is noteworthy that Hearst employed a woman as its architect.

Back on the coast road one is soon aware that you are experiencing a cliff-top drive more than comparable with Victoria's Great Ocean Road. The genesis of the road is in fact the same as that of the Great Ocean Road; both were constructed during the Great Depression of the 1930s as make-work projects for the unemployed. Geographically the 'The Big Sur'

(Spanish for 'south') is notable for being practically uninhabited and the few villages along the way exist only to serve the tourist trade.

The most notable man-made feature of the road is the Bixby Bridge opened in 1932. At 218 metres, it was one of the longest concrete arch spans in the world. At the time of my visit it was in the process of being strengthened to modern earthquake-resistant standards and it was when our bus driver was negotiating his way through the roadworks that I had one of the scariest moments of my long life.

Bearing in mind the absence of guardrails and the precipitous drop off the road, the manoeuvre of reversing the bus in order to get past an obstruction took it so close the edge that the view out the window was directly onto the rocks below! It was at that point that I realised why that particular tour was only offered in the northbound direction between Los Angeles and San Francisco. Driving on the right means that a northbound journey is undertaken on the side of the road furthest from the drop into the sea. The trip in the opposite direction in a tourist bus does not bear thinking about.

The Central Valley, Yosemite and San Francisco

The road from Monterey to the spectacularly beautiful Yosemite National Park passes over the Diablo Range and then crosses the wide San Jaoquin Valley that is the southern end of the California's Central Valley. This was somewhere I had wanted to see since university days. The journey across the valley takes one and a half hours during which its vast flatness extends to the horizon in all directions. It is covered with the irrigated orchards and labour intensive truck (market) gardens that give it the name 'America's Salad Bowl'. Water is brought from the snow-covered mountains of northern California by a system of massive concrete aqueducts and canals.

The ride across the valley also enabled me to see at first-hand the deterioration of the State's highway system under the regime of fiscal stringency that followed the passage of a Proposition (a form citizens-initiated referendum) designed to limit government debt, despite the clear need for expenditure to maintain, let alone improve, public infrastructure.

Indeed, the ride on the four-lane divided highway was so rough as to make taking photographs from the tourist bus all but impossible.

Once the Central Valley has been crossed, a two-lane two-way road commences its long winding climb into the Sierra Nevada Range. The road is notable not only for the general absence of guardrails but also, and more notably, for the presence of regular, closely spaced *turnouts*.

On the way along the Coast Road to Monterey I had noted numerous turnouts but I needed to confirm my understanding that they were *not* simply convenient places to pull off the roads to admire the view. Rather, and in line with the national model Uniform Vehicle Code, traffic law in California requires a driver who has accumulated a queue of more than five vehicles behind them to pull into the next available turnout and allow them to pass. Where turnouts are less frequent, drivers are reminded of their obligation by signs reading 'Slower traffic use turnouts' and advance signs such as 'Turn out ¼ mile'.

In light of the poor standard of so many rural main roads in Australia I had tried unsuccessfully while I was working in FORS to get the idea of a turnout law adopted in Australia, but was met with the response that they were only scenic parking spots. I have no doubt that a similar law in Australia would relieve the frustration that is behind much unsafe overtaking behaviour and complement the provision of the more expensive overtaking lanes that until recently tended only to be found in hilly areas. I was interested to see recently the provision of turnouts, but without the legal requirements to use them, on the curving Upper Sturt Road in the Adelaide Hills where there is a 60 km/h speed limit and continuous double lines.

The urgent passage of a turnout law has become even more desirable in the light of the advent of cruise control. This innovation, when combined with the desire on the part of the authorities in Australia to drive speeds down by every means possible, has had the unintended consequence of drivers setting their cruise controls at a speed *below* the legal speed limit. This is hardly a desirable outcome, leading as it does to unnecessary overtaking by drivers who simply wish to travel at the legal limit. In one notable case a Canberra driver wrote to the local paper lamenting that on his trip back from the coast he had been overtaken by more than 150 vehicles when travelling at the speed limit. One must ask whether he had a cruise control operating and simply thought that he was travelling as fast as was legal. It should be borne in mind that speedometers are only permitted to under-estimate the actual speed and the cruise control will therefore do likewise.

On the descent from Yosemite I counted no fewer than 22 turnouts and noted that the speed limit was 25 mph (40 km/h) at the top increasing to 40 mph (64 km/h) further down. Once again, guardrails were only in place where there was a significant risk of mishap. This may in fact represent an example of the importance of providing a consistent driving environment rather than seeking to simply make the task easier.

Once on the flat, the journey was soon along four-lane divided roads and then on the highway that runs almost the entire length of the State, north from the San Joaquin Valley in the south and through the Sacramento Valley to the north. Between them are the wetland deltas of the two rivers. The highway, which in places widens to ten lanes, bypasses the major population centres so that to reach San Francisco one turns off near Stockton.

The run into San Francisco crosses the Diablo Range at Altomont Pass, which is the site of hundreds of wind turbines erected on grazing land. The site is a propitious one because the afternoon sea breeze reaches the turbines at the very time when demand for power is peaking.

I found the entry into the suburbs on the flat areas to the east of San Francisco suburbs of interest for a number of reasons: the regional shopping centres again in park-like settings with cars parked in the shade of trees; a car yard exclusively devoted to hundreds of large and small motor homes; and the first encounter with the Bay Area Rapid Transit electrified railway network, in this case running at high speed in the freeway median.

The first sight of the CBD and the iconic Golden Gate Bridge came as we approached the Oakland Bay Bridge, the two halves of which are separated by a man-made island. Then, it was on to the surface street system replete with trolleybuses that I understand have remarkable hill-climbing ability. Of particular interest to me was the Embarcadero complex of high-rise office towers and open spaces that occupy land formerly the site of the Embarcadero Freeway on the edge of the CBD that was not rebuilt after it was devastated by earthquake in 1989.

The Mid-West by night

The final stop in my journey to the United States was Washington DC. Getting there on a flight that left San Francisco in the late afternoon and arrived at close to 1.30am provided me with one of the highlights of my trip. This was to look out the window of the plane and see, for an hour and a half, spread out below me, a carpet of lights extending to the horizon. At last I could understand how the population of the nation could be 300 million people. So closely spaced were the towns and cities below me that there were lighted highways between many of them.

How my flight across America by night contrasts with a trip from Brisbane to Canberra at night over the vast emptiness even of the Central West of NSW where it was uncommon to actually see three settlements, let alone towns in view at the same time. Perhaps the very density of settlement might explain why the United States could have mandated a 55 mph (88 km/h) speed limit during the oil shock of the 1970s. It was, however, the sparsely settled arid west states that were first to break with the lower limit, entertaining open road speed limits of 80 mph (126 mph). In an arid desert environment anything much lower would seem glacial, quite apart from the reduced traffic and thus the reduced accident risk. No doubt similar considerations influenced the Northern Territory to trial a road limit at 130 km/h that, incidentally, is the limit on grade-separated freeways in most of Western Europe that I would later see at first hand.

Megalopolis

The view from the air changes abruptly as one approaches the Appalachian Mountains, rather in the way that the view from the air changes as one leaves the Hunter Valley to fly over Barrington Tops. Before long, however, one becomes aware of a glow of lights to the north that soon becomes a carpet of lights even denser than the mid-west and marks the east coast of the United States and extends as far north as one can see. This is 'Megalopolis'.

Once the plane landed after a flight that seemed like being in the living room the whole time I spoke to the cabin crew and told them of my wonder at what I had just seen. The conversation took long enough for the flight attendants to suggest that the captain and co-pilot might be interested. I thus had the privilege of suggesting to them that they might draw the attention of passengers to the wonders below particularly for the benefit of people from sparsely settled populated places such as Australia. After crossing the Rocky Mountains I had thought that I might as well look out the window! What I might have missed?

Washington via the Beltway

On arrival at Dulles International Airport, situated at quite some distance from the CBD, I found that all the shuttle buses and taxis had already left. Another passenger told me that even his scheduled taxi had gone, but he was happy to share a ride with me into Washington. The only problem was that he lived in the outer suburb of Bethesda, in Maryland. Most of the seemingly endless journey took us along the famous Beltway that encircles around the western and northern edges of the metropolitan area. Many years before I had been told that on a car trip across America from west coast to the east coast a friend had "gone over, under or around every city they came to" except for Las Vegas where to drive The Strip is a highlight of any visit. The widened Tullamarine Freeway and the Eastern Freeway are the only things in Australia that rival the Beltway.

Getting to Downtown via the Beltway, however, had its other pluses. It gave me the opportunity to see what a typical American suburban home looked like. Lot sizes were larger, but what surprised me was the total absence of 'McMansions'. I had noted a similar situation in the tract (estate) housing coming into San Francisco. The houses were largish but not ostentatious.

The trip back from the suburbs to the hotel followed a railway that overpassed every crossroad. All had traffic signals, but some were, unbelievably, in flashing mode. By now a light fog had descended and I experienced again the terror of the driver racing through intersections where at any moment a similarly reckless driver might hurtle into view. This phenomenon had been a constant threat at any intersection in Australia with traffic lights until the flashing mode was done away with. This had followed the tragic death of the world famous orchestral conductor, Willem van Oterloo, in a collision at the intersection of Dandenong and Orrong Roads in suburban Melbourne where the signals were operating in flashing mode in the early hours of the morning. (That intersection was also noteworthy for the fact that every corner was in a different municipality.)

This may be an opportune moment to diverge from the narrative and reflect on the way in which the infrastructure deficiencies of Australian roads were swept under the carpet during the time when government inaction was cloaked in the propaganda rhetoric that it was all the drivers' fault and all would be well if everyone was just more careful.

The case of flashing yellow traffic signals represents simply the most tragic case of such obfuscation. As part of its continuing functions the Commonwealth Bureau of Roads (CBR), established in 1965, put in train a project to determine what measures could be put in place immediately that would make the road and traffic system safer. Top of the list had been to leave traffic signals operating 24 hours a day in red-yellow-green mode. The powers-that-be determined that the findings were much too volatile and not to be made public!

Europe

My trip around Western Europe began and ended in London. The trip from London to Dover for the cross-channel ferry ride takes one through the depressed area of South London on surface streets. Once in the open country, the divided highway begins and I was surprised to see that the highway was punctuated at fairly regular intervals by very large roundabouts. Towns were bypassed.

In the next seven days I would see parts of France, Belgium, the Netherlands, Germany, tiny Liechtenstein, Austria and Italy as far south as Sorrento. In all the tour covered 5,500 km almost all on grade-separated freeways known variously as autoroutes, autobahns and autostrada, all with a speed limit of 130 km/h, exceptions being the Netherlands (120), Italy (140) and some in Germany with no limit. Divided highways with only a median strip had a 110 km/h speed limit and a 90 km/h speed limit applied on undivided rural roads. This classification of roads and their speed limits was often drawn to the attention of drivers by signs at border crossings. All the freeways were notable for having not only median barriers but also side barriers as well. There was also a mandatory speed limit of 90 km/h on freeway off-ramps. In France the freeway limit also came down by 20 km/h in wet or misty conditions.

In the course of the trip I saw less than a handful of police patrols, only one reference to radar enforcement and that on an exit ramp, no other sign of speed cameras and a total absence of generalised sloganeering about safety. There was exemplary observance of lane discipline by all drivers, strict observance of speed limits by heavy vehicles on account of mandatory fitting and regular inspection of tachographs, and evidence of only two accidents, one a single vehicle accident on an exit ramp and the other involving a collision with a motorcyclist.

In most places the median barriers were double-sided with the space between the two halves planted with clipped hedges, shrubs or flowers. The French have taken this one step further by the alternating planting of small trees of various heights in the median barrier to reduce the monotony of the long journey across the plains between Paris and the Riviera which, incidentally, the government has regarded as worthwhile to facilitate not only by road, but also by high speed train, rather than to discourage.

The distinction between ordinary divided highways with at-grade intersections and grade-separated freeways is blindingly obvious but remains one that the authorities in Australia steadfastly refuse to acknowledge despite the clear difference in the potential for accidents. I have commented extensively on the mismatch between Australian enforcement practice and design speed on the grade-separated rural freeways that is limiting their potential to overcome the problems posed by the vast distances between our capital cities. Indeed I often wonder whether the authorities responsible for speed control policy even care that design speed equals *no surprises* for unimpaired drivers who travel at no more than the design speed.

It was also notable that as the traffic increased as one approached a city the speed limit came down first to 110 km/h and then to 90. The freeways frequently morphed into a ring road, again with a speed limit of 90. This is in marked contrast to the situation in the home of the speed camera – Melbourne – where one leaves the Hume Freeway via the Craigieburn

Bypass and then has to enter the Western/Northern Ring Road where a high-volume mix of heavy vehicles and cars is hurtling along at 100 km/h!

In the European cities, all of which have ring roads or are bypassed, I saw a similar regard for the tailoring of speed limits to match the conditions: a default limit of 50 km/h with speed zoning to 70 km/h on appropriately engineered surface arterials and 30 km/h on narrow streets in and close to the city centres. The most notable of the 30 km/h zones I saw was in Innsbruck immediately over the river from the CBD on which buses operated on a steep narrow curving street.

Riding a bicycle is common in European cities, most notably of course in the flatness of Amsterdam where the railing of every bridge over a canal is lined with parked bikes. (As it happened, the day I was in Amsterdam there was a tram strike and traffic in the vast space in front of the main railway station was barely moving.)

What is striking, apart from the absence of helmet-wearing, was the fact that pedal cyclists, at least in the cities, ride sitting upright – none of the 'head-down/bum up' characteristic of pedal cyclists in Australian cities. Cycling in Europe is a much more spontaneous activity with a more relaxed attitude to pedestrian/cyclist interaction partly as a result of the absence of the (uniquely Australian) requirement for riders to wear helmets. The provision of bicycle lanes is taken as a given. The absence of a requirement to wear a helmet also facilitates the operation of free bike-sharing systems. In cities, people can pick up a bike at one point, ride it to where they are going and drop it off at a point close to their destination. Pedal cyclists thus seem to be regarded more like high-speed pedestrians than members of a self-conscious, defensive, minority.

One notable feature of the freeways I travelled on was that a lot of money seemed to have been spent in order to eliminate anything that looked like a hill. Short tunnels are commonplace and the long hills and deep cuttings that remain even on Australia's best rural roads have been all but eliminated. This enables heavy vehicles to maintain their steady 100 km/h in the inside lane, leaving the other lane or lanes free for other vehicles to overtake before moving back to the inside lane. On very few occasions on the whole tour was the coach overtaken by a truck.

Major routes also appear to have been regularly rebuilt in order to flatten out the journey. Looking down from the long viaduct as the coach left Nice was like looking down from an airplane on approach to an airport such was its height. Along the French Riviera the freeway following the coast passes through more than 100 tunnels and a high bridge immediately follows many of these. The longer tunnels characteristic of the cross-country and cross-border routes are also notable for the safety exits between the twin tunnels that become more and more closely spaced towards the end of the tunnel. Presumably this reflects the greater risk of accident where traffic on the freeway slows down to enter the tunnel or begins to interact with traffic entering the freeway after leaving the tunnel.

Also in the mountainous area in the south of France I saw for the first time something that I had heard of for many years – an *arrester bed*. In some places the freeway would make a long steep descent into a populated area closer to sea level. To guard against the tragic consequences that an out-of-control truck or other heavy vehicle could cause there are arrester beds of very coarse aggregate designed to bring a vehicle to a stop off the travelled way. I was interested to see that this technology is being used in South Australia on the long steep descent of the South Eastern Freeway through the Mt Lofty Ranges into suburban Adelaide. Visually, one of those two arrester beds is particularly striking in that its end is in view as the road goes into one of the two tunnels on the freeway named for the famed Australian landscape painter Hans Heysen.

Of particular interest to an Australian was the way in which observance of speed limits on the freeways was encouraged by non-punitive means. Foremost of these was the French practice of reminding drivers of the reduced speed limit as the freeways leave the rural areas and morph into bypasses or ring roads by the addition of a supplementary plate reading 'Rappel' – remember. This stands in sharp contrast to the continual Australian reminders of the omnipresent speed cameras.

Words are inadequate to convey the ambience of Paris. From a traffic management viewpoint I noted some things that never appear to be commented upon.

One was that while we hear a lot about the wonders of the Paris Metro no one ever mentions the fact that in the very heart of Paris the River Seine is flanked on both sides by sub-surface arterial roads that pass under every bridge. It was in one of these long underpasses (*not a tunnel*) that Diana, Princess of Wales, was killed when the car in which she was travelling slammed into a pillar. Passing through that underpass it was astonishing to see that there was no guardrailing to separate the opposing traffic streams.

It was, however, an object lesson to observe how traffic negotiates the Arch of Triumph roundabout where twelve major roads intersect with a total absence of line markings. Drivers and riders simply make way for each other and without tooting. I recall hearing an ABC reporter who used the roundabout every day for five years recounting that in all that time he had never seen a crash there. Also of interest was that vehicles larger than a delivery van were banned from the inner parts of the city during most of the day with bulk deliveries made overnight.

My trip to Europe showed me above all that there are other ways of achieving the 'safe speeds' (that the National Road Safety Strategy makes so much of) other than the use of 'enforcement crunch'. These measures include a hierarchy of speed limits clearly matching the form and function of streets and roads, the use of side and median barriers on rural and semi-urban freeways and the use of visual cues to encourage safe speed choice.

Chapter 33

The Australasian College of Road Safety

Not long before I retired I attended a road safety conference in Armidale, New South Wales, under the aegis of the then newly established University of New England (UNE). In the mid-1980s, a general practitioner, Dr Brian Connor, a resident of Armidale, had become concerned at the large number of young people who were dying in road accidents in the New England region. He set about gaining support within the local community for the establishment of a driver-training centre at a site on the edge of the urban area. His able assistant throughout the process was another local resident, Colin Grigg.

This was a time when driving ranges were still regarded a useful way of improving the performance of young drivers. Their efficacy, however, had come under question in the United Sates where they had first been established. The most significant driving range in Australia was that in the northern Victorian city of Shepparton. The director of the range was a former police superintendent, Eric Montgomery, who delivered a paper about it at the conference. He sincerely believed that teaching novice drivers how to cope with skids and to retain control while manoeuvring under heavy braking helped young drivers deal with emergency situations.

There are two flaws in this line of argument; first, it is more important not to get into the situation to begin with and the second is that no amount of range training can provide drivers with the skills involved in *interacting* with other traffic. Most teenagers desperately want to get behind the wheel of a car and a driving range does enable this to happen in a controlled environment. The trouble is that it emphasises what is only a minor part of the art of driving safely – the manipulation of the controls - gears, brakes and steering – whereas it is interacting safely with other vehicles and other road users that is the crux of safe driving. How to operate the clutch and engage the gears on a manual car receives far too much time and attention. For this reason it is an abiding wish of mine that learner drivers will one day receive their initial instruction on an automatic car where the only control elements are accelerator, brakes and steering. Once interaction has been mastered, then is the time to be concerned with manipulation.

Nevertheless, I was surprised to find myself recommending in my report of proceedings that novice drivers in rural areas should receive training in safely getting off the paved surface and onto the gravel shoulder. Many two-vehicle accidents on rural roads, including some highways, come about when a driver finds the vehicle moving off the sealed part of the road with the nearside wheels in the gravel and the offside wheels continuing on the seal. Braking in this situation simply results in the vehicle spinning across the road and into the path of any vehicle approaching from the opposite direction. It is not surprising therefore that the provision of sealed shoulders is the most cost-effective countermeasure that can be applied on rural roads.

Personally, I remember as a novice driver being taught by one of my mentors to always be on the lookout for a place along a broken road edge that would be the safe to leave the sealed surface. At this time it was not at all uncommon for main roads in the outer suburbs of Melbourne to be so narrow that two vehicles could not pass in opposite directions without leaving the road. I have referred earlier to the bus crash on Warrigal Road in the 1940s that left seven passengers dead.

Even into the 1950s on what is now designated Warrigal Highway, with three lanes in each direction near Chadstone Shopping Centre, the road was so narrow that cars would have to move off the road in order to safely avoid a bus travelling in the opposite direction. One person even had an arm taken off by a vehicle coming from the other direction, on the Princes Highway East in the vicinity of suburban Clayton, an incident that was the trigger for the law that prohibits people from protruding parts of their body from a moving vehicle. These were of course the days when hand signals were still required even after traffic indicators were introduced (housed in the B pillar) or displayed semaphore-style from the driver's cab in the case of trucks. Indeed, hand signals were still required in New South Wales into the mid-1960s.

Another speaker at the UNE conference was the chief traffic engineer of the New South Wales Traffic Authority, Harry Camkin, still active in road safety, and a former president of the ACRS. He delivered what I still regard as the best exposition of the principles of cost/benefit analysis as applied to road accident countermeasures that it has ever been my privilege to hear.

I do not recall whether it had been Brian Connor's intention that an organisation be set up to promote road safety more generally but I do remember how the proposal for the establishment of the College was put forward at the conclusion of the conference on the Sunday morning. Various names were suggested and 'college' was chosen. Then came the need for an appropriate full title incorporating 'road safety'. Immediately the possible confusion with the Royal Australian College of Surgeons had to be addressed and avoided. A first attempt was the 'Australian Road Safety College' which instantly brought to mind the abbreviation for the singularly ineffectual Australian Road Safety Council. At my suggestion, the meeting changed the words around and the name by which the college was to be known was adopted.

The College has moved with the times and has developed policies across a range of issues, now including the road environment. The Journal of the college, published quarterly, includes both peer-reviewed and other contributions. (From 1988 to 2004 the journal was called *Roadwise*.) There are branches of the College in all states and territories and now also in New Zealand. Its headquarters are in Canberra with a permanent secretariat.

My association with the college has lasted from its inception to the present day. A year or so ago I was made aware that I was one of only three remaining foundation members. In addition to being the college's representative on the ACT Black Spot Consultative Committee I have also used my independence to make challenging contributions to policy development and to responses by the college to government action plans, both federal and territory.

Chapter 34

Together Again

On 18 March 2006, Peter Vulcan and his wife Joan hosted a reunion lunch at their home in Melbourne for the original team that had been brought together in 1971 and 1972 as the Road Safety Research Section to service the Expert Group on Road Safety (EGORS). All of the team were there except for one who had left the public service on medical grounds.

At the outset, back in 1971, Peter had made it clear that the section was to operate as a 'non-ranked team', and this included the two who provided the support services to the section. It is a testament to Peter's success as a leader that both were present at the reunion. What was also remarkable was that over the succeeding 35 years all the other team members had been continuously involved in road safety, some beyond retirement. Two became university professors with the younger succeeding the older as head of the Monash University Accident Research Centre (MUARC).

Nothing could have illustrated the egalitarian ethos better than the incident towards the end of lunch when Peter got up from the table to assist Joan with the tea and coffee. As he did so Laura said, "That's a good boy, Peter", to gales of laughter from around the table – the former typist to the former university professor!

A reunion is an opportunity to find out what people are doing, and to look back on what everyone has done in the interim. This might therefore be an appropriate time to summarise the subsequent careers of the team members.

Peter Vulcan, with a doctorate in biomechanical engineering, left the section after the second report of EGORS had been presented to the Minister, in late 1975, to take over as Chairman of Victoria's Road Safety and Traffic Authority (RoSTA). It was typical of his inclusive approach that his first action as Chairman was to visit every municipality in the state. He remained in the position for a number of years, leaving it to become the founding director of MUARC with the status of professor. In retirement he contributed his considerable technical and other skills to assist the work of the Kidsafe organisation.

Ian Johnston, who had joined the section in 1972 as its psychologist with a PhD in the perception of movement, went to the ARRB when the Office of Road Safety was transferred to Canberra in 1980. From there he went on to head up the non-engineering arm of RoSTA before returning to ARRB as Executive Director, overseeing its transition to the commercially based ARRB Research Ltd. His last career move was the one to MUARC.

Bob Ungers, the original 2IC, with a liberal arts degree, also went to RoSTA and was involved with driver licensing with particular reference to young drivers and speed control policy, retiring only recently.

Peter Milne, there at the beginning with a research background in transport economics, went to ARRB at the time of the Canberra transfer and became editor of its publications series covering internal research and external contributions, the position he continued in after he had formally retired.

Bob Heacock, who joined the team during 1972, moved to Canberra well in advance of the departmental transfer, but rejoined the ORS in Canberra to work in vehicle safety standards area. He too is now retired, but at the time of the reunion was doing consulting work in that area.

Pam Thomas, our clerical assistant, with a valuable library background, left the section after the second EGORS report and has forged a successful career in events management.

Laura Golino, section typist and Peter Vulcan's secretary, came to the section as a school leaver and soon established a reputation for her cheerfulness and dedication. On marriage, she left the section and was tracked down for the reunion running a cafe with her husband in Gippsland.

Chapter 35

Letting Go

At my time of life, I find myself faced with the sort of decisions about fitness to drive that were discussed in more or less academic terms by ACRUPTC and its Driver Licensing Sub-committee when I chaired it for a number of years. To some extent the issues relating to older drivers are a sub-set of medical fitness to drive which were addressed in the guidelines document produced by FORS.

The matters that cause concern in the case of older drivers at the individual level can come on in a catastrophic manner as with a stroke; come on gradually as with degenerative illnesses; or be so gradual as to be imperceptible, except to the observer who may be a concerned member of one's family or a close friend. Some may simply require medical intervention as in the case of failing eyesight that can be readily restored by small-incision cataract surgery.

I am fortunate to have been forewarned, so to speak. I know at least some of the things that might mark deterioration in my driving ability. Many older people simply do not drive at night, but my ability to do so safely was restored by cataract surgery. The difference that the removal of cataracts made to my night vision was extraordinary. Having brown eyes probably helps, but as I mentioned in the early part of this work I gained lasting benefit from having been taught how to focus on the side of the road so as not to be dazzled by the headlights of an oncoming vehicle.

In my younger days I had always wondered why it was that older drivers were forever going on about how fast younger people were driving. As I have grown older, I have realised that it was their *perception* that was giving them that feeling. I have noticed that driving at 70 km/h feels like what driving at 80 km/h used to feel like. This would appear to be related to the longer time that the ageing brain takes to process the visual stimulus.

Another thing I have noticed is that I no longer listen to the radio or to music routinely when I am driving. This would also appear to be related to maintaining an optimal degree of mental arousal. On one occasion when a tape came to an end, my speed rose from a legal 110 km/h to 120 km/h. One the other hand, I remember in earlier days on my way to tennis instinctively reaching for the volume control to turn the radio down when approaching a busy strip shopping centre; there the presence of trams and the high pedestrian activity demanded my full attention as I entered the street with a left turn and exited with a right turn. The attention currently being focussed on distraction seems to be crowding out consideration of speed adaptation and the maintenance of an optimum level of mental arousal.

In the same way, one seems to feel that curves and intersections come up more quickly especially in situations of low visibility. Using the air-conditioner can help by keeping the windscreen clear when it is raining. Visual changes, however, come on gradually and I would strongly urge older drivers to have their eyes tested not just for acuity but also for the detection of cataracts.

As it happened, I was quite happily mixing it with peak hour traffic on Melbourne's Citylink freeways in my late 70s and also with traffic on Sydney's notoriously narrow King Street Newtown, even at the time of day when people were 'unparking' at the commencement of the clearway restrictions. I continue to enjoy driving on the open road and on the winding alignment of the roads leading to the South Coast. I have, however, shown myself willing to take notice of my son's advice that I should no longer drive in Sydney. This would therefore seem like a good time to mention a few of the things that I have found useful to ensure safe driving as I have grown older.

Perhaps the easiest and least onerous concerns *route-choice*. Many years ago Max Lay, then head of ARRB, suggested that older drivers should plan their journeys in urban areas so as to *maximise left* turns and *minimise right turns*, avoiding if possible right turn entering movements onto main roads. Usually this means using a different route going out and coming back. Maximum use should be made of traffic lights that have right-turn arrows. It is also useful to be on the lookout for places where entering movements can be made when gaps occur as traffic is stopped by traffic lights. It is also useful to know, and pay special attention to, even avoid, the manoeuvres that may have left you feeling that you might have just had a near miss.

The coming of urban freeways that take through-traffic off the surface street system should also enable more right-turn arrows to be used at traffic lights without compromising capacity. Similarly, in view of the reduced light-gathering power of older people's eyes the presence of high-standard street lighting is of particular importance to the safety of older drivers.

Above all, however, it is important to let other drivers know what you are about to do by signalling in good time. Moving into the outside lane well ahead of where you intend to turn helps to avoid the conflict with following vehicles that can occur if you leave it too late. If you intend to turn at traffic lights, being in the outside lane one set of lights ahead is useful, provided of course that there is a right-turn lane where you intend to turn. When there are vehicles behind, tapping the brakes in advance of where you about to turn left gives following drivers the chance to slow down safely, especially if you are going to park or turn into a driveway. This is also a useful thing to do on rural roads when you are about to turn into a side road or pull over onto the shoulder.

One of the most useful contributions to the older driver debate has been a study conducted by the Centre for Research on Ageing, Health and Wellbeing at the Australian National University (ANU). This measured response times to visual stimuli against drivers' self-perception of their ability to drive safely. I was among the subjects and can speak highly of the researchers involved.

Broadly speaking, the ANU study showed that drivers at the lower end of the age spectrum *under-estimated* their ability and those at the upper end *over-estimated* their ability. What this shows to my mind is that the current practice in the ACT of requiring an annual medical check beyond 75 years of age without a practical driving testing steers a good middle course since most drivers in their late 80s voluntarily hand in their licences. It is likely that visual impairment will be picked up by annual medical examinations such as are in force in the ACT. The ANU study also showed that most drivers voluntarily relinquish their licences before they reach the stage of being a danger to themselves or others.

Nevertheless, as I said earlier, taking away anyone's licence to drive should only happen as a last resort, not as a routine procedure. The consequences for a driver's self-esteem and the additional burden placed on family and friends simply cannot be countenanced in a compassionate society. The emphasis so far as older drivers are concerned should be on positive measures that maintain mobility rather restrictive sanctions.

Not all older people, however, accept that they have lost their independence and continue to get about on their own. It's a 'sample of one' I know, but one friend whose licence was taken away on the ground of advancing age, complained to me that going to see her medical specialist involved getting *three trams* each way! Risks need to be carefully evaluated.

Even so, the rise in accident rates for elderly drivers puts them nowhere near the accident rate of the youngest drivers, but increasing frailty makes the injury consequences more severe, especially if they are in older cars.

Yet again I find a resonance with my earliest days with DST. One of the reports that I fell upon was of a study of the accident rates of delivery drivers employed by the Cadbury-Schweppes Company in the UK. This showed the familiar pattern of higher rates for younger drivers, flattening out to a lower rate between ages 35 to 54. Drivers aged 55 and over had an even lower accident rate, but when they had an accident it was more severe. Thus, it seemed that with age came enough experience to keep out of trouble but it also left them vulnerable to the sudden unpredictable event, perhaps because of a slowing of reaction time. In age as well as in youth, however, driving an automatic has the advantage of simplifying the driving task.

Measures to ease the transition for people who are retiring from driving should make the loss of independence as painless as possible. Governments around Australia have for many years given age-pensioners concessional travel on government-operated transport services and more recently extended that to include holders of seniors cards. Most recently the ACT government introduced a seniors *gold card* to give free travel on its buses to people over the age of 75 years with the qualifying age dropped to 70 in 2013. This is something I regularly make use of. Such measures will have an increasingly large role to play in encouraging older people to gracefully give up the driving privilege.

PART TWO

REFLECTING

Reflections

Australia's Golden Hammer –
Automated Enforcement

The Meaning of the Yellow Traffic Light

Pedestrians at Traffic Lights

Utility Poles

Government Disdain for Personal Mobility

The Railways – a Law unto Themselves

Compensation without Litigation

Uniform Accident Information

Exemplary Drivers

Madcap to ANCAP

Chapter 36

Australia's Golden Hammer – Automated Enforcement

With the silver bullets of occupant restraint and random breath testing spent, I fear that the Australian approach to reducing death and injury on the roads is entering what might be characterised as the phase of the Golden Hammer. Let me explain.

The term Golden Hammer has its genesis in the famous quotation from pioneering psychologist Abraham Maslow in his 1966 book *The Psychology of Science*. It has come to be known as *Maslow's Maxim* and has been paraphrased in many ways but the version that "When all you own is a hammer, every problem starts to look like a nail" gets the gist of it.

A flawed approach

The Australian approach to the road accident problem over the past 25 years has been characterised by an almost total emphasis, at least in the public mind, on the automated enforcement of speed limits by means of the speed camera. This has become Australia's golden hammer with speed as the nail. Leaving aside the two sliver bullets, almost all road safety *propaganda* is directed towards feeding the perception that speed, pure and simple (appropriate or otherwise in the circumstances), is the nail to be driven down by the hammer of what a former head of traffic police in

Victoria famously referred to as "enforcement crunch". This is not without its historic antecedent, as I will show later.

In 1999 I presented a paper entitled *Hit by Friendly Fire: Collateral Damage in the War Against Speed.* In it I pointed out three flaws in the Australian approach, especially in comparison to European practice. First, the enforcement net was being cast so wide as to catch too many drivers with good or perfect records of safe driving while doing nothing to deter those who do not, cannot or will not conform to the normal precepts of behaviour on the road; secondly, that such an approach turns its back on the benefits that would flow from the use of appropriate technology to reduce the risk of accident; and thirdly, missing out on the public support that a more understanding approach would bring forth.

It gets worse, however. The Australian approach barely gives lip service to the far greater contribution to the accident reduction made by improvements to roads and by traffic engineering measures as compared with speed limit enforcement. Only when a federal or state minister has 'an announcable', does the contribution to safety made by the duplication of major rural highways, the construction of city freeways or the implementation of local area traffic management schemes, get a mention. Only the Golden Hammer of speed limit enforcement gets credit.

The vast majority of drivers simply want to get from one place to another in a safe and expeditious manner and be protected from those who would do them harm. The authorities responsible for the current approach, however, cannot face the thought that they may be facing a 'rump' of irresponsible drivers whom they cannot identify and are powerless to stop. As a result, they find it far more convenient to make *everyone* feel responsible, especially when they have the technology to automate the campaign in the form of the speed camera.

No one would deny the need to find ways to control speed **that is excessive for the circumstances**. This, however, has ceased to be the focus of speed control in Australia. Rather, speed limit enforcement Australian-style employs strategies designed to put *all* drivers in a position where they are made to feel responsible for the problem, which is manifestly not the case.

When speed limit enforcement is bullying

The current approach in fact employs tactics that amount to nothing less than *bullying*, a phenomenon that is receiving quite a lot of attention in other contexts. The term is used advisedly. *What distinguishes bullying from other forms of intimidation is that the perpetrator is able to manipulate situations in such a way as to make it appear that the victim is only getting what they deserve.*

No matter how far out of touch with reality the speed limit is, in terms of accident risk or injury potential, the system is set up in such a way that drivers will be booked for simply responding to the conditions. This is bullying. Moreover, in line with the bullying approach, drivers will then be told that they should have just 'wiped off 5' like the propaganda campaign says, even if this means travelling *below* the limit, let alone the design speed. *At the other extreme, the blanket speed limit that applies on rural roads can actually lull drivers into going **too fast** for the conditions.*

The process of putting the blame on all drivers, whether responsible or irresponsible, begins with something as simple as the use of the slogan 'speed kills', rather than 'speeding kills', yet they are quite different concepts. When people are seeking to promote a controversial position on an issue the first step is to go through the dictionary, find appropriate words and ascribe to them the meaning that suits their purpose. So it is with the words 'speed' and 'speeding'. 'Speed kills' represents an appropriation of a self-evident truth, but its use denies the purpose of having roads at all, which is the movement of people and goods from where they are now to somewhere else. The corollary of 'speed kills' is not moving at all and that gets us nowhere.

At this point, the red flag brigade within the road traffic establishment ducks for cover protesting that it is a matter of balance. Indeed, it is, but how can we have balance when the basic premise of their campaigns is at variance with the legitimate need for movement. One might expect a legitimate balance to involve a bit more give and take, but in Australia the process is all one way – in the direction of ever more repressive approaches, having increasingly dubious validity. But why bother about ethics when there is a whole apparatus available to bully John and Joan Citizen into feeling that *they* are the problem?

Geoff Quayle

The grade-separated freeway as a case study

As if all this were not enough to call for a rethink of public policy in the field, the full value is not being achieved from the multi-billion dollar expenditure on grade-separated rural freeways. On such roads the risk of crash is close to zero for an unimpaired seatbelted driver and passengers. Not to allow grade-separated rural freeways to deliver their maximum benefit in a country of such vast distances represents a gross waste of financial resources. In view of the concerns being expressed about driver fatigue it makes no sense to unnecessarily prolong journeys. It would have made as much sense for the French government to have arbitrarily limited the speed of the Train Grand Vitisse (TGV) to 200 km/h rather than 300 km/h (at which speed these trains routinely travel without incident) on the grounds that the consequences of any accident would be less severe.

Nevertheless, it is on the grade-separated rural freeway that the bullyboy approach is most in evidence. *Responding quite rationally* to the conditions – as drivers are forever being exhorted to do – they drive a bit faster and they are pounced on, sometimes literally by police hiding on thickets of unmown grass or in the shadow of an overpass that, as we shall see shortly, is especially inappropriate.

The three distinctly different types of divided roads encountered outside the cities that are *perfectly obvious* to the people who build them and the people who use them: sections with at-grade (ordinary) intersections; sections where intersections have been replaced by overpasses and underpasses (proper freeways); and freeways where both side and median barriers leave a *virtually zero degree of risk for a properly restrained and unimpaired driver*. These differences should be recognised in the setting of different speed limits in each case (110 km/h as now, 120 and 130).

It is taken as a given, of course, that heavy vehicles should continue to be limited to 100 km/h on grade-separated rural freeways, effectively leaving the other lane or lanes available for general traffic.

Sadly, the authorities responsible for the classification of road-types, and hence of speed limits that are put in place, take *no account* of such differences. They apply to each the 110 km/h limit that was put in place back in 1974 for rural divided roads at the time of metrication, despite all the advances that have been made in road and vehicle engineering in the intervening years.

A similar view was expressed in 1987 by the then head of the New South Wales Traffic Police, K J Chapman, at a seminar on the Safety of 2-Lane Country Roads, only to be comprehensively ignored. He said,

> Freeways have a speed limit of 110 kilometres per hour. These roads are built to very high standards, are divided roads, have no intersecting streets, no roadside development or pedestrian activity. It seems ludicrous that there should only be a difference of 10 kilometres per hour in the speed limits between these roads and many of the roads they join.

It is surprising, too, given the contribution made by psychology to the revolution that occurred from 1960 onwards, that there seems to be little evidence of any understanding of speed choice. Ron Cumming pointed out long ago that driving is a self-paced task and presumably drivers will choose to drive at a speed at which they feel comfortable. Studies have shown that, all other things being equal, speed choice is influenced by whether the road environment is 'walled' or open and by the distance that can be seen ahead. It has been known for decades that speed choice is influenced by the rate of the flow of information across the retina of the eye – the further away the stimulus the higher the speed choice. This is a particularly important in Australia since much of our country driving is done on the 'wide open road' with unlimited visibility to the side and often ahead. Indeed, much of the driving on roads such as the Hume Highway, all now divided, takes place in such a setting.

Where all hazards such as trees in the immediate vicinity of the carriageway have been removed or where there is *nothing at all* off the road, raising the speed limit for general traffic on grade-separated rural freeways would be welcomed as a sign of good faith on the part of governments and would lend *credibility to the idea of driving according to the conditions.*

A few years back I wrote to the Minister for Infrastructure in the previous federal government saying that the current speed control policies were denying the community the full benefits from the multi-billion dollar expenditure made by the Commonwealth on National Highways. I suggested that the Commonwealth should require speed limits to be set in a manner that recognised the three classes of rural divided highway. The idea was politely rejected, but I was astonished by one piece of data that was given in justification of maintaining the status quo. It appears that, in response to calls for an increase in the speed limit on Melbourne's Western Ring Road, the limit was raised from 100 km/h to 110 km/h. The subsequent study showed that accidents had increased – surprise, surprise! Here was evidence from a *metropolitan* freeway carrying *70,000* vehicles per day where the speed limit of 100 km/h that *was already too high* being used to justify not raising the speed limit on a *rural* freeway carrying 10,000 vehicles per day!

Not long after, the Bureau of Transport and Communication Economics (BTCE) was given the task of coming up with an optimum speed limit for grade-separated rural freeways in Australia taking all factors into account, including the risk and severity of accidents, the value of time savings to individuals and businesses and fuel costs. The optimum speed for light vehicles, as opposed to heavy vehicles for which no change was recommended, was 120 km/h (a figure still below the European standard). Not surprisingly, that recommendation did not find favour with the road safety establishment. Monash University's Accident Research Centre (MUARC) was then commissioned to review the findings and this review recommended no change to the existing situation, so the status quo prevailed.

A disturbing aspect of the MUARC review was that it took no account of the psychological factors involved in speed choice in different driving environments. I was also surprised that the MUARC study should have taken issue with the concept of design speed when all that it means is that a driver who travels below that speed will not encounter any nasty surprises.

Worse still, it cast doubt on the wisdom of taking the 85th percentile speed as a guide to the speed below which a reasonable person might choose to drive - the speed below which 85% of drivers choose to drive The 85th percentile is of course no more than a statistically convenient way of recognising that 9 out of 10 people do the right thing. Nevertheless I have heard it said that relying on it is like "turning the asylum over to the inmates". Nothing could be further from the truth - the inmates are in the asylum precisely because they unable to behave in accordance with the normal expectations of the community.

On facilities built to the highest standards, collisions with roadside objects will be survivable for an appropriately restrained driver and passengers. Cross-median collisions are impossible when concrete or wire-rope barriers are in place, whilst bridge structures are protected by guardrail and light poles are frangible. In the absence of a barrier, the cross-median accident is generally non-survivable even at current speed, as is the wrong-way head-on. Similarly, collisions with a broken-down semi-trailer (that the MUARC report refers to) are recognised as being non-survivable at *any* speed and, although still possible, can effectively be dismissed in the rural freeway context given the provision of breakdown lanes.

It is not for nothing that the semi-arid and desert states in the USA were first to do away with the federally-mandated 55 mph speed limit imposed during the oil shock of the mid-1970s. These states permit higher open road speeds than the more populous east not just because traffic is sparse there even on the Interstate and other highways. It is important to remember that there has to be something to hit for an accident to occur, so the likelihood of an accident has to be considered as well as the likely injury level.

The US legislators who made the decisions to increase speed limits are not some bunch of rednecks but people who drive on the roads concerned and who have *carefully weighed the risks and the benefits and set speed limits accordingly.* Such considerations no doubt influenced the Northern Territory government to set the open road speed limit at 130 km/h, much to the chagrin of the road safety establishment, and most recently to conduct a trial, along a 200 km stretch of high standard road of abolishing it altogether. A similar approach should be considered in the case of high-standard outback roads that cover vast distances and present the twin challenges of enormous distance and monotonous driving environments.

A 'red herring' that is frequently lobbed into the debate about speed limits is to make much of the relatively small savings in time that would come from speed limits being raised. Leaving aside commercial vehicles (that are really outside the ambit of this debate), for a great many drivers, especially tourists, *the **actual** time of arrival is immaterial. The main object is to get the **tedium** over as soon as possible.*

The problem in urban areas

The situation in built-up areas is no better. The strict approach to speed control in built-up areas rests on data that is valid ***only*** in the context where it was collected and is of ***very dubious transferability*** outside of the city where it was collected – Adelaide. The ability for results to be replicated is one of the tenets of scientific inquiry.

Adelaide is unique not just in Australia, but quite likely the world, for a city of its size, for having, at the time the data was collected, no freeways within its urban fabric. The South-Eastern Freeway through the Adelaide Hills ends at the suburban edge, whilst the Southern Expressway begins some 12 km from the city centre. Only recently has another expressway been built across the outer northern suburbs to link the highways with the industrial areas and port facilities. The traffic mix on Adelaide's arterial roads must therefore be *unrepresentative* of that in any other capital city and of the provincial cities that have freeway-standard bypasses.

Two recent visits to Adelaide have shown me the adverse effect that such a situation has on driver behaviour. Especially noticeable is 'barging in' from side streets and exploiting minimal gaps in incoming traffic when turning right off main roads, whilst 'rat- running' - the use of local streets to avoid traffic lights and queues on the arterial roads - is endemic. Also noticeable is that there are fewer sets of traffic lights specifically installed to allow traffic to enter or cross main roads from 'distributor' streets or to interrupt continuous flow. As an example, on Portrush Road, the *only* arterial road running north from the end of the Southeastern Freeway, there are no traffic lights at any of the closely spaced intersections in the first 2.4 km. This is in marked contrast to Melbourne, Sydney and, even more so, to Canberra.

*The **accident risk** data from Adelaide, as opposed to the injury risk data, therefore, cannot be taken as representative of the speed/accident risk in any other city,* yet they have been used for many years to justify a policy of virtually zero tolerance and are repeated again in the Victorian review I referred to earlier.

This work has only one appendix. This is a detailed rebuttal of the conclusions from the report that, for 15 years, has been used to justify a zero-tolerance approach to what is disingenuously referred to as 'low level speeding'. Including that appendix gives me no pleasure, especially given the favourable recollections of Adelaide in the early years of my driving career.

It is somewhat surprising that data from *rural* South Australia by the same group of researchers responsible for the urban study of which I am critical pointing to the desirability of setting *a general* **90 km/h** *limit on rural side roads – which* **I would endorse** - have been ignored, except in Tasmania.

The claim that it was the introduction of speed cameras and attendant publicity that was responsible for the fall in number of road deaths in Victoria in the 1990s is also deeply flawed. Independent analysis of the situation by the Bureau of Transport and Communication Economics (BTCE) showed that one-third of the reduction could be attributed to the economic downturn during the recession of the early 1990s and a further one-third could be ascribed to road improvements. Most notable among the road improvements was the completion of the duplication of the Hume Highway between Wodonga and Melbourne, in addition to similar projects elsewhere in the State, as well as freeway construction in Melbourne including the Western Ring Road, the Northern Ring Road and the Citylink bypass.

A convenient myth

The most pernicious myth peddled in the current debate (if one can call it a debate) is that drivers will exceed any speed limit by some appreciable margin. Research from places with driving environments as diverse as Western Australia, New Zealand, California and The Netherlands, covering urban as well as rural settings, shows that *where a speed limit that is manifestly too low is raised speeds either remain the same or* ***fall.*** The difference is that the majority of drivers no longer found themselves on the wrong side of the law. Significantly, apart from the cases I have just mentioned, almost no research has been conducted into the effect of *raising* speed limits.

Monotony, boredom and fatigue

The sheer boredom involved in driving a car or similar vehicle on a grade-separated rural freeway at a speed manifestly below the design speed, with the attendant reduction in concentration and reduced alertness can also lead to the occurrence of the *very* sort of accidents that setting the current speed limit seeks to ameliorate. Similar considerations apply in any monotonous environment.

Whether the relevant authorities like it or not, research conducted earlier for the ORS by Monash University's psychology department into drivers' *unalerted* response times showed that drivers who were travelling faster had shorter response times than other drivers. This is consistent with Swedish research that showed that drivers felt fresher after driving quite a distance at a higher speed than they did after driving the same road at a lower speed. Fatigue is a problem not only for truckies but can affect anyone driving for a long time without taking a break.

Fatigue resulting from being on the road for too long at a stretch is, in characteristic Australian fashion, only being treated with sloganeering – 'Drive, Revive, Survive' with no regard for the underlying psychology. Added to this is the misallocation of police resources that could better deployed, for example, towards enforcement of safety requirements in the trucking industry.

The distinction between the three types of rural divided highways was, most recently, totally ignored in the *Vic Roads 2011-2012 Victorian Speed Limit Review*. The report also spoke disparagingly of the relatively small time savings that would flow from an increase in the limit that I have only been advocating for grade-separated freeways on the basis of an understanding of the 'perceptual' factors involved in speed choice in monotonous environments. To unnecessarily increase the length of journeys, where there is near-zero risk of accident, may bring on the very fatigue-related crashes we all wish to avoid, as well as reducing the incentive to take a break.

The dangers of automation

Cruise control is not without its problems either, since it depends on setting the speed in accordance with the speedometer reading (which by law cannot under-estimate the speed of travel). Moreover, concerns have been expressed in the commercial aviation sector about the dangers inherent in taking control of aircraft out of the hands of pilots.

Long queues of drivers who simply want to travel *at* the legal limit can build up behind a driver on cruise control. Even this could be tolerated if Australia adopted a turnout rule requiring drivers to pull into the regularly provided turnouts when a significant queue of vehicles, say five, builds up behind them, as is the case in the USA. On one of my recent visits to Adelaide I was interested to see that, despite the absence of an obligation to use them, turnouts are provided on the long curving grade on Upper Sturt Road on the southern edge of the Mt Lofty Ranges where the speed limit is quite sensibly set at 60 km/h and double lines are in place all the way.

General deterrence raised to an art form

With the development of automated speed detection devices, governments in Australia have raised 'general deterrence' (i.e. directed at all drivers) to an art form, whilst difficulties relating to privacy legislation have allowed governments to avoid the awkward question of determining whether the hundreds of thousands of motorists issued with traffic infringement notices each year throughout Australia are in fact the people having accidents.

Defenders of the present way of doing things describe breaches of the speed limit by less than 15 km/h as *"low-level speeding"* and even go so far as to say that this behaviour is mostly *"the preserve of normally law-abiding drivers"*. Then they conveniently mangle the language by equating this with "speeding", a term that should clearly be reserved for driving at a speed that is inappropriate to conditions. Then we have the recent newspaper statement by one former head of MUARC that "punishment is an important method of altering behaviour", adding that "it is very important that people are punished for their traffic offences, no matter how minor they are". Rather, I would say that *if the majority of the offenders are "normally law-abiding citizens", it is the limit that needs to be questioned, not the 'attitude' of drivers.*

There is a strong lesson in the decision of the then newly elected New South Wales government to turn off 38 speed cameras in Sydney on the basis that they are not doing anything for road safety. Moreover, no one seems to ask whether the speed camera sites that top the list for their contribution to revenue have characteristics that might cause drivers to exceed the speed limit. The drive to reduce the toll of death and injury on the roads is certainly not helped when normally law-abiding citizens feel, for whatever reason, that governments are only into the automated enforcement of inappropriate speed limits for the revenue it raises.

An alternative approach

Taking all the factors I have mentioned into account, it seems to me that the whole issue of how to set speed limits needs to be *turned on its head*. The prevailing attitude is that speed limits should be set based on "what is the lowest speed we can get away with", to use the words of an engineer from VicRoads at an ACRS seminar I attended in Melbourne in 2011.

I would suggest that a better question would be *"what is the fastest speed we can let people travel at, given the likelihood of a crash and the severity"?* Injury levels do rise with speed, but as I have said, there must be something unyielding to hit or something fragile to hit, as in the case with pedestrians who can, however, be better protected by other means.

A positive role could also be found for point-to-point speed cameras that would represent a compromise between the current approach and the expectations of drivers. On rural roads built to true freeway standards, or in isolated areas with no crossroads, a tolerance of 15 km/h (a breakpoint used in penalty scales) in excess of the current 110 km/h limit could be allowed provided that over a distance, of say 150 km, the average speed was below 110 km/h. As it happens, a tolerance set at that level would make legal the speed that was cited by K J Chapman as the 85th percentile speed for the Hume Freeway south of Sydney. Such a move would provide a real incentive to break the journey rather than boringly pushing ahead with a lower level of arousal and attendant loss of concentration. It would also give credence to the admonition to 'Stop, revive, survive'.

Summing up

The official attitude seems to be that everyone just has to slow down, irrespective of whether the speed they are doing is likely to cause an accident. This approach also relies heavily on the relationship between speed and accident severity. Action based on these premises fails to address whether there are other, more effective, ways of ameliorating the situation, e.g. median refuges for pedestrians in urban areas and barrier-protected safe overtaking opportunities on rural highways. Demonstration projects of the latter measure suggest themselves, for example, on the Kings Highway, Canberra's link to the coast, and on the Barton Highway link to Yass.

Let me say this just once and let me say it firmly - *I DO NOT AND NEVER HAVE ADVOCATED A WHOLESALE INCREASE IN SPEED LIMITS, ONLY THAT THEY SHOULD BE APPROPRIATE TO THE CONDITIONS.*

My almost *invariably misquoted* paper from 1999, *Hit by Friendly Fire – Collateral Damage in the War on Speed,* made specific reference to the fact that the blanket 100 km/h speed limit was manifestly **too fast** for the conditions on many rural side roads. The paper therefore recommended the **lowering** *of the speed limit on rural side roads to 90 km/h* with speed zoning above and below a new lower limit depending upon factors such as route (winding or straight), shoulder condition, roadside objects, road width and traffic volume. *Despite all this, I have even been accused of suggesting that some speeding is safe! That is not true.*

A 90 km/h limit on rural side roads is the norm in Western European countries under their strongly hierarchical approach to the setting of speed limits in accordance with the nature and function of particular roads, with 110 km/h on ordinary divided roads and 130 km/h on freeways. I should add that in the same paper I also supported a default *50 km/h urban* speed limit (since implemented) accompanied by appropriate speed zoning in 10 km/h steps above *and below* 50 km/h. *It is significant that an integral part of the European conception of Vision Zero is the 'self-explaining road',* something I discuss in a later chapter.

Leaving aside the introduction of compulsory seatbelt wearing in the early 1970s and random breath testing in the 1980s, it is modification of the driving environment that has driven the reduction of death and injury from the record levels of the late 1960s to levels that, while still a cause for grave concern, are lower than at any time since the 1940s. The miscreant minority, however, represent an intractable problem since they take no notice of speed limits and because acts of foolishness cannot be legislated against.

The current emphasis on the mass enforcement of speed limits is a blunt weapon that impacts on *all* drivers regardless of their record of safe driving or otherwise, the more so in view of privacy legislation that prevents of cross-matching of accident and infringement records. Moreover, many of the assumptions behind the emphasis given to speed limit enforcement throughout Australia, and the claims made for its success, do not stand up to scrutiny. As used in Australia, speed cameras simply slow down the people who are *not* going to have accidents and **punish them for not being perfect all the time,** whilst not slowing down those who will have accidents.

Automated enforcement and hectoring publicity are the road safety strategies of choice for governments that are not prepared to spend the money that is needed to provide roads of a standard appropriate to one of the most motorised countries on the world. But that is the nature of a golden hammer.

Recommended speed limits

Note: Heavy vehicles would be subject to a maximum speed of 100 km/h in all situations and be subject to any posted lower limit.

Urban areas

10 km/h	Shared Zones
	Passing stationary trams if clear to do so
40 km/h	Strip shopping centres
	School zones for one and a half hours in the mornings and afternoons

50 km/h	Residential streets
60 km/h	Arterial and sub-arterial roads
70 km/h	Divided arterials with frontage development
80 km/h	Divided arterials with service roads or no frontage development
90 km/h	Freeways with high traffic volumes and many entries/exits
100 km/h	Freeways with lower traffic volumes (in outer areas)

Rural areas*

80 km/h	Gravel side roads
90 km/h	Paved side roads
100 km/h	Undivided highways and main roads
110 km/h	Divided highways
	Undivided highways with low traffic volumes
120 km/h	Freeways (divided highways with full grade-separation)
130 km/h	Freeways with full grade-separation and median barriers
	Undivided highways in remote areas

* With speed zoning above *and below* default limit depending on factors such as route – winding or straight, shoulder condition, roadside objects, road width and traffic volume.

Chapter 37

The Meaning of the Yellow Traffic Light

In the course of writing this book one of the most notable things has been the extent to which matters that should have been disposed of long ago continue to plague both the public and the road safety establishment.

The meaning given to the yellow (amber in the old parlance) indication in traffic lights is one such matter. This is a vexed issue, so much so that in the home of the speed camera – Victoria – it is so hotly contested that a special commissioner has been given the job of investigating complaints not only about speed cameras not functioning properly but also the operation of cameras at traffic lights.

In the case of traffic lights, the commissioner's job is to determine whether or not drivers are being given a 'fair go' in respect of the timing of the yellow and red lights. His most recent report dealing with signal timings makes spectacular reading. Despite the responsible authorities being expected to have set the signal timings for the yellow light to take account of factors such as the speed limit on approach and the width of the intersection, the commissioner found that in a number of cases the yellow light was not even on for the old standard interval, of three seconds. Accordingly the authorities were required to return the money collected to those drivers who had been issued with traffic infringement notices because of this (although in a strange twist to his ruling the persons affected were still deemed to have committed an offence).

Given that the need to have a yellow indication *at all* has been reduced by the inclusion in modern traffic lights of an 'all red' period, the assigning of a *punitive* regulatory meaning to the yellow indication at traffic lights is a classic instance of *fanaticism*. One wit has described fanaticism as *"redoubling your efforts when you've lost sight of your objectives"*. None of this should come as a surprise given the Australian penchant for automating enforcement whether it is for speed control or compliance with traffic lights.

After all, the only reason there is yellow indication at all is to reduce the likelihood of conflict between vehicles when the light changes from red to green for traffic on the other road.

What then *should* the yellow light mean? In that most motorised place on earth, the USA, the framers of the Uniform Vehicle Code (UVC) that serves as a model for State traffic law, decided the matter in 1944. The UVC states that, *"the yellow light is a cautionary indication that the red light is about to appear"*. Of the fifty states, only eleven give it the meaning that Australia does and California, the most car-reliant place on earth, is not one of them. Back in 1978, Edward F Kearney produced a report for the National Highway Traffic Safety Administration of the Department of Transportation entitled *Differences among traffic laws in the United States.* (DOT 148-803). (This report continued the *Traffic Laws Commentary* published prior to 1972 by the National Committee on Uniform Traffic Laws and Ordinances.) Kearney states that,

> This obsolete rule [requiring a driver to stop for a steady yellow light unless it is unsafe to do so] was deleted from the Uniform Vehicle Code in 1944,
>
> A yellow light means caution, there is a change coming. It does not mean stop or go. To require a stop.... seems particularly difficult to justify. And with the yellow interval ranging from three to six seconds, it is often safe and customary to cross an intersection on yellow. Imposing a requirement might cause a lot of rear-end collisions.

Another American traffic engineer, Howard S Stein, working for the prestigious Insurance Institute for Highway Safety, had this to say on the matter writing in Transportation Quarterly in 1986,

> Most states have laws that regard the yellow light as a warning that the green light has ended and the red will appear next. Consequently, vehicles may enter the intersection throughout the yellow phase.

Stein then goes on to make a point that should be at the heart of the enforcement of any law relating to the approach of vehicles to an intersection when cross traffic is about to be given the conditional authority to proceed by a green light,

> Some states with this policy [yellow as warning] add the restriction that although vehicles are allowed to enter on yellow, **they are prohibited from being in the intersection when the signal turns red.** (*emphasis added*).

It is hard to believe, in view of the foregoing review of the situation that some jurisdictions in the US are taking advantage of the coming of automated enforcement to shorten yellow times. By doing so they are adding to local revenues because red light cameras are now snapping drivers. The situation is so concerning that it was raised in the US Congress by the House Majority Leader in 2001.

I should also point out that the addition of the all-red period is one of the most important developments in the whole history of traffic control. It makes the authoritarian approach adopted in Australia even more difficult to justify particularly in view of the unwarranted strain it puts on drivers every time they approach traffic lights showing green.

This will not be the first time that I refer to the inadequacy of Australia's urban road systems to cope with the demands placed on it. This inadequacy means that surface streets carry a mismatch of traffic that is conducive to accidents. This should be taken into account when placing obligations on the drivers of small vehicles to stop abruptly when they are sharing suburban roads with heavily laden semi-trailers and other heavy vehicles.

Before Sydney's M5 was built I recall the experience of driving from Strathfield to Liverpool with a semi-trailer either directly behind me, on one side of me, or in front of me. It is something I have told all my children as they started their driving careers: never put your foot on the brake when you see a yellow light come on without making sure you do not have a big truck behind you. This burden should not be added to the already difficult split-second decision-making within the so-called *dilemma zone*.

The word 'dilemma' has a particular resonance in the current context of the yellow light when the automated enforcement mix includes combined speed and red light cameras at traffic lights. The combination of the two adds a further dimension to the split-second decision-making when confronted with a yellow light. Remember, *a dilemma is not just about making a difficult choice: it is about making a choice when **neither** choice is a palatable one.* It is by no means unheard of for drivers, who have been observing the speed limit on their approach, to be slapped with a fine for momentarily exceeding the speed limit while traversing the intersection *with the signal still showing yellow* and no cross traffic able to legally move until the end of the all-red period.

To sum up, Australia should adopt the UVC meaning of the yellow signal as a *warning*, with it being an offence to be within the intersection when the red comes on.

Chapter 38

Pedestrians at Traffic Lights

The research I undertook in the course of writing the report *Safety of Older Pedestrians* included canvassing the views of numerous bodies representing the interests of older members of the community. At the top of their list of concerns was the inadequacy of the time given for them to cross the road at traffic lights.

The standard period for the display of the 'walk' signal is six seconds, followed by a period of the flashing red 'don't walk', during the display of which it is an offence to enter the road, as it is to disobey the steady red 'don't walk' signal that follows.

This practice was adopted at a time when traffic lights had fixed timings, changed in response to the approach of vehicles, or changed in response to the pedestrian push button. Each set of traffic lights operated *independently* which made it important for pedestrians to be given *sufficient* time to clear the intersection before waiting traffic was given the green light to proceed.

Today, traffic signals generally operate as part of a *co-ordinated signal system*, of which Sydney's SCATS (Sydney Co-ordinated Adaptive Traffic System) was the first. As I noted earlier, these systems not only improved traffic flow but also reduced accidents. Nevertheless the benefits in terms of safety and convenience that could accrue to pedestrians from systems such as SCATS have yet to be been fully exploited.

In a co-ordinated system, the length of the green time for traffic on each arm of an intersection is determined *ahead of the start of each phase* by computer programs using information transmitted from each intersection to a control centre about the number of vehicles at or approaching each intersection. In the old situation, where signals operated independently, the length of each phase could vary from as little as 20 seconds up to some set maximum. On main roads, the lights could remain green until the presence of a vehicle or pedestrian was detected on the side street, hence the need for pedestrians to be guaranteed a minimum crossing time by pressing the button.

Continuing to look at the pedestrian's need in the old way short-changes them and still persists even where the signals are operating under centralised control. Apart from the sheer frustration that all too often leads to crossing against the red, pedestrians are exposed to the elements from which vehicle occupants are sheltered.

As a frequent visitor to Sydney I have observed this to be the case in the CBD where a solution, if one can call it that, has been to increase police activity directed at pedestrians who disobey the lights or cross at inappropriate places. The worst thing about the present set-up is that it *undermines compliance*, which can have deadly results. Crossing against the signals – often, it must be said in perfect safety - can be seen all over the Sydney CBD. Such behaviour, however, can be extremely hazardous where pedestrians put themselves in conflict with vehicles that are proceeding in accordance with a green arrow. One newspaper article on pedestrian accidents included a map of the CBD that showed them to be so numerous as to render the marking of the streets superfluous – plotting them outlined the grid of streets.

A number of technical papers have been written in recent years on the pedestrian accident problem in the Sydney CBD. These papers contain all sorts of graphs and algorithms to take account of exclusive turn phases and scramble crossings (or Barnes Dances, named for their New York originator) as well as walk speeds. All this seems to me to be very much like *knocking down an open door*.

The entire situation could have been vastly improved by a simple change to the wording of the relevant Australian Standard that did not take co-ordinated traffic signals into account so far as pedestrians were concerned. The wording in regard to the 'pedestrian clearance interval' stated that the pedestrian must be given **sufficient** *time to complete their crossing* before the light changes; that is quite appropriate if signals operate independently of each other. A more pedestrian-friendly wording would have been "**need only** be given sufficient time to complete the crossing". The *Guide to Traffic Engineering Practice* that replaced the Australian Standard, however, does not lead to such simple amendment *but it should nevertheless incorporate a similar provision* (emphasis added).

A further serious problem has been identified for pedestrians crossing at traffic lights: the potential conflict with vehicles turning left. Irrespective of what the law says about drivers giving way to pedestrians, non-compliance by drivers for whatever reason is likely to have serious, or even fatal, consequences as highlighted by two recent fatalities in Sydney. A simple fix suggests itself - to delay the vehicle green signal for five seconds after pedestrians get their 'walk' signal. This is no different to the early-start priority given to buses and trams.

On main roads with long cycle times the 'walk' signal should come up routinely with the display of the vehicle green circle and, where warranted, on cross-streets if the cycle time is going to be more than the minimum. Indeed, on side streets the pedestrian should be able to call up the 'walk' signal if sufficient time still remains for a safe crossing. (This is no different to extending the time for vehicles.)

Examples of what I am advocating can be seen along Parramatta Road in Sydney's inner west and no doubt elsewhere and appear to be in evidence in at least parts of Melbourne's suburbs.

There is another way in which conflict with turning traffic could be managed, albeit a more radical one. This was put forward while I was still with FORS. Geoff Middleton, then senior traffic engineer with the Queensland Main Roads Department, made a strong case for restricting 'walk/don't walk' lights to intersections where there are exclusive turn arrows for vehicles. His article was published in the ARRB journal *Australian Road Research (vol 11, no.3).*

The other situation where pedestrians can be subjected to frustrating waiting times is in crossing a divided road. Pedestrians should be given the opportunity to cross to the median strip in that part of the signal phase when there is no conflict either with vehicles *turning away from them* to the right on a green arrow or with vehicles moving in that direction on the green circle (who are on the other side of the road). The pedestrian, having crossed to the median, can then complete their crossing while the turn arrow is operating in the other direction. Examples of good practice in this regard can be seen at the intersections on Northbourne Avenue in the Canberra CBD.

Chapter 39

Utility Poles

There has never been any doubt about the extent to which collisions with utility poles, and trees, are implicated in death and injury on the roads. Few aspects of the road accident problem generate such diametrically opposed views. Not unusually, one response is to trivialise the nature of the problem by making a joke out of it or saying "the pole was there in front of me". Crashes involving trees, however, can bring forth an even more emotive response than crashes involving poles, a response that rests on issues of amenity and environmental protection. To be sure, trees cannot be modified whereas poles can and should be.

Already we have seen a general movement among the engineers and others responsible for the design of roads towards the placing of guardrails around bridge abutments and on the entry approach to narrow bridges. Similarly we have seen the design of roadside reflective marker posts changed from wood to plastic. These will simply be pushed over if hit by a car, rather than presenting an unpredictable hazard in terms of where it will end up impacting the vehicle or its occupants. Today, too, traffic signposts and traffic light poles are designed to deform if they are hit.

When it comes to utility poles the situation becomes more complicated as these very frequently serve more than one function. Readers may have noticed that common usage still tends to refer to utility poles as 'telegraph poles' and this provides an insight into popular attitudes about the problem of crashes that involve them. The stringing of telegraph lines along poles beside the road well and truly pre-dates even the development of the horseless carriage (a k a the motorcar) let alone its widespread use. In the days of horse-drawn transport they would even have doubled as hitching posts. The poles would soon carry telephone wires as well and then gaslights and finally electricity wires and street lights, still pre-dating the motor age. Even more substantial poles made of steel would soon replace wooden poles as the means of supporting the overhead wires needed for the operation of electric trams, at least in Melbourne.

In the light of South Australia's general shortage of suitably long, straight termite-resistant timber, an even more solid object would soon line its roads – the 'Stobie' pole named for its designer. In terms of injury potential these things were (and still are) off the scale. Stobie poles consist of two steel H beams tapering upwards and filled with concrete. Placed at right angles to the kerb, they provide ideal and highly visible surfaces on which to place 'hail car [tram] here' or 'bus stop' signs and, more recently, street art. Yet again I had been sensitised to a safety problem early in my driving career through my regular visits to Adelaide.

In the United States, in 1969, the Insurance Institute for Highway Safety headed originally by William Haddon Jr, a medical doctor and engineer turned epidemiologist (and the first director of what became the National Highway Traffic Safety Administration), exposed the hazard presented by routinely lining roads and streets with solid objects capable of inflicting horrendous life-threatening injuries on the occupants of any vehicle that struck one of them.

Another figure, too often forgotten, who featured in the fight to render roadsides less hazardous was the American engineer Kenneth Stonex who pioneered the idea of designing out roadside hazards during his time as assistant director of the General Motors proving ground (1956 to 1971). In 1971, the Insurance Institute produced a film, *In the Crash,* highlighting the problem of what it termed highway booby traps. There can be no doubt that this film and the earlier work by Stonex galvanised the road engineering profession to rid roadsides of hazards that it was in their power to eliminate.

It is not surprising that *Roadside Objects* would be among the 24 reviews conducted for the Expert Group on Road Safety. By the time that review was conducted new designs for utility poles were being developed.

The first of these was the 'breakaway' mounting and this has become common; in this design the bolts are tightened to an extent that will enable a sufficiently forceful impact to snap the bolts off causing the pole to fall. Another development was the 'frangible' pole: in this design the pole is made of metal that will deform 'pocketing' the vehicle and absorbing the energy of the crash.

As part of the research program arising out of the EGORS national review, a study was commissioned by the ORS with the Mechanical Engineering Department of the University of Melbourne into *Collisions with Utility Poles*. The study was conducted by Professor Peter Joubert, Jim Fox and Malcolm Good and reported on in February 1979. The major outcome was the development of an accident-predictor model that identified accident risk on the basis of site measurements which, when used with estimates of the cost of accidents, could show when remedial treatments might be undertaken. Improving skid resistance and maintaining correct tyre pressures and tread depth were considered to be important countermeasures. Concerns about the use of breakaway poles, if there are likely to be pedestrians about, were shown to be unfounded. A presentation of the findings from the study included the comment that the passage of a severe storm across Melbourne could be tracked by team callouts to accident sites.

With some 1 in 10 urban road fatalities at that time resulting from a collision with a pole, a summary of the research report was tabled in federal parliament and distributed to local government authorities and relevant state bodies.

It soon became apparent that, in the light of the state of knowledge on the subject, an authority responsible for either erecting a utility pole, or allowing one to remain in a position, where there was a likelihood that it would be hit by a vehicle, might be liable to a claim for damages

The next step in the research was therefore to commission a study with the Law School of Monash University into *The Legal Implications of Frangible Poles*. The study was conducted by Judd Epstein and Lucy Hunter and the report setting out their findings was published in February of 1984. This looked at the problem from the point of view of the liability of an authority that used frangible poles. It found that they would not normally be held to be liable to compensate persons injured by them, but added more importantly that "Authorities who use rigid poles instead of safer equipment may be held liable in negligence in some circumstances". Such potential defendants were identified.

It is a matter of profound regret that work on the subject of utility poles and their placement that was undertaken by the Federal Office of Road Safety came to nothing. This was another outcome of the change in priorities that occurred under the Hawke-Keating ALP government that even then was looking to cut back on capital spending. I have already referred to the demise of black spot funding. It would be remiss of me not to mention the departure of David Murray, at about the same time. He had made the running in FORS on the modelling of the circumstances under which poles that posed a hazard could be identified for treatment, and went to work in the forward planning area of the South Australian Health Department.

I have spent some time detailing the story of how the subject of utility poles came to prominence and then passed from view. However, one of the researchers whom I mentioned, Malcolm Good, now a professor emeritus with the University of Melbourne, has relaunched the topic into the public arena. His comments formed part of an investigation by the Sydney Morning Herald reported on 13 February 2010 with the headline "Lost chance for non-lethal poles".

The response from the state authorities was as one might have been expected, despite the deaths of 170 people in the six years up to 2010 in car accidents that involved utility poles. Not surprisingly, the responses raised issues of harm to pedestrians and possible exposure to live wires. In reply, Professor Good maintains that the breakaway modification for timber poles that he and his colleagues designed in 1979 kept electricity cables hanging well above the ground. In the time since that investigation, a cone of silence appears to have descended on the issue and it needs to be lifted, urgently.

Astonishingly, the latest National Road Safety Action Plan 2015-2017 released in November 2014 makes reference to the need to *"Mandate pole side occupant protection standards for new vehicles"* whilst making no specific reference to utility poles under the item *"Review infrastructure safety programmes (sic) to establish best practice processes for identifying, prioritising and developing projects based in fatal and serious casualty reduction criteria"*.

Chapter 40

Government Disdain for Private Mobility

A distinguishing feature of transport policy in Australia in the 20th Century is that new provision for non-work-related personal mobility has never been regarded as a public good.

Extensive tram networks were developed in the late 19th Century, mainly to get people to work or to the CBD from what are today's inner suburbs, and reached their maximum extent just after the end of World War II. Travel demands in the new suburbs, however, were accommodated using rail infrastructure that had been provided almost solely for the movement of freight to and from country areas. Rail infrastructure was rarely augmented or extended. The same parsimony extended to road infrastructure as well.

This grudging attitude towards any expenditure that might facilitate personal mobility, let alone encourage it, also found expression in the characteristic way in which governments, federal and state, dealt with the emerging problem of road traffic accidents. These were seen to be purely the result of personal actions and no concern of governments. After all people didn't have to travel, except to get to work, and if they did so at other times and came to grief that was their problem for being on the road in the first place. The contrast with the United States is striking. An early federal government investigation of their road accident problem was entitled *Mobility without Mayhem*.

In more recent times, governments in Australia have been encouraged to continue their niggardly response to the documented inadequacy of road infrastructure by an environmental lobby that has nothing but contempt for motorised personal mobility.

Unfortunately for the safety of road users, the rise of environmentalism coincided with the realisation by the community at large that at least part of the accident problem in the cities could be overcome by taking high-volume traffic off the surface street system and onto freeways. This had been the case in all other comparably motorised countries and explained why at the same levels of motorisation the United States had a significantly lower rate of road traffic fatalities than Australia.

Worse still, governments tended to take the easy way out rather than issuing government bonds to provide the necessary funds. Instead they turned over the provision of such facilities to so-called public-private partnerships in the misplaced hope that such ventures would turn a profit for investors. The charging of tolls, however, meant that significant numbers of motorists who might otherwise have used the new freeways continued to use the surface streets, so denying the community the benefits in accident reduction and residential amenity they could have brought.

A prime example of this is Sydney's Cross City Tunnel. Linked as it is to the Eastern Distributor, it should have removed the majority of through traffic from the residential areas of South Sydney and most of the cross traffic from the CBD. Instead it has resulted in drivers finding new rat-runs solely to avoid the toll, with the result that further works were then needed to maintain traffic flow along William Street to which the Cross City Tunnel runs parallel. There, a reduction in traffic volume would have been a boon for public transport, quite apart from the effect on local streets in the area.

The contrast with the situation in Bondi Junction, not that far away, could not be more dramatic. There, the building of a bypass, Syd Einfeld Drive, enabled a section of Oxford Street to be turned into a pedestrian mall, whilst the area under the by-pass viaduct provides additional parking space. Similarly when the NSW Central Coast town of Wyong received its bypass there was a street party to celebrate. In a part of Melbourne with which I have been very familiar for many years, the opening of a section of the Monash Freeway enabled nearby Lower Malvern Road, that had previously carried much of the traffic, to have its four lanes reduced to two for general traffic with two for bicycles/parking.

In rural areas the chronic under-expenditure on rural highways and main roads was again apparent, especially where personal mobility was concerned. In contrast to the United States, and even the United Kingdom, railways in Australia were, almost from the beginning, public enterprises. They were built for the purpose of moving goods rather than people and, as Geoffrey Blainey pointed out in his iconic 1966 work *The Tyranny of Distance,* because motor competition increased the losses of the publicly owned railways, "Simply by spending meagrely on the building of bitumen highways, a government could check much competition from road hauliers".

We have already seen how this impacted on the mobility needs of people in outer suburbs of the cities. It is significant that to this day many coastal tourist resorts in Australia lack direct access by rail. The only practicable way to access these places is by road and the need to improve the nature of road access is only slowly being taken on board by government.

Successive studies of the Princes Highway to the south of Sydney, as well as the Pacific Highway to the north, have highlighted the tragic consequences of government neglect of the need to provide proper road infrastructure. It is noteworthy that even when the first National Highway program was conceived, the route chosen for upgrade between the Hunter Region and Brisbane was the inland New England Highway rather than the Pacific Highway. The South Coast region of New South Wales beyond Nowra is not served by rail at all, the neglect neatly symbolised by the line from Sydney ending at Bomaderry on the other side of the Shoalhaven River.

In Victoria the situation at the moment is no better with its two best-known seaside resorts, the Mornington Peninsula to the southeast of Melbourne and the Surf Coast to the southwest now having no rail service at all. The Victorian Government, however, has announced a study into building a new line to Torquay on the Surf Coast and rebuilding the link to Drysdale on the Bellarine Peninsula.

At least in Northern New South Wales and also in Queensland the main line to the north follows the coast, but passes to the west of the

Sunshine Coast. It is only in recent years that the Gold Coast regained its rail connection with Brisbane although its route lies inland from the tourist areas. It is ironic that its extension beyond Varsity Lakes has been delayed by opposition from environmental groups, so that it may be many years before the line reaches Coolangatta. To be fair, a substantial upgrade of the Gold Coast Highway to Surfers Paradise to freeway standard has taken place at the same time.

In Perth, the Western Australian government has done better with the new rail line to Mandurah, 68 km south, complementing its Northern Suburbs Railway. It is significant that both these lines were built in the median strips of freeways designed so that space would be there once sufficient rail patronage was assured, before which there were express buses.

Even recent developments such as Melbourne's Citylink CBD bypass, and its ring road, will never achieve their full accident reduction potential as long as governments rely on public-private partnerships to build them. Rather, 'shadow tolling' should be used to recoup the costs their private operators have incurred in building them. (Under shadow tolling governments pay the operators a set amount for each vehicle that uses the facility.) This would not only remove the disincentive that tolls represent, but also enable governments to do away with the constraints imposed under the current contracts that preclude governments from making improvements to public transport where that would reduce traffic volumes on the toll roads concerned.

Thousands of lives have been lost in Australia as a result of the paucity of road infrastructure in both rural and urban areas. It is surprising that any first world country should have so comprehensively ignored the need to provide safe travel for its people. Any motivation for change is also hindered by the endless, fruitless, arguments about freeways versus public transport, as though they were mutually exclusive. Each has a place in the urban fabric.

This might therefore be a good place to dispose of the notion that, once built, freeways fill up and deposit a bigger load of traffic somewhere else. This assumes, quite wrongly, that freeways have to *end* somewhere. In Australia this has been an endemic problem, but is not the case overseas as, for example, in Auckland or, even more significantly Toronto, which is often touted for its public transport focus. Toronto has not just one freeway that continues a rural highway, from one end of the metropolitan area to the other, but two, one along the lakeshore that passes close by the CBD and another 8-12 kilometres inland.

Moreover, hard data from a study into the effects of building the first section of Melbourne's Eastern Freeway gives the lie to the myth that freeways simply fill up anyway. Constructed in the Yarra River/ Koonung Creek valley, the freeway complemented two arterial roads, one to the south and one to the north. Before-and-after data for the very limited corridor *as a whole* showed an increase in traffic over the first year of operation of 4 per cent, 2 per cent of which was accounted for by the natural increase in traffic over the metropolitan area as a whole. On that basis it would take a very long time for the freeway to reach saturation, except for peak hours. That is when improvements to public transport such as a continuous median-side bus lane should be in place to provide a fast, attractive alternative to driving for city-bound commuters, as on Sydney's M2 Motorway for more than twenty kilometres (with stations) and on Adelaide Avenue/Yarra Glen in Canberra. Public transport was the big winner from the Eastern Freeway with a 24 per cent increase in patronage because express buses, of which there had formerly been none, now ran directly to the city down the freeway. This operation has now become Doncaster Area Rapid Transit, with DART its acronym.

For the future, governments must lay aside the debt-averse attitudes of the past that have seen our public infrastructure crumble or at best remain inadequate, and give the public the opportunity to invest in the future through retail bond issues. These could be aimed at 'mum and dad' investors individually as a secure source of retirement income ("guaranteed by the government") or at their superannuation funds. Bond issues were the prime source of funds for public infrastructure in the past. The improvement of safety on the roads is just one of the benefits that the public can expect to flow from the resumption of that approach.

Chapter 41

The Railways: A Law unto Themselves

Today's opponents of new urban road construction would do well to reflect on the cavalier attitude of the 19th century railway commissioners when it came to introducing their new transport technology into the existing urban fabric. Residents complained just as loudly about the land take for rail junctions. Examples can still be found in Melbourne suburbs. Nor was it for nothing that the expression 'born on the wrong side of the tracks' entered the lexicon. Indeed, there are places in our cities where there are more places where pedestrians can legally cross a freeway than there are over the railway in the same vicinity. I have already mentioned the arbitrary splitting of the street where I grew up. This, however, was a mere bagatelle compared to some other intrusions into the urban fabric.

Such intrusions are built into the fabric of Melbourne's suburbs and indeed the whole State. One of the more notable is to be found in the Melbourne bayside suburb of Brighton where the railway runs diagonally through the busy intersection of New Street, a main arterial, and Dendy Street, the Middle Brighton shopping strip. (Dendy Street was named for a developer prominent in the land boom of the 1880s and is the location of the original Dendy cinema.) More than a century was to pass before the crossing gates were replaced and the whole intersection turned into a roundabout with two sets of boom gates, and this is not the only such location.

An even more spectacular example, in view of the importance of the roads concerned, could be found in the southern suburbs of Adelaide next to the Emerson railway station. This is where South Road (a major north-south arterial) and Cross Road (the east-west link leading from the Adelaide Hills to beachside Glenelg) intersect. The railway line slices diagonally through the intersection. An overpass was built on South Road in 1984 but there is still a level crossing on Cross Road.

In my memory, the most notorious intrusion of all lay on the outskirts of Melbourne where Boronia, now very much a suburb, had grown up around the intersection of Dorset Road (running between the towns of Croydon to the north, and Ferntree Gully to the south) and the Mountain Highway. Here again the railway cut straight through the middle. Despite constant pleas for something to be done to stem the stream of accidents, nothing more than the usual crossbucks ('Railway Crossing') were in place. It would take the deaths of seven young people who were returning from a church camp in the Dandenongs when a suburban train wiped out the bus in which they were travelling for flashing lights to be installed. As a result of a huge increase in traffic volumes, the intersection has now been bridged and a new station built below ground level. This has also taken place at other rather less hazardous locations where traffic delays alone warrant grade-separation. Such improvements are a good example of why, all other things being equal, the rate of traffic accident fatalities per 10,000 vehicles falls as motorisation (the number of vehicles per thousand of population) rises.

The elimination of level crossings on major highways in rural areas rarely receives the credit it deserves in reducing the toll of death and injury, eliminating as it does the risk of collisions between trains and road vehicles. This represents an excellent example of *taking drivers as they are rather than trying to change behaviour.*

It is not surprising that angled crossings abound in rural areas, particularly in soldier settlement areas of northern Victoria where roads running on the boundaries of properties form a grid pattern. A railway, however, serves the quite different purpose of moving freight, and people, by the most direct route that can be economically constructed between origin and destination. This arrangement poses great difficulties from a safety perspective and I have acute personal experience of this.

Even as a passenger I tend to be aware of what lies ahead, at the same time doing my best to enjoy looking at whatever lies out the window. One day I was being driven to and from Shepparton, a rural city in Victoria's Goulburn Valley, for a work visit to Radio Australia and felt completely at ease with the departmental driver. The transmitter site is a little distance from the CBD and getting to and from it involves crossing the Tocumwal railway line at an oblique angle. The crossing, at that time, was marked only by the standard 'railway crossing' crossbucks signs. On the way back as we drove across it, the driver and I were completely unaware of the approach of a diesel-hauled passenger train. We were barely over the crossing when a flash of dark blue appeared in my peripheral vision. Neither the driver nor I had perceived the train against the background of the SPC fruit cannery with its long low grey buildings just over the crossing. "Looked, did not see" took on a whole new meaning in accident reports when I became involved with road safety.

Even in the early 1970s good practice with regard to level crossings could be found in unlikely places. In 1970, on a work trip to Hobart I had decided to fly there, but to travel back as far as Launceston by the passenger train that was still operating, and on to Melbourne by overnight ferry. As the loco-hauled train with its low-slung cream and red, streamlined carriages slowly wound its way up out of Hobart it felt like Melbourne's Puffing Billy with air-conditioning, but on a wider gauge track. From a road safety perspective, however, I was impressed by the fact that every single level crossing in the midlands, and there were many, was equipped with flashing lights though not bells.

From an ergonomic point of view, drivers of road vehicles approaching angled level crossings with only warning signs face a particular hazard. From two of the four directions, the train will be approaching from behind them. One idea to deal with this problem was to create S-bend approaches so that the road crossing is made at right angles to the railway track. That, however, does not solve the worst part of the problem. This relates rather to the difference in the speeds of a train approaching at high speed and a driver proceeding *cautiously* on the look out for trains. Any train travelling at high speed will only be seen in peripheral vision and if there is no change in the visual angle, a collision is inevitable. Means therefore have to be found, not so much to *slow* the road vehicles but rather to cause *deceleration* so as to change the visual angle. (Therein lies part of the success of priority control at local street intersections.) Transverse markings and rumble strips can reduce speeds at crossings.

Other solutions may exist, however, in specific situations. In one well-publicised case involving a rural school bus, investigations showed that there was only one train a day in each direction and the potential for tragedy could be eliminated by simply rescheduling the train away from the time the school bus used the crossing.

People who cross railway tracks on foot (or on bicycles) also merit more consideration. Astonishingly, the problem for them has been that until quite recently, in an number of jurisdictions, the part of a level crossing that is provided for pedestrians to cross the tracks away from vehicles did not fall within the confines of an 'intersection' between a 'road' and a 'railway' as they defined 'an intersection' for the purpose of road traffic accident data collection! As a result such crossings were a no-man's land when it came to reducing the dangers.

As it happens, railway authorities had long ago used crib crossings so that people would be looking one way and then the other as they crossed the lines, a measure later adopted widely in the design of median refuges on roads. The crib crossing, however, was hardly a solution if a pedestrian had waited for one train to pass only to find, too late, that a train was bearing down on them from the opposite direction, having been hidden by the train they had let pass. Following numerous tragic and well-publicised fatalities, some involving children, railway authorities have added or incorporated pedestrian boom gates into the boom gate set-up in urban areas.

I am only too aware that a small number of drivers do play Russian Roulette with trains and thus turn any approach to a crossing into a potential nightmare for the train driver. In the 1970s, when the level crossing problem was at its worst, the Road Trauma Committee of the RACS, headed by Dr Gordon Trinca, organised a seminar on the topic with speakers from all the authorities concerned. These included a specialist in the field, Eric Wiggglesworth, from what is now the RMIT University. A film was shown taken from the driver's compartment of a Melbourne suburban train on the Dandenong line. At crossing after crossing, all equipped with flashing lights and bells, it was like watching a Mack Sennett movie from the silent era – will the car stop in time - or will this be the nightmare event that every train driver fears. Nor is the cost in human terms borne only by any survivors, the victims and the families and friends, the train drivers involved take years to get over the trauma. Today, all of the crossings on the Dandenong line have been equipped with boom gates, another instance of expenditure on infrastructure removing a problem, meaning that all but the most foolhardy are protected from accident.

Unfortunately, a new problem has been created at level crossings close to signalised intersections, due at least in part to a lack of liaison between rail and road authorities. Crashes involving fatalities have occurred in the recent past and both involved vehicles being hit by trains while waiting in a queue that extended back over a boom-gated crossing waiting for nearby traffic lights to change. Such situations could have been anticipated and appropriate controls put in place.

The whole problem of level crossing accidents merits further attention from another angle altogether as passenger train speeds routinely increase to 160km/h. Large numbers of heavy commercial vehicles are coming on to the roads that have the potential to cause great harm to passengers on the train, not to mention the drivers in their now exposed position on high-speed trains such as the XPT. No longer are train crews shielded from harm by the long boilers of their steam locomotives. In the past, because might was on the side of the train, the operating authorities could smugly dismiss the potential harm to road users as being their own fault for being there in the path of the train. This danger is now officially recognised by the Australian Transport Safety Bureau. In the time before I retired my attempt to include reference to it was summarily removed from a draft ministerial briefing on level crossing matters.

The tragic, and well publicised, collision between a semi-trailer and a passenger train near Kerang in Victoria that killed eleven people, all on the train, in 2007 was a sharp reminder of the dangers. To their credit the Victorian government took immediate steps to mitigate the risks at the location concerned and elsewhere with the swift roll out of boom gates. By February of 2014, 50 crossings had been treated in this way. At most of the locations there had formerly been the traditional flashing lights and bells, but at some there had been only Stop signs or Give Way signs. Similar programs to that in Victoria are being put into effect in other states.

One more question remains to this day. Is there anything that has not been tried before that can be used to reduce the level of injury and damage when a train collides with a road vehicle? In its second report the Expert Group on Road Safety clearly thought there was, and recommended a study to "examine the feasibility of mounting energy-absorbing devices on the front of locomotives". Over the ensuing 40 years there has been no action on this matter.

Also ignored was the EGORS recommendation for the evaluation "by means of a large-scale field trial, the effect on accidents of fitting flashing warning beacons to mainline railway locomotives". It is ironic that the main competitors to freight trains - semi-trailers – present no doubt to drivers of other vehicles on rural roads of their approach because of the display of highly conspicuous supplementary lights, front and sides. Indeed, even the much simpler idea of placing reflectors or reflective tape on railway vehicles has never been taken up.

Perhaps an anecdote from the time I joined the DST will indicate just how long it takes to achieve accident reductions when more than one opinionated body is involved. The department's functions included advising the Minister on matters arising out of the workings of the then Commonwealth Railways, the operators of the Transcontinental line among others. Someone in the railways had come up with the idea of trialling the use of reflectors on the side of a number of wagons to increase their conspicuity at night. A trial did take place, but only on the condition that the wagons were to be clearly marked "never to be allowed into interstate traffic", so that was the end of that approach.

I close this chapter with an interdisciplinary thought or two. Railway authorities have for many years used fluted steel panels to increase impact resistance and so protect passengers in crashes between trains and in derailments. The carriages that were torn apart in the Kerang accident mentioned earlier had only plain steel panels, having been built to a 1930s design. Passengers were thereby exposed to an avoidable risk; the modern 'V/locity' country carriages do have fluted side panels.

Which leaves me with one parting thought regarding the railways. How is it that the operators of luxury long-distance passenger trains are allowed to simply hang a car-carrier wagon with all its exposed metal parts on to the back of the train ready to impale anything that happens to run into the back of it. A radio black spot and fog may have precipitated the Glenbrook disaster where a commuter train ran into the back of the Indian-Pacific express, but what about the car-carrier? Semi-trailers have been equipped with under-run protection for years. It would seem reasonable for a car-carrier to be designed more like a carriage, without protruding parts.

Chapter 42

Compensation without Litigation

Among the aspects of the cultural landscape within which the motor vehicle operates is the idea that for something to go wrong someone must have been negligent to a degree, and, in order to obtain compensation for a wrong, that negligence must be proved. It became clear early in the motoring century that the consequences for all but the wealthiest citizens of a judgement to that effect going against an individual in charge of a motor vehicle would be financially catastrophic. Hence we now have to take out compulsory third party injury insurance (CTP), paid along with our motor vehicle registration fee. Taking this concept further led some states in the USA to introduce so-called *No Fault* compensation schemes, a move that has been taken up to varying degrees elsewhere.

A few years before I joined DST, Justice Sir John Barry of the Supreme Court of Victoria had delivered an address to the Southern Tasmanian Bar Association with the title *Compensation without litigation*. In this 1963 paper he questioned the participation of the legal profession in the system by which compensation was delivered under the then existing CTP arrangements, given that the defendant was protected from personally paying up should the judgement go against him, noting that many of the cases were in fact settled out of court. Reference was also made to the general question of cost.

Delays, often running into years, were also commented upon in the review of Insurance in relation to road safety that was undertaken by Professor P S Atiyah as part of the EGORS National Review in the early 1970s. Indeed, the system was seen to provide little incentive for cases being to be quickly brought to court.

The legal system is not given to rapid change and so it was to our near neighbour, New Zealand, that the newly-elected Whitlam ALP government turned when it sought to introduce a more equitable, and *nation-wide, accident compensation system, not just for road accidents, but for all forms of misadventure.* To conduct the review Mr Whitlam turned to the man who had been the architect of the scheme administered by the New Zealand Accident Compensation Commission, Mr Justice Woodhouse. His recommendations were for a similar scheme to be adopted in Australia, but time caught up with the Whitlam government and the recommended scheme was quietly laid to rest in 1976 by the incoming Coalition government under Malcolm Fraser.

Sensibilities were sufficiently disturbed by what was contained in the Woodhouse Report, and other sources such as the EGORS National Review, that the states and territories did bring in modified no-fault schemes that at least gave immediate access to funds for the purpose of hospital and continuing medical treatment. In 2014 the ACT government announced that it will introduce a no-fault scheme to pay for lifetime care for Canberrans catastrophically injured in motor vehicle accidents. The ACT is in fact buying into the scheme already operating in New South Wales. Such reforms are welcome.

There has also been all-party support for the introduction of the National Disability Insurance Scheme that will go some way to addressing some of the issues raised, but it is time for a wider review with the aim of providing a national compensation scheme covering all forms of misadventure.

Chapter 43

Uniform Accident Information

It has been said that 'information is power'. The vital importance of accident information in the formation of road safety policy was recognised as long ago as 1974 by the conduct of the Road Accident Information Seminar under the aegis of the Expert Group on Road Safety. I have mentioned earlier that one of the foremost recommendations in the second report of EGORS in 1975 was for federal government assistance for the creation of uniform records that included the accident involvement history of drivers and motorcyclists as well as their traffic infringement history.

In its 1982 report on the training and licensing of drivers the House of Representatives Standing Committee was particularly scathing about the failure to integrate the different records relating to drivers saying at para. 276, that,

> *The Committee cannot accept that it is possible to link traffic violations to a driver, but not accidents.*

The committee went even further, making the disturbing finding, totally ignored, that,

> *Convictions, although raising significant revenue, do not relate well with accidents.*

The committee then recommended in para. 279 that driver records should contain at least the following basic information:

- *licence application information, including name, address, age, sex and licence test reports;*
- *involvement in reportable traffic crashes;*
- *conviction for traffic violations;*
- *licence sanctions taken whether by court, or licensing authority; and*
- *all vehicles registered in the name of the licensee.*

The succeeding 40 years have seen no progress on this front in any state or territory, with the exception of Queensland.

In a submission I made in 2013 to the ACT Auditor-General's Inquiry into the operation of speed and red light cameras I stressed the need for this information to be available and urged her to make representations to the Privacy Commissioner for this data matching to be allowed. Currently it is not. My argument is simple. I would have thought that *being able to tell whether the people who are having accidents are the ones who are receiving traffic infringement notices or not would be the cornerstone of any well-directed enforcement operation.*

In terms of what gets into the mass data system the situation is no better. The statistical material put out by the Australian Transport Safety Board (ATSB), for instance, merely describes the problem and fails completely to give the intelligent layman any indication of the nature of the problem or how it might be tackled. As an example, the bulletin gives figures on accidents classified by speed zone but with no cross-analysis by type of road configuration. Similarly, there is no classification by location – mid-block or at intersection – or by type of traffic control. This is because the various jurisdictions cannot agree on the definition of what is an 'intersection'.

A former Assistant Commonwealth Statistician, Fred Bagley, who died a few years back, put his finger on the root cause of the problem at the Road Accident Information Seminar in 1974 - that road accident information is a *by-product* of the enforcement system.

An attempt was made by FORS in the 1980s to gain agreement, with a document entitled *Common core of road accident information*, but like so much else it foundered. One item that would have been useful was 'point of impact on the vehicle', but the list of 16 items was hardly onerous. Attempts to devise a system of vehicle identification numbers (VINs) that coded for vehicle characteristics that would have been useful to accident researchers also came to nothing.

The situation, however, has improved markedly in respect of fatal and serious road accidents. Data from a variety of sources such as hospital and coroners as well as the police represents a valuable research resource. As I see it, however, such research as is undertaken receives little publicity and at times seems overwhelmed by information about the recall of particular road safety campaign messages.

Before leaving the subject of accident information there is one more point I would like to make. This concerns the omission in Australian data collections of any reference to the concepts of 'at fault' and 'not at fault'. I am well aware that the concept that the occurrence of any accident could have one 'cause' was rightly anathema to the new breed of road accident researchers when they were seeking to expose the prevailing, simplistic, view of accident causation. Their emphasis was rather on 'contributing factors' in accordance with the epidemiological approach presented in the form of the Haddon Matrix.

Traditionally, statistical bulletins used to include data relating to 'cause and responsibility'. As we have seen, data entering the mass data system is *by-product* of the enforcement system where police use the accident report primarily in order to determine whether a participant in an accident should suffer some sort of penalty as a result of their actions. To not include information relating to the imposition of a penalty in the mass accident database would seem to be odd to say the least.

Indeed, research reports from the USA dealing with the effectiveness of driver licensing practices make continual reference to drivers being the 'at fault' or 'not at fault' participants in the accidents. I have referred more than once to the needless restriction that the non-inclusion of accident involvement in driver records places on research that might shed light on the true state of play out there on the roads. The gaping hole in the knowledge base is a classic case of 'the baby having been thrown out with the bathwater'.

The type of research reported on at seminars in Australia and New Zealand in 2011 by Professor Thomas Dingus, director of the Virginia

Tech Transportation Institute, for example, would simply not have been possible in Australia. This showed, for example, that 10% of drivers create roughly 50% of the crash risk. Whilst it may be difficult to identify such drivers ahead of time, is should not be difficult to track them once they have entered the database.

One is left with the inescapable conclusion that the road safety establishment in Australia simply does not want to know who is really responsible for the problems out there on the roads, given the fixation with automated enforcement that impacts on all drivers irrespective of their accident record.

Chapter 44

Exemplary Drivers

In the course of writing this memoir and discussing aspects of it with a number of people, I have become increasingly aware of the fact that many had never had an accident in their lives, despite having picked up traffic infringement notices for exceeding the speed limit. This is not the place to revisit that issue to which I have devoted a lot of attention already. Nevertheless, I have to ask myself, what are these exemplary drivers doing right and, whatever it is, can it be passed on? Do exemplary drivers represent a source of information that is being wasted?

That question exercised the mind of Michael Austin in his book *Accident Black Spot* that was published in 1966 and which made such an impression on me at the time. Indeed, he included amongst his recommendations that research should be undertaken into "the reasons why some drivers are able to drive for a lifetime without having an accident". In all the years since I have never once come across such a study and I must ask, why this is so?

One episode in *Fawlty Towers*, the one in which Basil Fawlty goes on about not mentioning the war, ends with the German psychiatrist telling his wife as they leave that "you could run a whole conference on that man". I could write a whole chapter on my wife's *technical* failings as a driver and, indeed, on her failure to observe the niceties of the traffic code. Nevertheless, in a driving career of more than 60 years including driving across town to work virtually every working day for almost thirty years, first in Melbourne and then in Canberra, she has received only one traffic infringement notice and been involved in only two very low-speed rear-enders.

So neither technique, nor letter-of-the-law observance of traffic rules, seems to be a factor. Perhaps the traffic system is so forgiving that minor indiscretions do not result in accidents, but the time period is too long for that, so, I would prefer to concentrate on what she might be doing *right* that has kept her out of trouble.

What I do know is that she never drives after consuming alcohol and that she wore a seatbelt even before it was compulsory. Perhaps most importantly, she keeps a sharp lookout ahead and behind and I have been grateful, and not just as I have grown older, for her having seen people or vehicles that I have missed in my wider and longer visual field. She says she doesn't even enjoy driving whereas I regard the opportunity to operate such a wonderful thing as a car as one of the best things in life.

It is clear that the driving task produces a different level degree of arousal in us. I am generally under-aroused by it and so give myself little challenges where it is safe to do so, such as slowing down without touching the brakes to get to the traffic lights just as they change or to get down to the new speed limit when approaching a town. On the open road, seeing a semi-trailer in the distance sets me thinking about my strategy to overtake it without getting right up behind it whereas that is just what Jennie would do. Similarly, I tell her that at the design speed of a divided highway there will be no surprises to demand a sudden control response, but that does not stop her slowing down approaching a crest or when driving around left-hand curves.

Perhaps the reason why the resource that exemplary drivers represent is ignored comes back to the traditional way of looking at whey accidents occur. Accidents are not meant to happen and if they do someone must have messed up. People only come to the attention of the authorities when they do something wrong and if they do not – well, they're not supposed to do the wrong thing are they, so why bother about them? The trouble with that line is that the people with accident-free records have been out there while the miscreants are doing their thing, but somehow seem to have avoided them. How, no one knows and no one seems to want to find out. Moreover, enforcement as carried out in Australia, with its emphasis on automation, means that the net catches everybody – so everybody must just be doing the wrong thing!

Michael Austin made another recommendation that may be relevant to the case of the exemplary driver and that was for "The use of near-misses studies as a means of determining accident causation factors". I feel that there is a vast amount that could be obtained if only there were some way of looking at the accidents that were averted. I make no secret of the fact that I have had near misses, but if I take the time I can recall almost all of the situations concerned, and hopefully have learnt from them. Perhaps this is the area where a study of exemplary drivers could begin. How have they avoided trouble or what did someone else do so that the accident was avoided, and what did they learn from the encounter?

As I recall, there was some research done in the UK in the 1970s that indicated that there was often a two second window of opportunity to avoid an encounter turning into an accident. Thomas Dingus, whom I referred to in the previous chapter, goes so far as the say that. "If you are awake and looking at something you almost never hit it". He warns of the danger of fatigue being a "much larger (i.e. 20%+) crash risk problem than previously thought… [and] …true for both light and heavy vehicles". I have already expressed my view that people need to be given real incentives to take a break and not have journeys prolonged unnecessarily.

So, is too much emphasis placed on technique and on observing the letter, rather than the spirit, of the law? For many of us, it began when the first thing we had to do was master clutch and gear change and remember to push the clutch pedal just before we stopped. That is why I was delighted to hear that a granddaughter of mine was learning to drive in an automatic car. Think of the contrast – just put the T-bar in drive, press the pedal on the right to make it go and the other one to make it stop and let`s go out and learn to interact with other road users and with the road environment.

The identification of exemplary drivers would not be difficult if only the driver licence record included accidents as well as violations. Whether the purists in the road safety establishment like it or not, the police *do assign responsibility* or otherwise for an accident as an integral part of their *prosecution* of offenders and so it is not unreasonable for 'at fault' or 'not at fault' to be included in the licence record as well.

I can only repeat Michael Austin's call from all those years ago for a study into the reasons why some drivers are able to drive for a lifetime without having an accident.

Chapter 45

Madcap to ANCAP

I have already mentioned that I joined the road safety revolution at precisely the right time. An important aspect of the revolution was the growing understanding that the design of vehicles could be modified in such a way as to protect their occupants from injury in the event of a crash, and even to reduce the likelihood of crashing. Until that time cars were taken to be a plaything for the rich that had become available to the masses to use for more practical purposes.

One of my continuing concerns with this whole work was that I would not be able to do justice to those areas of the field of road safety with which I had not been directly concerned, most notably in relation to heavy freight vehicles and also bicycle and motorcycle safety. Nevertheless these areas do receive good coverage in technical journals and in specialist magazines. I would, however, like to reflect on some of the notable advances in the design of the motorcar that I have seen, particularly in the latter part of my driving career.

It is not generally recognised that Australia was in the forefront of safety in vehicle design long before the more widely publicised seatbelt wearing initiative of the early 1970s. So far had such work advanced that the first Australian Design Rules were passed into law before the better-known Federal Motor Vehicle Safety Standards in the USA.

I became very much aware of this almost as soon as I joined DST. Only days before, a leading newspaper had prominently run a story about the formulation of the Design Rules, giving some credence to the idea that they might produce "funny looking cars". This could have been a reasonable concern, given the small size of the Australian motor vehicle manufacturing industry, but more importantly it reflected the traditional resistance to change within the industry. Indeed, it has been said that the biggest players were initially the most resistant, but once government showed its determination, the same big players would be the first to support design initiatives because they would be in a better competitive position to accommodate change.

The two biggest manufacturers in the United States had not long before been made to squirm when they were confronted with the revelation of their responsibility for design flaws that led to the Corvair scandal and later the Pinto scandal. The racy General Motors sports sedan, the Corvair, lacked the handling characteristics to match its performance and was spectacularly involved in rollover crashes, whilst the Ford Pinto was a small sports sedan that was considered unusually prone to catch fire in rear-end collisions.

So dire was the situation that Nader was moved to produce a second edition in 1972 containing over 100 pages of new material. A passage from page 201 of the first edition, however, has a disturbing echo today as the Australian road safety establishment seeks to contend with a slippage in our standing in world road safety rankings,

> Today almost every program is aimed at the driver – at educating him, exhorting him, watching him, punishing him, compiling records about his driving violations and organizing him in citizen support activities.

One of the early tasks that I was involved in shortly after joining DST was an investigation into the integrity of car roof structures in rollovers. This study made use of records made available on a confidential basis by the State [motor vehicle] Insurance Office, the body that administered the compulsory third party injury insurance scheme. The investigation showed conclusively that the strength of roof structures even then was quite adequate across the majority of cars.

Perhaps the most significant finding of the Adelaide in-depth study of 1963 – 1965 was that pedestrians were not being run over by cars: rather they were being *run under*. On impact people would be thrown onto the bonnet, slide up and impact the windscreen with the head and be catapulted onto the roof, and then fall to the road.

The implications for vehicle design to reduce pedestrian injuries are immediately apparent. The aspect that most clearly needed to be fixed was the impact with the windscreen - replacing glass that would shatter into lethal shards with tempered glass that shattered into small pieces on impact. The solid nature of such a windscreen, however, meant that the victim would still be impacting something very solid. The solution came in the form of laminated glass in which a plastic inner layer is sandwiched between two pieces of shatterproof glass. Not only does this lessen the impact forces but it also 'pockets' the head.

(In notable transfer of technology, the Australian Standard (1288-2006) that covers glass in buildings now requires that automotive safety glass be used in windows that reach close to the floor and in certain other situations such as places where glass could be mistaken for a doorway or other opening.)

It was not long before it became apparent that the bonnet of the car might also be made in such a way as to 'pocket' the pedestrian on the bonnet thus reducing the likelihood of impacting the windscreen. One English engineer has said that with an appropriate bonnet and enough clear space left in the engine compartment pedestrians could be protected from serious injury in frontal impacts of up to 40 km/h.

The Swedish Vision Zero concept (of which more later) envisages reducing the speed limit to the even lower figure of 30 km/h in places where there is a high level of interaction between vehicles and pedestrians. Indeed, a 30 km/h limit was put in place in busy Swanston Street in Melbourne when it was reopened with wider footpaths and one lane of general traffic in each direction. (Swanston Street, between Flinders and Bourke Streets, has now been closed to all traffic except trams and bicycles). A 40 km/h speed limit has been put in place in parts of Canberra's town centres and larger local centres following two successful trials.

A notable change to the look of vehicles has been the elimination of bonnet ornaments, the lowering of the parked position of windscreen wipers so that they are below bonnet level, and the development of rules relating to the body profile so as to eliminate contact with sharp edges. A famous example of the potential danger was seen on one Holden model that was nicknamed the 'kidney scooper' for the pointed ends of the headlight surrounds, a design error that was quickly corrected.

Attention was also given to the initial point of impact – the bumper bar - typically at a height that the knee of an adult victim would be struck with serious consequences for subsequent mobility. A small child would be more likely hit on the body, resulting in even more serious injury. Minor rear-end collisions are, not surprisingly, the cause of many claims for repair of damage, so much so that in the USA a standard for energy-absorption was formulated for avoidance of damage in collisions. There was also concern that bumper bars could vary in height and position. The part of the leg where they might impact pedestrians also needed to be taken into account since injuries to the knee are especially disabling. However, one of the most obvious changes to the appearance of vehicles has been the elimination of the bumper bar as separate from the rest of the body.

Another feature distinguishing today's cars from those I grew up with is that nowadays one steps down into the passenger compartment with the floor pan sitting below the side rail rather than level with its top. This change gives greater protection in side impacts while the doors themselves have been strengthened with sidebars. I was recently surprised to see the return of the running board to a new 'four-wheel-drive' vehicle, having disappeared by the mid-Fifties as slab-sided design took hold.

To co-ordinate work in the area of vehicle design to reduce injury or *secondary safety*, ATAC had put in place the Australian Motor Vehicle Design Advisory Panel. Attention had been given much earlier, on a state-by state basis, to regulating the sort of things that motor vehicles needed to make them safe to take on to the roads such as brakes, steering, lights, tyres and the like – so-called *Primary Safety* or design to reduce accidents. Indeed, one of the first committees established by ATAC in 1947 was the Australian Motor Vehicle Standards Committee (AMVSC), comprising representatives of government and industry.

Two particularly important changes have been made that improve primary safety. These are anti-lock brakes and electronic stability control that have become available on all but the most basic models. These, along with disc brakes, are a far cry from the early days when cars could be trumpeted for having 'four wheel brakes'. Even my first car, the A40, only had what were called 'hydro-mechanical brakes" which meant that only the front brakes were hydraulically operated while the back brakes had a mechanical linkage to the brake pedal. In those days the brakes had pads that operated by pressing against the inside of a steel drum at the centre of the wheel (drum brakes). Pads were made from composite materials frequently including asbestos because of its heat resistance. At root, because a brake is a device for turning the energy of motion into heat, that heat must be dissipated; otherwise 'brake fade' will occur when the drums can no longer dissipate the heat. Disc brakes operate by having a clamp that grasps a rotating disc and therefore can dissipate heat more readily. Motorcycle brake discs are now perforated for this reason.

Even the way in which a car is steered is different. When I learned to drive there was a trade-off between the number of turns of the steering wheel one had to make to turn a corner and how precisely the road wheels would track. Light steering meant turning the wheel a lot, but more direct steering was heavier. My 1960 Ford Falcon needed 4 turns from lock to lock. Various systems of steering were developed in the early days with names like 'worm and sector', 'recirculating ball', and 'rack and pinion', of which the latter was the most direct but heavier. Then an Australian engineer, Arthur Bishop, came up with a system, now adopted almost universally -'variable ratio rack and pinion' – that was both light and precise, the more so with power steering. Today also, a car is not so much steered as guided; gentle pressure in the '10 to 2' hand position keeps it going straight, whilst minimal hand movement and a little shoulder movement will take it around highway curves.

In regard to secondary safety, I would direct readers to other sources of information that describe in detail the work done over decades starting in the 1940s, especially in the US by the Cornell Aeronautical Laboratory and in the UK by Road Research Laboratory. These efforts built on US Air Force Colonel John Stapp's rocket-sled deceleration experiments with himself as the seatbelted subject that had shown the feasibility of 'packaging' people to absorb the forces involved in crashes. Even earlier, World War I pilot Hugh de Haven survived being shot down by falling into a haystack and then spent a lifetime working on how to package people in vehicle crashes. It is to the credit of those involved that a Special Subcommittee on Traffic Safety of the US House of Representatives conducted an inquiry that led to a recommendation for installation and use of seatbelts as early as 1957.

I therefore commend readers to the excellent exposition of the seatbelt story and vehicle safety research generally that is contained in a monograph by one of my former colleagues, Peter Milne, entitled *Fitting and Wearing of Seat Belts in Australia: the History of a Successful Countermeasure*, published by the Federal Office of Road Safety, Department of Transport as report OR2 in April 1985. This is an update of Peter's original 1979 report.

I will also leave it to others to tell the story of how the airbag, now almost commonplace, came upon the scene to complete the packaging of people in cars so that they can survive what was formerly the unsurvivable.

One sub-group in the population of vehicle occupants stands out in terms of the attention that it has received over the past few decades – children and infants. What I found interesting was that the USA baulked at making seatbelt-wearing compulsory but was prepared to require children to be in properly designed car seats. The danger posed by reversing vehicles has also been addressed, first by the requirement for truck-type vehicles to have reversing beepers and more recently the development of reversing cameras. The need to protect children around reversing trucks was foreshadowed in Michael Austin's book *Accident Black Spot*.

A group of vulnerable road users – pedestrians - is likely to benefit from the inclusion of light emitting diodes (LEDs) into the frontal light displays on motor vehicles, especially in dull or rainy conditions. Their use to supplement traditional turn indicators by adding them to the outside mirrors should assist drivers interacting with each other.

Looking at the motorcar as I have seen it develop over more than the 60 years I have been driving, it is perhaps the development of the Australian New Car Assessment Program (ANCAP) that rates the safety of new cars, and the prestige associated with receiving a high rating, that best sums up the transition of the motorcar from a madcap plaything to an essential adjunct to modern life, whatever form that it may take in the future.

Resolution

THE SEASONS OF SAFETY

VISION ZERO – THE PHILOSOPHY FOR
THE FUTURE, NOT JUST A TARGET

PROTECTING THE REVOLUTION

Chapter 46

The Seasons of Safety

"For everything there is a season,
and a time for every purpose under heaven"
(Ecclesiastes, 3, 1)

Even before thinking about writing any sort of history, I had begun to ask whether there was a 'theory of everything' that could guide future actions towards making road usage safer. In an unpublished paper entitled *The Seasons of Safety* I put forward the idea that the way in which new countermeasures were developed to reduce death and injury on the roads could be seen as following a coherent, even deterministic, pattern. Any understanding of the past that puts the present in context should enable us to predict the nature of new developments.

The pattern that emerges can be seen to reflect the five phases into which an accident event can be divided. For an accident to occur there must first have been an *intention* to make a journey by road. The participant must then *encounter* other road users (or a situation beyond their ability to control). One of these encounters may result in an *incident* that may or may not turn into a *crash* that may or may not result in *injury*. Any successful countermeasure will act *between* these phases to prevent the event from moving from one phase to the next. This is the basis of *causal chain strategy* – that if the chain can be broken at *any* point, and by *any* means, accident or injury will be avoided. That idea is not new, but I have taken it in a new direction.

The model shows that countermeasures applied by governments can be seen as having followed each other in the same order as the five phases of an accident. For example, the earliest interventions - road rules and driver licensing – make their impact at the *intention/encounter* interface. Before making good the *intention* to make a road journey by venturing into traffic people can reasonably be expected to have acquired the requisite skills and to have knowledge of what is expected of them as they *encounter* other road users. This is the first dimension of the model and it can be traced through the phases in succession.

The second dimension of the model is that almost everything that governments did in the beginning, including their use of road safety propaganda, involved *doing things to road users or requiring things of them* as a means of reducing the potential for accidents to occur.

Indeed, road safety stalled at the *intention/encounter* interface for the first half of the motoring century. Road accidents were seen as a problem to be combatted by enforcement of rules and by road safety propaganda urging road users to display an unattainable degree of perfection in all circumstances and, in Australia, with little help.

In an earlier chapter I pointed out that whereas governments in other motorised nations invested heavily on road infrastructure and traffic control devices, governments around Australia did almost nothing. At best they installed traffic lights only where the free-for-all endemic under the give-way-to-the-right rule became intolerable, spent minimally on street lighting, let even the major highways fall into disrepair and failed altogether to provide adequate transport infrastructure in the rapidly growing cities. These failings were the major contributor to giving this nation the unenviable distinction in 1970 of having the world's highest per capita rate of road traffic accident fatalities.

At this point the model has already highlighted *the* major flaw in the way in which Australia dealt with the road accident problem for most of the 20th century. Action at one whole interface where one would expect to find governments intervening – **between *encounter* and *crash* - was simply missing**.

Even though comparably motorised countries had moved to act at the *encounter/crash* interface, it was only in the 1960s, largely in the light of work done by pioneering researchers in the United States, that attention started to be focussed on what it was inside the vehicle, or outside it, that occupants were making contact with that was injuring them – at the interface between *crash and injury.*

A new, scientific approach to the problem of road accidents had arrived. Indeed, large numbers of people even retrofitted their cars with seatbelts before their use was made compulsory, starting with Victoria in 1971. By this time, the fitting of seatbelts in front seats had been mandated under the Australian Design Rules whilst Victoria had required motorcyclists to wear helmets even earlier, another world first.

One must be grateful that within the engineering profession there were people such as John Lane, Ron Cumming, Peter Joubert, John Permezel, Jack McLean, David Herbert, Michael Henderson, and Peter Vulcan who recognised that in the Australian context only action at the *crash-injury* interface was going to stem the tide of injury accidents. This marked a sea change in thinking about the road accident problem.

Armed with the new knowledge about accident and injury reduction, however, road users themselves began to make demands on governments to protect them from accident or injury – *to do things for them.* A new range of countermeasures started to be implemented, beginning at the *crash/injury* interface, resulting in the development of mandatory standards for the inclusion of other safety features in new cars.

With the nature and complexity of the road accident problem being better understood, governments accepted the responsibility to *do things for road users* as well as *to* them. At this point the theory takes a twist. The progression of new countermeasures still followed the pattern of the phases, but in *reverse order.*

At the *crash/incident* interface, for example, turn arrows were incorporated into traffic signals. At the *incident/encounter* interface, street closures began to be put in place and street lighting improved. Likewise, to improve the driver's field of view, requirements such as those for the demisting of windscreens were put in place. Finally in this half-cycle, governments started directing public education towards *encouraging* more responsible drinking, a measure acting at the *intention/encounter* interface.

The model, however, has a third dimension. By the early 1980s governments had accepted a range of responsibilities aimed at making road usage safer, but society as a whole was becoming increasingly intolerant of deviant behaviour on the part of groups of individuals who put people at risk. The cycle of countermeasures therefore starts over again only this time governments direct their attention not at road users as a whole but start *doing things **to** particular **groups*** whose behaviour is deemed unacceptable and again they start at the *encounter/incident* interface.

Random breath testing was introduced in the early 1980s backed up by publicity to heighten the fear of apprehension. Motorcyclists were required to drive with headlights on in the daytime so as to improve their conspicuity. Off-road training for motorcyclists was introduced as well as heavy vehicle pre-licence training and the half-cycle ends with requirements for the use of approved child restraints

Groups, such as motorcyclists, who had been the target of pre-licence training, however, soon began to make demands for *things to be done **for** them* - for standards to be set or modified to meet their specific needs as in the case of motorcycle brakes, and the demand for an improved standard for helmets. While changes to the driving environment had been most evident in urban areas, country drivers, as a group, have benefited from the sealing of road shoulders, a measure that operates to reduce the likelihood of an *encounter* resulting in a *crash*. Motorcycle awareness campaigns took the cycle back to the *intention/encounter* interface by the late 1980s.

A third cycle began around 1990 and, as the model would predict, the new countermeasures were concerned with ***sub-groups***. As an example, at the *intention/ encounter* interface the maximum permissible blood alcohol concentration for novice drivers and riders was reduced to 0.02 and also for the operators of heavy vehicles.

This time around, when we come to the *incident/crash* interface we see a development that is inconsistent with what the model would have predicted at that stage – namely, the deployment of huge numbers of speed cameras across Australia.

By their very nature, often capturing a momentary lapse by drivers and riders from a level of perfect performance that is not demanded, or expected, in any other everyday activity, speed cameras make ***all*** drivers and riders their target including those with impeccable driving records.

That this occurred at a time when attention was being directed at deviant minorities is incomprehensible as a piece of public policy. For such a situation to be tenable, speed limits would also have to *perfectly* reflect the risk of crash – which they manifestly do not – being set too low on rural freeways (in view of the near zero crash risk) and too high in many urban settings. Speed cameras, however, produce a neat revenue stream and enable police activity to be credited with accident reductions that rather are the result of road improvements. Indeed it might be said that speed limit enforcement is the strategy of choice for governments that are not prepared to expend the necessary funds to make road usage safe for the majority of drivers and other road users, a trait noted earlier.

It is significant that the design features built into modern roads simply make the driving task more predictable, taking drivers as they are and doing things for them rather than to them. This is a far more productive approach than hectoring them about 'attitude'. In the future, enforcement must be concentrated on the *minorities* who cannot, do not or will not conform to reasonable standards of behaviour on the roads – a *group* of road users. Traffic law enforcement should not impinge on the vast majority of road users who simply want to get from point A to point B as expeditiously as possible without harm to themselves or others. This is the theme of the conference paper I presented in 1999 with the challenging title *Hit by Friendly Fire - Collateral Damage in the War against Speed*.

Returning now to the cycle and moving to the *crash/injury* interface, helmet use by pedal cyclists when using roads was made compulsory. We see *infant* restraints being mandated and the fitting of seatbelts in long-distance coaches.

The cycle then continues back through the phases with moves for pedal cyclists to be allowed to ride on footpaths. Significantly, because the drivers involved are a *minority* group compared to the majority who manage not to impact off-road objects, calls to do something about the hazard presented by inappropriately placed utility poles have largely gone unheeded. At the *encounter/incident* interface the need for pedestrians to be given a better go at traffic lights starts to take effect with longer walk times. At the end of the cycle, road safety public education campaigns begin to be directed to sub-groups, e.g. to women drivers to make them aware that they may be more affected than men after consuming the same number of standard drinks.

The model has yet another dimension. This relates to the length of time that each cycle has taken to complete. In broad terms the first cycle began at the start of the motor age with governments demanding compliance from drivers *collectively* until around 1970. Then came the road safety revolution with demands for governments to take action based on emerging knowledge of the nature of the problem. Around 1980 the focus changes to *groups* who by around 1985 started making demands of their own. Around 1990, the focus of government turned to *sub-groups*. Within five years sub-groups start making demands of their own. This takes us to the year 2000. It can be seen that each of the cycles took less time than the previous one to work through - 80 years for the *collective* cycle, ten years for the *group* cycle, but only five years for the *sub-group* cycle.

This is where the model indeed has one more card to play which points towards a completely new approach to road safety. The cycles can also be presented as a sine wave, of decreasing frequency, each cycle focussing on smaller and smaller groupings of road users. I thank my former colleague, psychologist Gary Hampson, for suggesting that the successive cycles be looked at in this way.

The shortening of the length of time that each cycle takes to work through also points to the possibility that at some stage, maybe not too far distant, the interests, the needs and failings of *all* road users would come to be considered *concurrently* in policy formation and so enable *policy gaps* to be identified. There are signs of this approach in the concept of road safety audits being undertaken before newly built or reconstructed roads come into use.

For the future, the attention currently being paid to the increasing numbers of older drivers, as the baby-boomers reach retirement age, provides a precise indication of the predictive power of the model.

First, came the idea of doing something **to** the sub-group of older drivers who had reached a certain age. This was a matter of determining fitness to drive as measured by a medical report, clearly designed to show whether an older driver who, having expressed the *intention* to keep driving, was still fit for the *encounter* with other road users. The next concern was whether a driver was actually capable of performing the task in such a way that *encounters* did not lead to *incidents* or, worse still, to *crashes*.

Most recently, however, has come the recognition that older drivers are likely to be driving older vehicles that may lack safety features that make crashes less likely and protect their occupants in the event of a crash. Doing something about this would require doing something *for* drivers rather than *to* them, which represents the first step in the *reverse* half-cycle of countermeasure development. The next step in the half-cycle is the efforts to reduce the likelihood of accidents by making road layout and traffic control more user-friendly (something that would benefit all road users).

The final stage in the process, so far as older drivers are concerned, is withdrawing from driving. This represents a return to the *encounter/ intention* interface. The numbers of older drivers will soon increase sharply as the baby-boomers enter their retirement years with higher expectations than earlier generations, pointing to an even greater need for adequate and equitable travel alternatives. This is exactly what the model predicts: the need for a social framework that will prevent this new cohort of drivers from becoming a problem to themselves and others. The ACT already offers free bus travel for people once they reach 70 years of age.

Even more recently another even smaller sub-group has emerged that demands attention – *commuter cyclists*, as opposed to recreational pedal cyclists. This sub-group eschew the use of cycleways, seeing them as too indirect and claim it as their right to use the arterial road system, even in the ACT where riding on ordinary footpaths and shared paths has been permitted for as long as I can remember. Earlier on I mentioned the use of barriers to restrict pedestrian movement across busy roads to places where it is safe to cross. The opportunity may therefore exist for cycle lanes to be separated by kerb-type barriers, or a shorter form of the rumble strip used in Melbourne along tramlines to keep them free of other traffic. Certainly the tripping hazard they might present to pedestrians would be absent, whilst preventing the appalling crime of 'dooring'. The fact that a word has come into use to describe the practice is an indication of the tensions surrounding the issue. Perhaps too it is time to look again at not allowing cyclists to ride two abreast on busy roads.

In the first enunciation of the model in 1995 the reduction in cycle length was seen as pointing towards the eventual adoption of what has been referred to as a ***systems approach***. On the other side of the world in Sweden, however, a similar but even more comprehensive approach to the reduction of death and injury on the roads was taking shape - ***Vision Zero.*** This represents a completely new approach. Vision Zero is the way ahead and the one to which the model has been pointing. What it should mean for the future of road safety is the subject of the next chapter.

Chapter 47

Vision Zero – the philosophy for the future, not just a target

Vision Zero represents a new, comprehensive approach to cutting the road toll that was approved by the Swedish parliament in October 1997. It *takes people as they are*, with all their capabilities and weaknesses, and seeks to work *with* them to achieve the goal of eliminating serious or fatal injury on the road, employing whatever measure will prove most effective in solving a particular accident problem. It accepts that people will make mistakes, *and not just out of carelessness or disregard for others*.

At the heart of Vision Zero is the idea that all the elements of the road system will be designed in such a way as to eliminate crashes that involve fatal and serious injury. This means that roads will be designed in such a way as to induce safe driving behaviour and appropriate speeds that will enable pedestrians, cyclists and cars to operate safely together in shared zones. Roadsides will be designed so that the consequences for straying off the travelled way will not involve serious or fatal injuries. The means to do this have been available for decades. Vehicles too would be designed to not only offer a high degree of protection to their occupants in a crash but also not inflict fatal or serious injury to vulnerable road users – pedestrians, motorcyclists and pedal cyclists – with whom they may come in contact. The means to modify bonnet design so as to eliminate serious injury to pedestrians at speeds up to 40km/h were known about more than two decades ago. Then there is the full separation of cyclists from other traffic and of local from through traffic by means of overpasses and underpasses. Similarly, the separation of opposing traffic streams by wire–rope barriers can produce freeway-standard safety on '2+1'rural highways.

The idea that the system should be adapted to the capabilities and limitations of people rather than the other way around has therefore been at the heart of this book. It had in fact been completed when John McPherson, a friend from DST days more than 40 years ago, drew my attention to an article that appeared in *The Atlantic* magazine's City Lab section on 20 November 2014 with the challenging title 'The Swedish approach to road safety: the accident is not the problem'.

In the view of Sweden's top road safety strategist a position in the Swedish Transport Administration, Matts-Ake Belin, a key architect of Vision Zero, the main barrier to its implementation was the entrenched attitudes in the road safety establishment. First there were the economists whose benefit/cost orientation did not readily accommodate the idea of zero (that would, by extension, supplant the notion of reaching some optimum level of accidents). More serious, however, was the problem encountered in dealing with "our expert friends". To quote Belin,

Because most of the people in the safety community had invested in the idea that safety work is about changing human behaviour. Vision Zero says instead that people make mistakes, they have a certain tolerance for external violence [crash forces], let's create a system for the humans instead of trying to adjust humans to the system.

Belin goes further, and the contrast with the Australian approach becomes even starker,

If we can create a system where people are safe, why shouldn't we? Why should we put the whole responsibility on the individual, when we know that they will talk on their mobile phone, they do lots of things that we might not be happy about? So let's try to build a more human-friendly system instead. And we have the knowledge to do that. But to do that we need those who build to actually accept this philosophy.

Belin also takes on the issue of enforcement and here again we see the contrast,

> I will say enforcement plays of course a role in Sweden, but not so much. We are much more going for engineering than enforcement. If you have a very dedicated police staff.....I don't think you will get a safe system. You can reduce risk, but you will not achieve a safe system.
>
> And when it comes to safety cameras, which is what we call them, ...they are not about catching people – it's nudging people.....it's because we have a history of crashes [in an area]. And we have increased compliance on these roads from 50 to more than 80 or 90 percent. And we don't catch people at all. We reduce the speed, but we don't catch people and we don't earn any money. It's an investment for us.

Acceptance of the philosophy of Vision Zero is clearly a two-way street. The Swedish decision with regard to rural freeways is a clear indication of the idea of taking community along and garnering their more general support for measures needed to reduce risks elsewhere, such as 30km/h zones in parts of urban areas.

My fear is that Australia will pay lip service to the notion, but continue its reliance on punishment using the words 'Vision Zero' as no more than an aspirational target while doing more of the same only with greater severity. There is already evidence of this in the title of one Victorian event 'Towards Zero'.

Justice, it seems, has been relegated to the back seat, so wide is the enforcement net cast. Indeed, in these environmentally conscious times, an apt metaphor would be that the by-catch far exceeds the haul of the desired species.

Of particular relevance in the current Australian context is the importance placed in Vision Zero on ***the self-explaining road.*** A normally law-abiding person in charge of a motor vehicle will receive sufficient cues *from the surroundings* to encourage them to behave appropriately to the circumstances. The authorities here, however, prefer to engage in bullying - refusing to make the obvious distinctions between the various classes of rural roads - and then prosecuting drivers for *driving according the conditions.* Point-to point cameras merely magnify the hypocrisy. **Simple justice demands that speed limits be self-evident,** something that is inherent in Vision Zero.

Indeed, if the Vision Zero principle of the self-explaining road were taken seriously in Australia, enforcement as it is currently practised would become unnecessary. The police could then focus on the real villains – those who cannot, do not, or will not abide by the accepted rules of the game.

The refusal on the part of the road safety authorities to give ground on the issue of grade-separated rural freeways in the face of overseas experiences reflects not only a blinkered approach but is also an instance of the contempt they show for their fellow drivers. This is why I have devoted so much time to it. The decision by safety-conscious Sweden to *increase* the speed limit on the safest sections of its rural freeways to 120 km/h was welcomed by none other than Claes Tingvald, a former director of the Monash University Accident Research Centre and now the Road Safety Officer of the Swedish Highway Administration.

The Australasian College of Road Safety and others in the road safety fraternity in Australia have already expressed concern that the decline in the number of deaths and injuries on our roads may have levelled out and that Australia is losing its place as a world leader in road safety. There is good reason to be pessimistic unless governments in Australia are prepared to wholeheartedly embrace the underlying philosophy of Vision Zero rather than some bowdlerised version of it that looks down the blind alleys of the past.

Vision Zero and all that it stands for represents a revolution in thinking comparable with to that which saw the number of road deaths fall from 3798 in 1970 to 1153 in 2014. This meant that the per capita mortality rate from road traffic accidents in Australia has fallen by more than 80% since 1970 despite the level of motorisation (as measured by the number of vehicles per 1000 people) having almost doubled. This achievement should never be forgotten, but it has depended for its success on the *scientific analysis of the problem and countermeasures derived as a result,*

The silver bullets of mandatory helmet and seatbelt wearing and random breath testing have been spent and so a levelling out in the rate of decline in the accident rate is inevitable ***in the absence of some new approach****.* Setting targets based on novel and intrusive countermeasures such as are being contemplated in the National Road Safety Strategy represent not a recipe for success but a self-fulfilling prophecy of failure.

Chapter 48

Protecting the Revolution

At the start of this work I said that the study of history should help us not to repeat the mistakes of the past. Looking back over the past ten years I fear that we are entering an era whose philosophy looks, sadly, like the one that was in full swing when I first became a driver.

Government authorities of the 1950s were well aware that the escalating number of deaths and injuries on the roads was a problem, but chose to take the view that if everyone would just be more careful all would be well. Governments felt no need to do more than hector road users about it all being their own fault if they came to harm.

The revolution in road safety that saw the toll of death and injury on the roads reduced dramatically in early 1970s happened when the attention of road safety authorities came, finally, to be focussed on what it was in vehicle interiors and the outside environment that people were hitting in crashes and so causing them to be injured. Until that time road safety efforts had acted on the principle *that if only people would take more care* all would be well on the roads.

Today, we see a similar attitude being adopted by road safety authorities in Australia that *if only people would slow down* all would be well on the road. Using this as the *dominant* strategy in Australia it makes it easy to overlook the other things that *reduce the risk of crashing* in the first place. Not only has this alienated public opinion but also failed to be matched by the hoped-for *major* fall in the number of fatalities.

Despite this, the reaction of the authorities is to do more of the same and indeed simply intensify the degree of surveillance. One of the best-known events in Australian history bears testimony to the futility of relying on ever more 'enforcement crunch'. The attitudes to speed limit enforcement in Victoria, that have influenced the rest of the country, bear an eerie parallel to the disputes over miners' licences during the gold rushes of the 1850s that led up to the Eureka Stockade. To quote from Geoffrey Blainey's 2006 book, *A History of Victoria,*

> Whereas the government in Sydney handled the gold crisis with masterly commonsense, the new government in Melbourne continued to handle its own gold crisis with less skill.
>
> Governor LaTrobe retired to Europe and was replaced by a starchy and aggressive governor, Commodore Charles Hotham. He inherited La Trobe's inept policies on how to cope with the invasion of diggers but did not change the policies. A man of the quarterdeck, he simply enforced them. As nearly half the miners of the 77,000…… succeeded in evading the licence fee, Hotham eventually ordered the police to hunt for unlicensed diggers twice a week.
>
> The subsequent rebellion was crushed, but public opinion was not. Thirteen miners, including an American Negro, were tried for high treason. The jury refused to convict them.

More than a hundred years after the Eureka uprising in 1854, Harry Camkin, a former head of the New South Wales Road Traffic Authority, wrote a conference paper entitled *A Tale of Two Cities.* In it he contrasted the *overt* use of speed cameras in New South Wales with their *covert* punitive use in Victoria.

A century and half later, in the court of public opinion, a jury of *peers* would be unlikely to convict a driver for 'speeding' whose only offence has been to exceed a speed limit that they agree (by their own actions as drivers) is manifestly too low. I am unable to track down the reference but it has been said that a law that is broken by half the population is either badly framed or unnecessary. As to the aftermath of the Eureka Stockade, self-government was granted to the colony of Victoria a year later.

Nevertheless, an official document on road safety that recently crossed my desk entitled *Strategic Goals and Objectives* placed primary responsibility for 'Safer speeds' under the heading of 'Enforcement', rather than under 'Encouragement' or 'Engineering'!

The Australian approach implies that *all* drivers are potential miscreants who will only be kept in line by draconian law enforcement. This is to take a very poor view of one's fellow human beings. In an article in The Age (19 January 2004) Professor Claes Tingvall, a former Director of MUARC, mused about how depressed most road safety experts are and how contemptuous of the ordinary citizen.

Indeed, some of what we are seeing represents a throwback to the pre-scientific era in road safety to infer that decent law-abiding citizens turn into selfish uncaring monsters once they get behind the wheel of a motor vehicle – shades of the Walt Disney cartoon *Motor Mania!* Distressingly, the expression *the nut behind the wheel*, a classic relic of the pre-scientific era in road safety, has even been given an airing in the media, a situation not aided by continual references to the need to change driver behaviour or *attitude*. More than fifteen years ago an OECD (Organisation for Economic Co-operation Development) report expressed the view that,

> Road safety practitioners should carefully consider whether the attitude concept is of any real help in clarifying actual road safety problems or guiding the choice of measures to improve road safety.

The time has clearly come to enlist the goodwill of the vast majority of drivers by no longer casting them as potential law-breakers every time they venture onto the roads. It is paradoxical that governments can accept the need for a forgiving roadside environment that benefits all, but are so unforgiving of momentary lapses from the *standard of perfection* that is inherent in automated enforcement of speed limits.

Concern about speed cameras is coming to be seen as part of a wider concern about the whole concept of automated surveillance of human activity. No lesser journal than the New Scientist (7 September 2013) ran an article with the title "Penal Code", with the sub-title, "We're creating a world where all-seeing algorithms can punish every wrongdoer, but do we want that?" To quote from it,

> If the enforcement algorithm believes a fine is due, no human being will see the letter sent out... [but] ... The law was not written for the 'perfect enforcement' of tireless all-seeing algorithms ..,. [and] ... If individuals know they are likely under surveillance, they have decreased autonomy and are less likely to engage in important behaviour necessary for human development.

Recent slogans such a 'Road safety is everyone's responsibility' deflect attention away from the need to deal with what remains of the road traffic accident problem. This is to protect those who want to do the right thing from the predations of those who, for whatever reason, seem unable to do so, and at the same time design out, or attend to, unexpected hazards. This would benefit all drivers, but most of all the increasing number of elderly drivers. Above all, governments must be seen to be working *with* the responsible majority and not *against* them.

The major difference to driving I have seen in the past thirty years is that it has been made *more predictable* for those of us who simply want to get from A to B as efficiently as possible without endangering others or ourselves. Despite this, there are those well placed in the road safety fraternity who will think that any deviation above *any* speed limit should punished on the ground that any increase in speed above the limit will increase the severity of accident, *as though there were no other ways of making road usage safer.*

Australia is known worldwide as for its leadership role in reducing the menace of drink-driving and by introducing compulsory seatbelt and helmet wearing legislation. The spectacular effectiveness of these generally accepted measures, however, must not be allowed to crowd out the subtle and continuing effect of *adapting roads, traffic control and vehicles to the capabilities of people rather than the other way around.*

Leaving aside random breath testing – directed at *a minority* - and improved occupant restraint, head protection, better crashworthiness and other vehicle improvements, the reduction in the risk of accident has been achieved most notably by the duplication of major highways, the building of urban freeways, local area traffic management measures, traffic control at intersections and high standard street lighting. This is where gains will be made in the future, not by some despairing retreat into the attitudes of the past.

-0-0-0-

Appendix

My Rebuttal of C N Kloeden, A J McLean, V M Moore & G Ponte
Travelling Speed and the Risk of Crash Involvement
FORS Report CR172, 1997

1. ADELAIDE HAD NO URBAN FREEWAYS (aside from the South-eastern Freeway through the Adelaide Hills) at the time the study was undertaken. This made it UNIQUE among mainland capital cities in Australia and THIS CASTS DOUBT ON THE APPLICABILITY OF THE RESULTS TO OTHER STATE CAPITAL CITIES and to towns elsewhere where bypasses exist.

2. For this reason, the results are questionable because the composition, nature and behaviour of traffic on its *entire* [surface] street system is therefore unlikely to be representative of other cities whether the roads are arterial or local.

3. Vehicles whose speeds were measured in the study were *travelling at free speeds.* On arterial streets, especially during periods of heaviest traffic, their drivers are likely to include platoon leaders and those who had been hurrying to catch the lights but were just too late to catch the green.

4. Drivers who have just entered the traffic stream are also more likely to be travelling at a higher speed in order to attach themselves to the platoon *that held up their entry* and especially on the approach to traffic lights that are about to change from green to yellow.

5. Drivers who have just entered the traffic stream will almost certainly include *'rat-runners'* who are more likely to use the local street system in the absence of urban freeways.

6. Rat-runners are likely to be found in larger numbers because of the predominately grid road layout of Adelaide, so that the composition of traffic and the behaviour of drivers on the *local street system* are unlikely to be representative of that in other capital cities.

7. The grid pattern of the street layout in Adelaide makes it likely that local streets and sub-arterials will be used for a greater proportion of any journey than in the hillier environments found elsewhere, as in Sydney and Brisbane where side streets may be relatively short.

8. Traffic on the *arterial road system* in Adelaide is also unlikely to be representative of that in the other mainland capital cities in respect of:
   composition – more heavy vehicles
   trip purpose – more vehicles making longer cross-town journeys
   behaviour – greater likelihood of driver frustration as a result of less predictable journey times and more delays as a result of accidents.

Implications

Taking the results of the study at face value makes those drivers *elsewhere* who are *unlikely* to be involved in accidents the scapegoat for the inadequacy of the Adelaide road system. Without the safety benefits of even a skeletal freeway system in its capital city, South Australia now has a road accident fatality rate that is consistently above the average in grave contrast to the situation in the 1950s when it had by far the lowest rate.

Indeed, the study has taken on a life of its own elsewhere and is afflicting drivers throughout Australia. **This is especially the case in Victoria where the results are probably less applicable than anywhere else in Australia** since the opening of Melbourne's City Link (completing a freeway route from one side of the metropolitan area to the other), the western and northern sections of the Metropolitan Ring Road (now connected directly to the Hume Freeway) and the provincial city bypasses.

Victoria's 'Wipe off 5' campaign can be seen as an attempt to justify the reduction of the enforcement tolerance to 3 km/h – the width of speedometer needle – on the ground that no one should even be doing 60 km/h, thus making the de facto general limit 55 km/h, or 45 km/h on residential streets. Such a reduction of the enforcement tolerance also discriminates against drivers who cannot afford newer and more expensive vehicles in which digital displays replace speedometers and warning devices can be set to alert the driver that he or she has exceeded the speed limit.

Taking the results of the Adelaide study at face value also ignores speed zoning on arterial (non-freeway) urban roads above the general limit. The use that has been made of the *speed/accident relationship*, however, gives the impression that this relationship is a *general* one, whereas it **can be applicable only to the very specific case where the speed limit has been correctly set at 60 km/h,** and perhaps even then only in Adelaide and other urban centres lacking adequate bypass routes.

None of the above denies the increased risk of injury as impact speeds increases.

What is argued against is the use of the deeply flawed and unrepresentative Adelaide data to justify the **zealous application of a near-zero tolerance approach to 'otherwise law-abiding drivers'** for small infractions above the 60 km/h speed limit.

Moreover, such an approach fails to take into account other more effective ways of preventing *the likelihood of accidents* in the first place, notably by the use of median refuges, peak hour clearways in strip shopping centres, and disincentives to the use of side streets as rat-runs.

Abbreviations

ABCB	Australian Broadcasting Control Board
ACRS	Australian College of Road Safety
ACTION	Australian Capital Territory Internal Omnibus Network
ACRUPTC	Advisory Committee on Road User Performance and Traffic Codes
ADRs	Australian Design Rules
AMVSC	Australian Motor Vehicle Standards Committee
ANCAP	Australian New Car Assessment Program
ARRs	Australian Road Rules
ARTCC	Australian Road Traffic Code Committee
AMVSC	Australian Motor Vehicle Standards Committee
ARRB	Australian Road Research Board
ARSC	Australian Road Safety Council
AS	Australian Standard
ARTCC	Australian Road Traffic Code Committee
ATAC	Australian Transport Advisory Council
BAC	Blood alcohol concentration
CBD	Central business district
CBR	Commonwealth Bureau of Roads
CRB	Country Roads Board (Vic)
DCA	Department of Civil Aviation
DMR	Department of Main Roads (NSW)
DST	Department of Shipping and Transport

EGORS	Expert Group on Road Safety
FORS	Federal Office of Road Safety
HORSCORS	House of Representatives Standing Committee on Road Safety
LATM	Local area traffic management
MCG	Melbourne Cricket Ground
METCON	Metropolitan Intersection Control
MITERS	Minor Improvements for Traffic Engineering and Road Safety
MUARC	Monash University Accident Research Centre
NRTC	National Road Traffic Code
ORS	Office of Road Safety (later FORS)
PACERS	Publicity Advisory Committee on Education in Road Safety
RACS	Royal Australasian College of Surgeons
RSB	Road Safety Branch
RSRS	Road Safety Research Section
RSSA	Road Safety and Standards Authority
RoSTA	Road Safety and Traffic Authority (Vic)
SCATS	Sydney Coordinated Adaptive Traffic System
SLATMASS	Sandringham Local Area Traffic Management and Safety Study
STATCON	State-wide [intersection] Control (Vic)
TARU	Traffic Accident Research Unit (NSW)
TERSIP	Traffic Engineering and Road Safety Improvement Program
UVC	Uniform Vehicle Code (USA)
VIN	Vehicle Identification Number